BRITISH ARCHITECTURAL SCULPTURE 1851-1951

BRITISH ARCHITECTURAL SCULPTURE 1851–1951 *John Stewart*

LUND HUMPHRIES

To William and Elizabeth

First published in 2024 by Lund Humphries

Lund Humphries
Huckletree Shoreditch
Alphabeta Building
18 Finsbury Square
London EC2A 1AH
UK

www.lundhumphries.com

British Architectural Sculpture 1851–1951
© John Stewart, 2024
All rights reserved

ISBN: 978-1-84822-665-4

A Cataloguing-in-Publication record for this book is available from the British Library.

All rights reserved. No part of this publication may be reproduced, stored in a retrieval system or transmitted in any form or by any means, electrical, mechanical or otherwise, without first seeking the permission of the copyright owners and publishers. Every effort has been made to seek permission to reproduce the images in this book. Any omissions are entirely unintentional, and details should be addressed to the publishers.

John Stewart has asserted his right under the Copyright, Designs and Patent Act, 1988, to be identified as the Author of this Work.

Front cover: One of Gilbert Bayes's exquisite reliefs on James Miller's Commercial Bank depicting *Industry*.
Credit: Roger Edwards.

Frontispiece: One of sculptor Henry Poole's groups of Mermen and Mermaids on Cardiff City Hall.
Credit: Author's Collection.

Copy edited by Pamela Bertram
Designed by Jacqui Cornish
Proofread by Patrick Cole
Cover designed by Paul Arnot
Set in Arnhem Pro and Portrait
Printed in Bosnia and Herzegovina

CONTENTS

Acknowledgements   6

Introduction   7

1   To the Victor the Spoils   9

2   One True Christian Style   27

3   *Et in Arcadia Ego*   56

4   Harmony Attained   79

5   The Power and the Glory   112

6   The Changing Scene   144

7   A House Divided   169

    Epilogue   193

Notes   195
Bibliography   202
Index   204
Picture Credits   208

ACKNOWLEDGEMENTS

This has been one of the most interesting and challenging books that I have written, taking me as it has out of my comfortable world of architectural history, into the world of sculpture. Fortunately, I have had several excellent guides on my quest, whose publications on British sculpture have proved invaluable. The first of these is, of course, the great Rupert Gunnis whose magisterial *Dictionary of British Sculptors, 1650–1851*, though it largely precedes the period of this book, nevertheless provides its foundation. The second is the equally venerable Benedict Read, whose *Victorian Sculpture* not only covers the first half of this book but, just as importantly, provides an invaluable insight into the sculptor's world. The third is the sculptor, Albert Toft, whose *Modelling and Sculpture* explains in detail the techniques of his art; the fourth, Susan Beattie, whose book on *The New Sculpture*, remains the classic work on this outstanding period of British sculpture in which architectural sculpture played such an important part; the fifth, Penelope Curtis, for her writings on modern British sculpture; and finally I'd like to thank and pay tribute to all the contributors to the remarkable series of books that seeks to chart the *Public Sculpture of Britain* as part of the Public Monuments and Sculpture Association's National Recording Project.

The Library of the Royal Institute of British Architects, and in particular their collection of periodicals which provides contemporary coverage of the entire period of this book, has (once again) proved to be invaluable, while the British Library has provided back copies of both *The Studio* and the *Art Journal*.

The extensive collection of photographs used in the book are almost all new and previously unpublished, and, as befits a book on British architecture and sculpture, they cover the entire country. Their acquisition alone has been a substantial undertaking, and in addition to my own photographs, I have been assisted by too many others to mention individually, but to all of whom I am grateful, and by Peter Clarkson, Philip Wright and Maggie Jones in particular, who have each provided a number of excellent images. That leaves my photographer 'in residence' in Glasgow, Roger Edwards, who has generously photographed the wonderful architectural sculpture across that great city at my behest, often returning again and again in different (and often very indifferent) weathers, and at differing times of the day, to capture the subjects of this book – many thanks once more.

And finally, once again, my architect wife, Sue, for her continual support and encouragement, research, compilation of the index and companionship on numerous visits around the country.

INTRODUCTION

Now rarely noticed, high above the street, often stained, occasionally providing a home for moss, lichen or even worse, the odd buddleia (and far too often netted to keep pigeons at bay), are some of Britain's greatest works of art. The richly carved sculptural detail on our historic buildings, not to mention the major allegorical groups, sculpted tympana, pediments and statues, which formed such a significant element of traditional architecture, are the work of master masons, exceptionally gifted stone carvers, and perhaps surprisingly, some of the country's most important sculptors. The term for this work is 'architectural sculpture' and though perhaps we do not yet generally appreciate it, we are fortunate in Britain to have one of the world's finest collections of this art form.

Personally, despite a life-long interest in architecture, a pretty long architectural education and a 35-year career as a practising architect, even I had never come across the term 'architectural sculpture' until after I retired from practice and started to write on architectural history. It was only while carrying out research for my double biography of the late 19th/early 20th-century Scottish architects James Miller and John James Burnet that I first began to understand just how the richly carved ornamentation and sculpture on their buildings was created. I began to recognise which parts of their buildings were executed by local stonemasons and which demanded the sculptor's art, and increasingly, how the architects, masons and sculptors worked together to produce what appeared to be entirely integrated works of art. Both Miller and Burnet enjoyed long-term working relationships with a number of sculptors who were responsible for the complex and very beautiful carved stonework which was such an essential element of their architectural language. In Burnet's case, he collaborated again and again with both Sir George Frampton and Sir William Reid Dick, while Miller worked almost exclusively with Albert Hodge until Hodge's early death, and afterwards with Gilbert Bayes; and in the case of all these outstanding sculptors, architectural sculpture was one of the principal outlets for their extraordinary creativity and craftsmanship.

For almost the entire history of British architecture up until the 19th century, architectural sculpture had been the ultimate achievement of the master mason who, usually directed by an architect, had provided the carved decoration on the nation's buildings. Fine Art sculptors rarely contributed to this process as they had no intention of playing what they saw as a minor role within an artistic partnership. Their lives were spent producing busts, monuments, medals and statues in their studios, for patrons who were usually either royalty or at least came from the upper classes, and they had no intention of competing with master masons for commissions nor, perish the thought, of clambering around scaffolding on a building site in the depths of winter. Even by the middle of the 19th century the division between Fine Art sculptors and architects was almost absolute, as architect John Seddon confirmed in 1851, writing that: 'artists of either class are content to grope on blindly in their own narrow course, utterly careless of the sympathy of their fellows'[1] (although he did identify the contemporary pediment frieze of St George's

Hall in Liverpool, designed by architect Charles Cockerell with assistance from sculptor Alfred Stevens and carved by William Grinsell Nicholl, as a notable exception). As the 19th century progressed and Britain's wealth increased exponentially, this situation began to slowly change, however, and one or two of the country's finest sculptors began to add architectural sculpture to their range of works; and consequently (rather disturbingly), they often met a group of outstanding stone carvers who were making a remarkable social progress in the opposite direction. By the end of the century, we find numerous architects and sculptors working together consistently, enjoying shared artistic ideals and fruitful collaborations, with the vast and then apparently ever-expanding British Empire providing them with what seemed to be unending opportunities to jointly pursue their shared art (fig.1).

This coming together of fellow artists reached its zenith with the formation of the Art Workers' Guild in 1884 and in the consequent contributions of the leading members of the New Sculpture Movement to the architecture of the late 19th and early 20th centuries, so much so that, by the time of the outbreak of the First World War, long-term artistic partnerships between the best British architects and sculptors had become the expected norm. It was also around this time that the first experiments in Modernism were taking place in Britain, and they too offered an early promise of shared ideals between a new generation of sculptors, who included Jacob Epstein, Henry Moore and Eric Gill, and their contemporaries in architecture (albeit against a strong and vital conservative mainstream, which maintained an expectation that all major public and private building would still be in traditional styles). Soon, however, these hopes were largely dashed, as the sculptors retreated once more to the private worlds of their studios, while their fellow architects pursued a stripped-down Functionalism in which there was rarely any place for any form of applied art or decoration. By the end of the Second World War, Modernism reigned supreme and a recording of the *decree absolute* between the two parties appeared imminent.

This book provides an overview of British architectural sculpture throughout this period, from the Great Exhibition of 1851, which celebrated Britain's ascension to the position of leading global power, to the Festival of Britain of 1951, which offered a vision of a new social democratic future. It is neither a comprehensive record of the British architectural sculpture of the period, nor a gazetteer. It is limited to architectural sculpture and excludes free-standing statues, most tombs and funerary monuments, bridges, ecclesiastical monuments in churches and (with some regret) most of the nation's outstanding collection of war memorials. It does, however, trace the development of the practice of architectural sculpture; the techniques involved; the relationships between architects and sculptors; and the works of the remarkable sculptors, masons and humble stone carvers who contributed to the extraordinary quantity and quality of the outstanding British architecture of this period.

1   One of sculptor Harry Bates's winged caryatids on architect John Belcher's Institute of Chartered Accountants' Hall

I
TO THE VICTOR THE SPOILS

A panoramic painting in the Royal Collection by David Roberts (1796–1864), shows Queen Victoria and Prince Albert on a raised dais beneath a suspended blue baldachin in the centre of a great glasshouse, built in Hyde Park in Central London (fig.2). The painting commemorates the 31-year-old Victoria declaring open 'The Great Exhibition of the Works of Industry of All Nations' and while all Britain's major international competitors were indeed well represented amongst the many exhibitors, they were simply there for comparative purposes, as it was Victoria's Great Britain which, through its innovation, industry and military success, had by that Thursday, 1 May 1851, achieved global dominance. As she wrote in her journal that evening: 'This day is one of the greatest & most glorious days of our lives, with which, to my pride & joy the name of my dearly beloved Albert is for ever associated!'[1] For it had been her beloved Prince Consort who, through his enthusiastic promotion of the exhibition, followed by his Presidency of the Royal Commission for the Exhibition of 1851, had more than any other individual been responsible for the creation of the extraordinary scene that surrounded her that day.

Soon to be nicknamed the Crystal Palace, the great glass and steel vaults under which the ceremony was taking place were themselves an awe-inspiring example of British architecture, engineering and industry. Designed by Joseph Paxton (1803–65), they had been manufactured and constructed in a mere nine months using the very latest British cast-iron and sheet-glass technology to create the largest glass building ever constructed in the world. It was a bold, self-confident and suitably innovative celebration of the unique position that Victoria's small island nation had achieved. Her country had been the first in the world to undergo an industrial revolution. Englishman Thomas Newcomen's invention of the atmospheric steam engine in 1712 had provided a new source of power which over the next hundred years led to the industrialisation of numerous manufacturing processes previously carried out by hand. The effect was to produce an entirely unprecedented step-change in productivity, outstanding economic and population growth, a shift of resources from agriculture to manufacturing, and consequently, the dramatic expansion of Britain's towns and cities.

The scale of the changes that had taken place were breathtaking. Coal powered the new steam engines and the British soon found that they were sitting on a vast supply of it. Between the start of the 18th century and 1851, coal production had increased from 6 million tons to 62 million tons per annum, with much of this used to smelt iron, and thus iron production had increased over the same period from 12 thousand tons to 2 million tons per annum. In 1750, Britain had imported around 2.5 million pounds of raw cotton for processing; by 1851 the total imports were 588 million pounds, all of which was then processed by steam-driven machines. A network of canals moved goods and raw materials around the country, and private railway companies had already linked all the major cities. The population had increased from 6 million at the start of the 18th century to 16.8 million by 1851, and while London was now by far the largest

2   David Roberts, *The Inauguration of the Great Exhibition: 1 May 1851*, 1852, oil on canvas, 86.4 × 152.4 cm (34 × 60 in)

city in the world with a population of over 2.3 million people, Glasgow, Manchester, Liverpool and Birmingham were now also all amongst the world's top ten.[2]

Industrial innovation, however, was only part of the reason for Britain's pre-eminent global position. Since the start of the 17th century, it had been in a race with its fellow European superpowers to colonise as much of the globe as possible, and it was a race that by 1851, Britain had also largely won. By 1750, Spain's South American empire was in decline and it was France who was to be Britain's challenger for supremacy of continent after continent, but it was Britain's military might which proved superior again and again, with India effectively won for the British in 1751 and Canada in 1763; and while the loss of the American colonies in 1783 following the War of Independence was a blow to British prestige, at the time it was more than compensated for by the unopposed acquisition of Australia and New Zealand, which soon progressed from penal colonies to become a valued part of the growing empire. The Cape of Good Hope on the very southern tip of Africa had been taken from the Dutch to protect the British sea trade route to India, and from there the expansion of its empire north into the continent was soon underway. The key to maintaining and trading effectively with these vast overseas land holdings was naval sea power, and with the crushing of the French fleet at the Battle of Trafalgar in 1805, Britain's control of its maritime trading routes was also finally assured. By 1851, Britain had secured access to a considerable proportion of the world's natural resources and created a vast, tightly controlled market for the goods of its many manufacturers – and, as with every empire before it, it had begun to celebrate and proclaim its wealth and power in its arts.

The Great Exhibition was not only an opportunity for Britain to display its manufacturing and technological progress – the arts were also prominent, although here British dominance faltered rather, with its imperial rival France taking centre stage. By 1851, Paris had succeeded Rome as the artistic capital of Europe and it was to there, and not London, that any self-respecting (and suitably wealthy) young artist would go to study. While Britain was pursuing its industrial revolution in the late 18th century, France had undergone a much more radical political and social change with the revolution of 1789, which overthrew the *ancien régime* and led to the execution of King Louis XVI and his Queen, Marie Antoinette, and the establishment of the First French Republic in 1792. This gave a considerable impetus to what was already emerging as a very significant break with tradition in the arts. Teaching began to replace traditional pupillage in many areas and exhibitions allowed artists to sell their work directly to the public, rather than relying on commissions from wealthy patrons. The impact, particularly on painting and painters' choices of subject matter, was immediate and many abandoned traditional portraiture or religious themes in favour of contemporary scenes, landscapes, or even the portrayal of humble rural life. Jacques-Louis David (1748–1825) painted the revolutionary, Jean-Paul Marat, murdered in his bath; Eugène Delacroix (1798–1863) studied and painted the colour and vitality of the Arab world; and soon English painter William Blake (1757–1827) offered his own fantastical visions. As E.H. Gombrich perceived, the unity of tradition had disappeared:

> The patron's taste was fixed in one way: the artist did not feel it in him to satisfy that demand. If he was forced to do so for want of money, he felt he was making 'concessions', and lost his self-respect and the esteem of others. If he decided to follow only his inner voice, and to reject any commission which he could not reconcile with his idea of art, he was in danger of starvation. Thus a deep cleavage developed in the 19th century between those artists whose temperament or convictions allowed them to follow conventions and to satisfy the public's demand, and those who glorified in their self-chosen isolation.[3]

3   The Sculpture Court in the Great Exhibition

Of all the arts, sculpture, largely by its nature, remained truest to its traditional subjects and values, namely: portraiture of royalty, the upper classes and military heroes, the saints and religious scenes from the Bible, the Greek gods and their myths, heroic tales from ancient Rome with their exemplars of valour and self-sacrifice, and allegorical subjects illustrating virtues or vices. Certainly, contemporary events were also celebrated in statuary, but well within the bounds of respectful traditional portraiture, with the teaching of sculpture consistently Classical and the art of antiquity and Renaissance Italy a constant reference point. The Great Exhibition reflected this and included a substantial display of sculpture with entries from 86 sculptors, which very comprehensively represented these traditional themes in busts, funerary monuments, ideal works and public statuary, in a wide range of materials (fig.3).

As was then to be expected, the royal family took precedence amongst the subject matter, both historically, with portrayals of both *Queen Elizabeth* and *King Charles the First* (by James Philip Papera), and in their contemporary incarnation, with a bust of *Her Majesty Queen Victoria* (by John Ayres Hatfield) and another full-size *Figure of Her Majesty* (by R. Hall) in elmwood. In addition to the much-sculpted Victoria and Albert was a series of statues in porcelain of her children – each representing one of the seasons, with Princess Alice as *Spring*, the Princess Royal as *Summer*, Prince Alfred as *Autumn* and the Prince of Wales as *Winter* – by Mary Thorneycroft, one of a small band of contemporary female sculptors. Next in line came the national

13

heroes, with *The Duke of Wellington* (by Henry Ross) still leading the charge nearly 40 years after the Battle of Waterloo, and a vanquished equestrian *Napoleon* (by John Hatfield) maintaining their rivalry. In both cases and as with the other military figures who were busy extending Victoria's empire, the fashionable Neo-Classical aesthetic demanded a certain level of flattery to achieve a suitably heroic end product, with these role models often presented as at least a superior class of being or, in extremis, as Greek gods swathed in togas.⁴

This Classical theme was further extended in numerous 'Ideal Works' which sought to link the emerging British Empire with the grandeur that was Greece and the glory that was Rome (indeed the exhibition was a significant opportunity for sculptors to present these works as there was generally much less demand for them amongst private patrons who, in most cases, would rather commission sculpture to celebrate their own achievements and immortalise themselves). These included scenes from Classical literature and mythology such as *Cupid Stung by a Bee, Complains to Venus* (by James Legrew) as well as more intentionally inspiring subjects such as *Dying Gladiator* (once more by the extremely industrious John Ayres Hatfield); and of course there were the usual representations of the virtues and vices such as *Innocence* by the outstanding sculptor of the age, John Henry Foley. For most sculptors these more abstract subjects represented rare opportunities to express the poetry that they believed was within them, and they were regarded professionally as being amongst the highest achievements of their art; but even these works, despite their high aspirations, were not immune to criticism from an increasing number of devout Victorians who favoured what they regarded as Christian Gothic and condemned Classical works as pagan art.

For this pious and fast-expanding flock, only scenes from the Bible proved acceptable; or, if led ever so slightly astray, perhaps subjects from English literature or Shakespeare's plays might fall within the bounds of acceptability. They were well represented too within the exhibition, with *Christ Blessing Little Children* carved in oak by J. Walker, a series of sculptures by Richard Cockle Lucas in ivory including *The Descent from the Cross* and *The Raising of Lazarus*, *The Expulsion from Paradise* by Edward Bowring Stevens and *Titania* by Felix Martin Miller (and despite the apparently religious or literary nature of these works, it was quite remarkable just how many still involved naked female bodies).

Beyond this category we descend into what, to 21st-century viewers, is that most difficult to understand or appreciate world of sickly Victorian sentimentality which so dominated the art of the period and, beyond the portraiture, actually comprised the second largest class of sculpture in the exhibition. *Little Nell and her Grandfather* in plaster by William Brodie, *An Infant* in wax by Peter Rouw, *The Babes in the Wood* by John Bell, *The Pet Dove's Return* in marble by James Farrell, and so the list goes on of angelic children, loyal pets, cheeky cherubs, nursing mothers and noble, aged parents in plaster, wood, bronze, porcelain, wax and marble to the fascination and delight of the visiting hordes; and it was these works, along with portrait busts and funerary works, which largely sustained British sculptors throughout most of the 19th century.

Of funerary monuments, there were a few examples such as the *Design for an Intended Monument to the Late Lord George Bendinck* by Thomas Milnes, but this was – though lucrative – very dangerous ground for serious sculptors, for here they might meet master masons climbing up the professional ladder from below. Tombs for dukes and duchesses, memorials in cathedrals or private chapels, were opportunities for great art, but moving out into the common ground of cemeteries and graveyards could only be done with the greatest of care, lest one's hard-won reputation as an artist should be compromised, while to contribute architectural sculpture to a piece of architecture, and thus be subservient to the concept of another artist, was regarded as simply beyond the pale by the country's leading sculptors in 1851.

Amongst this vast array of exhibited sculpture, there was one which perhaps more than any other both captured the spirit of the age and best portrayed the craft of the Victorian sculptor. It was sited, not in the sculpture gallery, but as the centrepiece of a trade stand. It was *The Eagle Slayer* by John Bell, which had been cast in iron by the Coalbrookdale Company of Ironbridge in Shropshire, where Abraham Derby had first smelted iron ore – the raw material of the industrial revolution (fig.4). It was a typical 'Ideal Work' portraying one of Aesop's fables – a shepherd straining every sinew to fire an arrow at the eagle that had killed the lamb which lay at his feet. (To raise the artistic bar even higher, Bell even provided his own poem to further support his interpretation of the work.) What struck a chord with the majority of visitors, most of whom were from the emerging middle class, however, was less the shepherd's desperation for revenge or the technological innovation – this being the first cast-iron sculpture ever produced – but much more the image of Man desperately striving onward and upward to achieve his goal, thus personifying the Victorian practical dynamism which was fuelling the country's extraordinary achievements.

This was, in fact, far from the first occasion on which Bell's sculpture had been exhibited, as it had already appeared in one form or another since its first showing at the Royal Academy's summer exhibition of 1837 (exhibit No.1176), where it appeared as a white plaster cast. Bell had, like most of his contemporaries, first modelled the sculpture full-size in clay, with even the most successful Victorian sculptors such as Baron Carlo Marochetti (1805–67) and John Henry Foley (1818–74) working in this way, as none of them could afford the expense of either working directly in marble or casting their own work in bronze. Their aim was to exhibit their work in clay or more usually plaster, hoping that a suitably minted patron would then commission them to execute it in a more permanent and much more expensive material, while paying them to undertake the conversion process.

Clay had many advantages for the sculptor, most notably that it was cheap, and even more importantly that it could be used again and

4   John Bell, *The Eagle Slayer*, c.1851, painted cast-iron, height 256 cm (100 ¹³⁄₁₆ in), width 132 cm (52 in)

again. But it did need to be kept moist in a tank, tub or air-tight box to avoid it drying out, and once modelled, it had to be stored in a moist environment, otherwise it cracked or shrank. Larger pieces, such as *The Eagle Slayer* which was actually super-lifesize, had to be modelled around a supporting structure of wood and wire and kept moist to avoid (as often happened) fully modelled limbs dropping off (fig.5). Working in this atmosphere was a constant threat to the health of

5 A mould for a large figure

sculptors, as the critic John Ruskin later recalled: 'Munro the sculptor, like all sculptors, lives in a nasty wood house full of clay and water tubs, so I can't go without catching cold.'[5]

Once the sculpture was completed in clay, a plaster cast was usually made, with plaster built up in layers until a sufficient thickness was achieved to create a self-supporting plaster mould when dry (after which the clay within would be reused). The inside of the mould was then coloured (often yellow ochre or blue), before liquid plaster was poured in to recreate the solid object. This work was usually carried out by the sculptor and his assistants in the studio, but for larger or more complex works, specialist 'plastermen' were employed to undertake this stage, with the moulds often made in sections and reinforced with iron rods, depending on the scale of the work. The sculptor now had a perfect plaster version of his original clay model to which he could make any final adjustments before exhibiting his creation, and then hopefully attracting a patron to finance a lasting version. Importantly, the copyright of the work of art remained with the sculptor, and while one patron might request a marble version, the artist was then quite likely to offer the work again for reproduction in bronze, or even on occasion with smaller works, in porcelain. Indeed, as the century progressed and more and more people could afford to exhibit sculpture in their own homes, many works were scaled down for domestic display using a variety of machines and techniques.[6]

If the work was to be produced in marble, it was quite usual for the sculptor to be paid to travel to Carrera in Italy to select their material. The design was transferred to the block by a complex process using a 'pointing machine' with a steel needle which was calibrated to a fixed axis which would transfer measurements from the plaster cast into the marble block, drilling holes to the prescribed depth. Once the measurements had been transferred, either stone masons or assistants would cut away the stone until the measured points were reached, at which point the sculptor would take over the production of the final work of art.

In the context of architectural sculpture, clay models would often be submitted to allow the selection of a sculptor or sculptors to undertake a commission; and once selected, following consultation and discussion with the architect, the sculptural elements of the building were modelled in clay for his approval (in the 19th century, it was always 'his' approval). In some instances, architects would have the clay models raised into their final position on buildings before agreeing to their final execution in stone or terracotta, to ensure that both the forms and their proportions in relation to the overall composition were acceptable. Normally, the final stone version would be created either in part or entirely by stone carvers, whom the sculptor would supervise, often applying merely a few finishing touches themselves.

Bell's Royal Academy plaster cast had previously attracted the attention of the Earl Fitzwilliam who commissioned a marble version for Wentworth Woodhouse (then the largest private house in England); Bell was able to submit this marble version as an example of his work in 1844 to aid his selection as one of the sculptors for the extensive sculptural work at architect Sir Charles Barry's new Houses of Parliament buildings, before its eventual casting in iron for the Great Exhibition (for which Bell was further commissioned to provide a vast cast-iron canopy to enclose the sculpture, supported on slender oak trunks complete with acorns and leaves, above which now hovered the eagle, pierced by the shepherd's arrow); and such was the success of the exhibit at the Great Exhibition, that numerous further versions were commissioned in bronze – all in all, a very successful return on Bell's speculative plaster original. His submission for appointment as one of the principal artists to work on the Houses of Parliament also proved successful, and it is to that symbol of British democracy, Victorian taste and extensive architectural sculpture, which was under construction at the time of the exhibition in 1851, that we now turn our attention.

While the design and construction of the Crystal Palace was both an experiment in new technology and a proclamation of British industrial leadership, it was by no means typical of the country's architecture in the middle of the 19th century. By 1851, the 'Battle of the Styles' between Gothic and Classical architecture was well and truly underway, as architects and their patrons sought to represent the values, achievements and aspirations of Victorian society in buildings of one style or the other with:

> many of the ensuing skirmishes focused on the comparative qualities of these two civilisations: the Romans' superior rationality, learning, order, *virtu*, etcetera; pitted against the medievals' faith, hope and charity . . . The question was, or seemed to be: which of these much older cultures should Britons look to, as the main inspiration of their architecture – and perhaps their lives.[7]

It was a conflict that would rage until the end of the century, with Britain's ever-increasing wealth providing the combatants with a constant supply of opportunities to fire their salvos.

Until the start of Victoria's reign, Classicism had held sway, being employed for every type of building from the town and country houses of the upper classes to the Georgian terraces of the expanding towns and cities, and it continued to exhibit an extraordinary resilience, receiving a new injection of vitality as a result of the exploration of Greek antiquity which had been underway during the latter part of the 18th century. Architect Charles Cockerell (1788–1863), for example, spent much of his seven-year-long 'Grand Tour' in Greece studying, sketching and measuring the monuments which were then emerging from centuries of neglect. As we know, a considerable quantity of ancient sculpture was then in the process of being relocated to London, including half of the surviving sculpture of the Parthenon (The Elgin Marbles), which went on display in Robert Smirke's great, Classical, new British Museum building during the 1840s. What better way to express the might and virtue of the new British Empire than to allude to its illustrious imperial predecessors, whose exquisite temples came to be regarded as man's greatest architectural achievement? By the 1840s and 1850s this had developed into a new Graeco-Roman phase which exhibited Britain's wealth and power throughout the country in a series of magnificent secular buildings, ranging from Decimus Burton's (1800–88) and Charles Barry's (1795–1860) London clubs, including Burton's Athenaeum of 1827–30 and Barry's Reform Club of 1837–41, to William Playfair's (1789–1857) National Gallery of Scotland of 1850–54, and culminating in Harvey Lonsdale Elmes's (1814–47) and Charles

6 Britain's greatest Neo-Classical building, Harvey Lonsdale Elmes's and Charles Cockerell's St George's Hall, Liverpool, 1841–54

Cockerell's St George's Hall in Liverpool of 1841–54, which remains Britain's most magnificent Neo-Classical monument (fig.6).

In the other corner were the Goths. Gothic architecture (or *Gothick*, as it was then known) had been used in the 18th century largely for picturesque effect or 'aristocratic whimsicality'[8] in country retreats or follies, but in the first few decades of the 19th century it emerged as something of a moral force, inspired by Augustus Welby Northmore Pugin (1812–52) – architect, devout Catholic and, most significantly, polemicist. Through his writings,[9] Pugin offered Gothic architecture as the only true 'Christian Style', thus proposing a return to an 'Age of Faith' that would both be free of Greek or Roman pagan contamination and act as an antidote to the intemperance and increasing materialism that he perceived in British society; and it was within this stylistic battleground that an architectural opportunity of national importance arose in the 1830s.

The Houses of Parliament – or to give it its correct title, The Palace of Westminster – had been the seat of British democracy since the 13th century, but for most of this period it had been a democracy of a very limited kind. In 1832, however, the Representation of the People Act had signalled the first significant broadening of the franchise to the growing middle class. It was a hugely controversial reform and had been bitterly opposed by the then Prime Minister, the much-sculpted Duke of Wellington; and as if to confirm the moral rectitude of his and his supporters' position, almost the entire Palace of Westminster was destroyed by an act of God in the form of a massive fire on the night of 16 October 1834, just two years after the passing of the act.[10] Both Houses of Parliament were lost and by the morning of the 17th, only Westminster Hall and a few other buildings such as the Jewel Tower and the Undercroft Chapel remained on the smoking, charred and blackened site.

A Royal Commission was established in 1835 to oversee the rebuilding of the Palace, and there immediately ensued a vigorous and at times

extremely heated debate between the Goths and the Classicists as to the most appropriate architectural style for this most symbolic of national buildings. In June, the commission publicly rejected the Classical style (on this occasion as being too closely associated with Republicanism) and confirmed that an architectural competition would be held the following year to select a design and an architect to undertake the rebuilding, in a suitably English 'Gothic or Elizabethan' style. From a total of 97 proposals, that of architect Charles Barry (1795–1860) was selected the following year.

Barry, like a number of his contemporaries, was neither a committed Goth nor Classicist and was equally at home producing architecture in either style, having already completed several Gothic churches and numerous Classical city buildings before entering the competition. Such was the scale and national importance of this commission, however, that he played something of a trump card by enlisting the assistance of Pugin himself – the high priest of Gothic – thus combining his own skill in planning and experience of the design of major buildings with Pugin's unique grasp of medieval detail, which proved to be an unbeatable combination.[11] The result of this marriage of convenience was a new public building which successfully captured the contemporary British public's imagination, offered the world a new symbol of Britain as the historic home of democracy, and provided an exemplar for other British architects as to how the Gothic style could be applied to major civic buildings (fig.7). (This massive design and construction project was finally completed in 1868, some years after both Pugin's early death in 1852 and Barry's in 1860, having almost driven Barry to distraction during the latter years of his life.)

No sooner had Barry and Pugin been selected than a further Royal Commission was established – under the chairmanship of Prince Albert himself – to promote and encourage the integration of the Fine Arts within the buildings. As noted above, British sculptors were invited to submit examples of their work, with John Bell, William Calder Marshall and John Henry Foley being chosen to execute the majority of the statuary inside the building. Prince Albert played a very active part in this process over the next few years, including on one occasion when the commission was considering who should be appointed to carry out the major group of *Queen Victoria Flanked by Justice and Clemency*, having a note passed around the meeting saying: 'His Royal Highness thinks Mr Gibson should have it', and it was thus that one of Albert's favourite sculptors, John Gibson (1790–1866), was selected. The quantity of statuary provided within and without the buildings was quite staggering, with most notable London-based sculptors eventually gaining commissions by the time of the completion of all the decoration in 1876. But it is the extensive architectural sculpture, integral to the building and essential to the architecture, which particularly interests us. When it came to the appointment of architectural sculptors, most were within Barry the architect's personal gift and he already had in mind the man who would lead this vast task of detailed design, sculptural modelling and stone carving.

While supervising the construction of his design for King Edward's School in Birmingham (1833–7) Barry had come across a young stonemason, John Thomas (1813–62), who: 'was employed here carving some ornamental bosses from wax models when, being delayed for the want of an original to work from, he designed one himself. This was shown to the architect, who saw at once that the designer was a man of superior abilities.'[12] Thus Barry instructed that Thomas should execute all the remaining stone and wood carving at the school – a task which took him three further years. Thomas, who had been orphaned at 13, was steeped in the Gothic, having spent much of his apprenticeship with a local stonemason restoring lettering and sculptural detail on various ancient gravestones around his native Gloucestershire, after which he joined his brother, an architect in Birmingham, with whom he mastered technical drawing. Barry (like a number of architects subsequently), took this young artist – 'who was basically a glorified stonemason'[13] – under his wing, sending him on a tour of Belgium to study medieval Gothic architecture, before starting work on the Houses of Parliament. On Barry's recommendation, Thomas was appointed as one of the master masons in 1841, and in 1846 was confirmed as 'Superintendent of Stone Carving'.

Thomas's responsibilities were extensive – supervising all the carving on the building, including both the statuary which was carried out off-site as well as the carved architectural detail which proceeded along with the construction of the building. Thomas was:

7   The extraordinary depth and quality of the architectural sculpture on the Palace of Westminster, 1840–76

himself responsible for a prodigious amount of work, including the statues on the north and south fronts, the panels with the arms of the Kings and Queens of England from William the Conqueror to Queen Victoria, the statues and bosses for the Victoria Tower and the bosses in St Stephen's Hall. He later made the bronze statues of Stephen Langton, Archbishop of Canterbury, and William, Earl of Salisbury, for the House of Lords.[14]

We are fortunate to also have a record of the procedure for the execution of the stone carving as described by Thomas Garland, one of Thomas's team, in Alfred Barry's *The Architect of the New Palace of Westminster*,[15] who confirmed that:

> there was generally a small drawing made in Mr. Barry's office showing the general design, which was enlarged by Mr. Thomas and others, and the models were then made in the shops full size, Mr. Barry invariably giving his personal attention to them before they were carved . . . I certainly never received any instructions from anyone except from Mr. Barry and Mr. Thomas, the foreman never allowing anything to be cast for the carver until he had given his formal approval.'[16]

(This would suggest that Pugin's contribution to the detailed design of the building related almost entirely to the completion of the interiors, with Barry leading the design of the Gothic stone detailing, along with Thomas.) And so, it was young Thomas, and his extensive band of many hundred stonemasons, who were responsible for the carved sceptres, labels, badges, shields, coats of arms, inscriptions, bosses, angels, lions, griffins, and every other element of stone decoration on this vast Gothic palace (fig.8).

Like a number of other successful stonemasons turned architectural sculptors, Thomas went on to undertake further work that would traditionally have been within the realm of Fine Art sculptors, and indeed, his achievements on the Palace of Westminster were noted by Prince Albert himself who described him as an 'unassuming self taught genius in his way'[17] and commissioned him to carry out a considerable amount of architectural sculpture for both Buckingham Palace, including two large reliefs of *War* and *Peace*, and Windsor Castle, where Thomas was responsible for the decoration of numerous rooms. By the 1850s, Thomas was recognised as one of Britain's leading architectural sculptors and, like so many of his fellow craftsmen, expended an astonishing energy constantly travelling the country to provide decoration to buildings from Bristol (the Fine Arts Academy of 1857 and the West of England Bank of 1858) to Edinburgh (the Life Association Building of 1855–8 and the Freemasons' Hall of 1858), while also managing to provide the Great Fountain at Castle Howard in Yorkshire, two lions on Brunel's Menai Bridge in Wales and life-size wooden figures of British judges for the Dining Hall at Lincoln's Inn in London. As his remarkable abilities became more publicly acknowledged, commissions for statues and busts soon followed, including *Thomas Attwood* in Birmingham (1858) and *Queen Victoria* in Maidstone (1863); and by the end of his career he was even being invited to undertake that highest category of sculpture – Ideal Works – including *A Naiad* for Queen Victoria herself, and finally undertaking several architectural commissions in his own right, such as the design of Somerleyton Hall in Suffolk which was rebuilt between 1844 and 1857 for self-made Victorian businessman, Sir Samuel Morton Peto.

While there were few stone carvers or masons who could match John Thomas's meteoric rise from orphaned apprentice mason to sculptor to the Queen, the journey from stone carver to architectural sculptor (and occasionally on to Fine Art sculptor) was one which many talented craftsmen achieved during the 19th century, such as the equally capable (and industrious) Albert Hodge (1875–1918), who rose from the humblest of beginnings on the tiny Hebridean Isle of Islay in Scotland, or Joseph Armitage (1880–1945), the son of a Yorkshire house painter, both of whom

8   The kings and queens of Britain beneath their Gothic baldachins on the Victoria Tower

went on to become leading architectural sculptors in their day. Their career paths were various, but usually included an apprenticeship with a firm of monumental masons and study at a regional school of art, which, if they were particularly talented, was often followed by further study in London and occasionally in Paris or Rome (fig.9) (though many of their contemporaries remained as employees of the many masonry companies, and within this context, still contributed architectural sculpture of a very high order). George Gilbert Scott, who became one of the most prolific of all the Gothic Revival architects, consistently engaged the London firm of Farmer and Brindley Limited on almost all his commissions, from the Albert Memorial in London to Manchester Town Hall, stating that William Brindley himself was 'the best carver I have met with and the one who best understands my views',[18] while the Glasgow firm of J. & G. Mossman Limited dominated sculpture in the city throughout the 19th century, providing much of the city's statuary as well as architectural sculpture, while also taking a leading role in the development of the teaching of sculpture at Glasgow School of Art and contributing significantly to the establishment of the Glasgow Fine Arts Institute.

For every young stonemason who was working his way up from what was then regarded as the lowest level of artistic society, there were also a small number of sculptors who, having been trained in the Fine Arts, also deigned to undertake architectural sculpture under the direction of architects, or occasionally in genuinely creative partnerships with them. For this class of architectural sculptors, the career path was entirely different. During the 19th century, the teaching of sculpture in schools of art such as the Royal Academy in London was constantly bemoaned by its practitioners. Unlike architects, who would pay to undertake a contractual pupillage with their masters, most sculptors learned as assistants in the studios of their successful elders and were paid for their work – indeed, without their own patrons, this was the only route to earning a living as a trainee

9   A typical stonemason's yard

Fine Art sculptor. In most cases, their days were spent along with the stone carvers, plasterers and figure carvers – supporting the work of the master sculptor, and in some cases (as with many employed masons), assistants were either content to spend their career as such or, unable to secure their own commissions, often working in the studios of several sculptors to increase their income.[19] But for most, there were always opportunities to contribute to the finished works, with some assistants even specifically hired for their specialist skills, whether in sculpting drapery, hair or foliage, for example. For the master sculptors, assistants were a necessity if they were to build up their workload and business, with some studios such as that of Sir Francis Chantrey (1781–1841) at its peak, resembling something close to a production line, as he attempted to keep up with the growing demand for his outstanding portraiture.

The quality of teaching in the studios was, as one would expect, hugely variable, with some sculptors, such as Edward Hodges Baily (1788–1867) and William Behnes (1795–1864), producing several prodigious assistants, whereas other assistants were largely exploited; and indeed, there were several instances of successful sculptors whom it was believed relied a little too much on the contribution of their assistants. This issue was brought to court in one instance when sculptor Richard Claude Belt (1851–1920) was accused of passing off the work of his assistants Thomas Brock (1847–1922) and Pierre François Verhyden (1843–1919) as his own (it being claimed during the hearing that his studio was fitted with a trap door down which they were forced to scurry if a patron turned up unexpectedly!)[20] The situation was complex, with many talented assistants lacking their employer's contacts and patrons, or the funds to survive on their own; several outstanding sculptors, including Brock and Albert Bruce-Joy (1842–1924), were only able to establish their own studios by continuing ongoing commissions inherited on the death of their principal. Being around the studio did, however, mean that assistants encountered potential patrons: visits to artists' studios by the upper classes were quite social events during the 19th century, as Mrs Adams-Acton, the sculptor's wife, confirmed: 'Society people, knowing nothing about Art, would come crowding to the studio in constant succession, making ridiculous remarks.'[21] Overall, however, and bearing in mind the inadequacies of the schools of sculpture, the role that working as an assistant contributed to the practical education of a sculptor far outweighed the many injustices of the system.

Overlaying all this artistic activity was, of course, a still relatively rigid class system. The upper classes had always been the main patrons of sculpture, and they continued to be so throughout the 19th century; but the century was also typified by a quite remarkable rise in the wealth and influence of a newly enfranchised middle class which soon led to a consequent boom in commemorative sculpture. Most sculptors still aspired to work for the upper classes, with the royal family continuing to be the most valued patrons, but socially, the sculptors themselves were generally looked down upon, as their efforts involved manual labour. This snobbery persisted within the profession with architectural sculpture often seen simply as stonemason's work – but for an aspiring and talented assistant with few social contacts and an employer who showed no sign of impending mortality it frequently offered the only route to independent work and the prospect of a return to portraiture and ideal works at a later date.

The other attraction to pursuing a career in architectural sculpture was, as we have seen in relation to the rebuilding of the Palace of Westminster, that while Prince Albert may have led the selection of sculptors for the extensive programme of statuary within the building, it was the architect Charles Barry who commissioned John Thomas to oversee all the architectural sculpture. There were numerous other similar, more modest opportunities throughout the length and breadth of Victorian Britain as the social gulf between many sculptors, master masons and architects was not so great. It was predominantly architects who were the patrons of architectural sculptors (albeit that they often had to convince their client of their preferred sculptor's merits), with many architects and sculptors establishing mutually advantageous long-term relationships and even close friendships throughout the 19th and early 20th centuries. As well as Barry's working relationship with Thomas, there was the brilliant Alexander 'Greek' Thomson's reliance on sculptor John Mossman (for whom he even designed a studio), William Burges's consistent use of Thomas Nicholls, and, in the 20th century, John James Burnet's work with William Reid Dick (for whom he also designed a studio), as well as Herbert Baker's encouragement and promotion of Charles Wheeler, in this latter case with Baker even financing Wheeler's Grand Tour of Europe in the same way that Barry had done for Thomas a century earlier.

And so, by 1851, we find this motley group of talented British sculptors, master masons and stone carvers, from an astonishing variety of backgrounds, busily working alongside the nation's architects, with mallet and chisel or modelling clay in hand, poised, ready to celebrate and commemorate their country's astonishing commercial, industrial and military success in exquisitely carved stonework.

2

ONE TRUE CHRISTIAN STYLE

If the Great Exhibition had been a celebration of Britain's new-found global supremacy, then the rebuilding of the Palace of Westminster became its icon – the 'Mother of Parliaments' from where Victoria's mighty empire was effectively ruled – and thus its Gothic architecture became inextricably linked in the minds of most Britons with democracy (albeit still of a very limited form), an evangelising Christianity (which they aimed to promote to heathens around the world), an imaginary merry, medieval England (which was almost entirely fictitious) and the moral superiority of the British (to which as much of the rest of the world as possible ought to be subjected). It was a powerful concoction of values and aspirations which turbo-charged the Gothic style into a leading position.

If Pugin had kindled the flame, it was to be the hugely influential art critic John Ruskin (1819–1900) who would become the torchbearer for Gothic architecture throughout the remainder of the 19th century and who through his books and pamphlets would offer it as an antidote to all the evils of an industrialised society. Like Pugin, his writing was powerful and persuasive, and his arguments and instructions would not only sustain the Gothic Revival but also hugely influence the Pre-Raphaelites as well as the later Arts and Crafts architects, artists and craftsmen, and indeed many of his pronouncements, such as 'truth to materials' and 'the honest expression of structure', would provide much of the moral tone of Modernism a century later. Though neither a sculptor nor an architect, such is Ruskin's importance that an understanding of the man and his writings is required, as they provide a constant undercurrent to much of what follows.

The son of a father with whom he shared a love of the romantic works of Byron, Shakespeare and Sir Walter Scott, and an evangelical Christian mother, after winning the Newdigate Prize at Oxford University it seemed that young Ruskin might be destined for a life as a poet, but with the publication and success of the first volume of *Modern Painters* in 1843 at the age of just 24, there opened up the new prospect of a career as an art critic. His extensive travels with his parents to the Lake District, Scotland and throughout Europe developed a love of nature, a particular fascination with geology and a life-long love affair with both the Alps and Venice which eventually extended his writing to cover geology, mythology, ornithology, literature, education, botany and political economy as well as painting, sculpture and architecture. In *Modern Painters* he rejected the picturesque conventions of the Old Masters – or the 'pestilential art of the Renaissance', as he described it[1] – and sprang to the defence of J.M.W. Turner, arguing that he and his fellow contemporary landscape painters were honestly and accurately portraying nature in all its beauty, and thus more genuinely honouring God's work.

Pugin had already established the powerful link between Gothic architecture and a return to the religious piety of the Middle Ages as an antidote to the ills of Victorian society, but it was to be Ruskin, with the help of the Ecclesiological Society within the Anglican church, who would wrestle Gothic architecture from Pugin's Roman Catholic clutches and offer it as the natural expression of evangelical

10 One of Ruskin's watercolours of Venice

of the devil, while in *The Stones of Venice* of 1851–3 (fig.10) he traced the cultural history of the Republic of Venice, offering its transition from a culture founded on faith to one based on rational thought as the principal reason for its decline: 'The Rationalist kept the arts and cast aside the religion. This rationalistic art is the art commonly called Renaissance, marked by a return to pagan systems . . . Instant degradation followed in every direction – a flood of folly and hypocrisy.'[3] And when it came to architecture: 'the harm which has been done by Claude and the Poussins is as nothing when compared to the mischief effected by Palladio, Scamozzi, and Sansovino . . . we shall find in it partly the root, partly the expression, of certain dominant evils of modern times.'[4] This acted both as a further justification for the superiority of Christian Gothic architecture over that of the Renaissance and also as a warning to Britain, whose moral and spiritual health he believed to be corrupted by its pursuit of industrial Capitalism and what he saw as its shoddy mass-produced products.

His model for the British Empire (as a committed Imperialist) was the Christian Venetian Empire rather than the pagan empires of Greece or Rome, and he went on to develop his philosophy in considerable detail with Renaissance architecture ('dead architecture'),[5] Roman Catholicism, mass-production and industrialisation portrayed as the contents of Pandora's box, while Gothic architecture ('Living Architecture'),[6] Anglicanism, individual craftsmanship and honest labour were offered as being self-evidently God's work. He rejected 'The use of cast or machine-made ornaments of any kind'[7] and proclaimed that: 'All the stamped metals, and artificial stones, and imitation wood and bronzes, over the invention of which we hear daily exultation – all the short, and cheap, and easy ways of doing that whose difficulty is its honour – are just so many new obstacles in our already encumbered road.'[8] He was appalled by almost every element of the industrialising society which was developing around him, with even the nation's new railways not escaping his scorn as they 'transmute a man from a traveller into a living parcel'.[9]

Anglicanism. The Anglican Ruskin was always keen to distance himself from the Catholic Pugin, dismissing him in *The Stones of Venice* – which was first published in the year of the Great Exhibition – as 'not a great architect but one of the smallest of conceivable architects'.[2]

His moralising tone (which was to become a fundamental element of his criticism) was further developed in *The Seven Lamps of Architecture* of 1849 in which he cast machine-made products as the work

Fortunately for Ruskin's architectural followers, he set out exactly what was required to keep them on the true path to righteousness – as he explained in the second book of *The Stones of Venice*: 'I believe, then, that the characteristic or moral elements of Gothic are the following, placed in the order of their importance: Savageness, Changefulness, Naturalism, Grotesqueness, Rigidity and Redundance',[10] with each element then further defined in voluminous detail. Gothic architecture had not merely to be replicated, but revived as a living language, practised by a new noble class of craftsmen who would provide their own creative contributions to the production of works of architecture in much the same way that their forebears had done in constructing the great Gothic cathedrals. And so, the architects with whom they would collaborate were instructed to: '1: Never encourage the manufacture of any article not absolutely necessary in the production of which *Invention* has no share. 2: Never demand an exact finish for its own sake, but only for some practical or noble end. 3: Never encourage imitation or copying of any kind except for the sake of preserving record of great works.'[11]

He encouraged the picturesque, the asymmetrical and an architecture which responded to human needs and local conditions, which honestly replicated nature, honestly expressed the building's materials and structure, and which was built by hand by honest craftsmen.

When it came to suitable architectural sculpture, Ruskin, as we would now expect, was not short of opinions and instruction, both as to suitable subject matter and the process of its execution – out were swags, heraldic symbols, inscriptions, scrolls, bands, garlands, armour, instruments and tools, to be replaced on all occasions by the replication of natural forms with 'all noble ornamentation (being) the expression of man's delight in God's work'[12] and thus 'all most lovely forms and thoughts are directly taken from natural objects' 'and also the converse of this, namely, that forms which are *not* taken from natural objects *must* be ugly'.[13] As expected, he provided schedules of suitable examples in *The Stones of Venice Vol 1*:

1. Abstract lines
2. Forms of Earth (Crystals)
3. Forms of Water (Waves)
4. Forms of Fire (Flames and Rays)
5. Forms of Air (Clouds)
6. (Organic Forms) Shells
7. Fish
8. Reptiles and insects
9. Vegetation (A) Stems and Trunks
10. Vegetation (B) Foliage
11. Birds
12. Mammalian animals and Man.[14]

But simply replicating the forms of nature was not sufficient to satisfy Ruskin – to achieve beauty and suitably honour The Lord, the works should also be executed by craftsmen who must be free to express their own creativity, as he believed had been the case in both medieval Venice and England, thus: 'Ornament, as I have often before observed, has two entirely distinct sources of agreeableness: one, that of the abstract beauty of its forms, which, for the present, we will suppose to be the same whether they come from the hand or the machine; the other, the sense of human labour and care spent upon it.'[15] He even went as far as to state that, 'so long as men work *as* men, putting their heart into what they do, and doing their best, it matters not how bad workmen they may be, there will be that in the handling that will be above all price';[16] and that 'I believe the right question to ask, respecting all ornament, is simply this: Was it done with enjoyment – was the carver happy while he was about it?'[17] It was to all intents and purposes a proposal to reintroduce medieval guilds of skilled craftsmen as an antidote to the industrialised methods of construction typified by the Crystal Palace. Rather astonishingly, such was the power of his rhetoric that he soon developed both a messianic flock of supporters within the general population (with Ruskin's pious beliefs chiming with their own) and – despite the inherent conflict

11   The central hall of the Oxford University Museum of Natural History, 1855–60

between his proposed methods of execution and the industrialisation of the building construction process which was then underway – a very considerable number of followers within the architectural profession.

At around the time of the Great Exhibition, events were coalescing in Oxford which were to provide Ruskin with just the opportunity that he sought to provide a practical example of his revitalised Gothic architecture. The university's Honour School of Natural Science had been founded in 1850, shortly after which Sir Henry Acland – then the Regius Professor of Medicine at the university – proposed that a new museum should be constructed to bring together the study of science within the colleges around a permanent exhibition of geology, zoology, minerology, anatomy, physiology, astronomy and medicine, thus offering students the opportunity to study 'Nature as the Second Book of God'. During an earlier visit to Dublin, Ruskin had admired the work of architects Thomas Newenham Deane and Benjamin Woodward and of their stone carvers, the O'Shea brothers, James and John, and their nephew Edward Whelan, on their new building for Trinity College. Ruskin thus proposed their appointment to Acland for what was to become the Oxford University Museum of Natural History. While Deane and Woodward's Gothic architecture proved generally acceptable to Ruskin, it was the O'Sheas' carving of flora and fauna that in his view was quite exceptional. Funds were raised for the building and construction commenced in 1855.

The Natural History Museum building really ought to be even better known than it is as, despite its rather dour and worthy exterior, it has one of the finest Gothic Revival interiors in Europe. The plan is straightforward (and sadly for Ruskin almost entirely symmetrical), with a central top-lit nave and two side aisles within a main central court, off which are the more modest teaching spaces and repositories for the university's collections. Almost certainly heeding Ruskin's diktat that there should be no 'deceptive concealments of structure',[18] Woodward produced an elegant skeletal steel and cast-iron frame which soared upwards into a series of Gothic arches, decorated with steel branches and leaves, below a delicate, glazed roof (fig.11). Unfortunately, Ruskin had already decreed that 'true architecture does not admit iron as a constructive material',[19] but if the building's structure was somewhat compromised (in Ruskin's view), the O'Sheas' architectural sculpture within the surrounding masonry was exactly what he aspired to, both in its exquisite craftsmanship and in terms of its consistency with his doctrines. Here were the moral elements of Ruskin's Gothic, carved in stone atop the polished column shafts of various British rocks – themselves an acknowledgement of the vast range of God's creation. Each column capital was entirely unique and together they offered an extraordinary range of flora and fauna (based on specimens provided by the university's Botanic Gardens) which were further developed to include birds and small mammals within the branches and stems (figs 12 and 13). It was a virtuoso display of the sculptor's art – sharp, precise, finely detailed and full of surface intricacies – and possessed an anatomical and botanical accuracy that makes each of these

12   A column capital in the Oxford University Museum of Natural History

13 A column capital in the Oxford University Museum of Natural History

minor masterpieces as fresh today as when they were first carved. As an expression of Ruskin's ideals they were never bettered; and in contrast to most other Gothic Revival sculpture, they were entirely the original work of exceptionally skilled craftsmen, rather than simply copies of earlier medieval designs.

Thomas Woolner, the only member of the Pre-Raphaelite Brotherhood who was a sculptor, provided the external surround to the main entrance and numerous other sculptors, including Alexander Munro and Henry Weekes, completed the statues of eminent men of science which ring the ground floor arcades, but sadly, while the O'Sheas completed their work on the interior of the building, most of their planned further carving on the exterior was suspended, thus adding to its rather stiff and puritanical expression. The reason for their eventual departure from the building site is the stuff of legend and explanations range from rather too naturalistic carved combinations of monkeys and cats to one of the O'Sheas shouting 'monkeys' at a member of the university's Convocation when asked what he was carving. The rather prosaic reality, however, was that the project was simply over budget. The university instructed the sculptors to leave the site, and when the O'Sheas continued in their efforts to complete their commission, they were accused of defacing the building and carrying out unauthorised work. As a parting gift they did, however, manage to add caricatures of the Members of the Convocation as parrots and owls over the main entrance (with Acland later having the offending faces removed). This was, perhaps, just one of the risks of employing independently minded craftsmen.

The O'Sheas and Whelan went on to work with Woolner on Alfred Waterhouse's Manchester Assize Courts, which was sadly destroyed during the Second World War, but their fine carvings of further capitals – which on this occasion portrayed various gruesome forms of medieval punishment such as *Ye Punishment of Ye Wheel* and *For Scolding Women* – fortunately survived and were accommodated within the replacement building. Such was Woolner's admiration for their work that he employed one of the O'Sheas to carve the corbels in his own studio in London, writing to the critic Francis Turner Palgrave that, 'O'Shea is doing his work like a man, and the corbels are bursting forth into violets, roses, thistles, ivies, geraniums & other things lovelier than their names … such rapidity of workmanship I never saw, he does 3 corbels a day!'[20] Ruskin attempted to further promote James O'Shea as a Fine Art sculptor but with limited success and so, much to his disappointment, O'Shea returned to his native Ireland, where he spent most of what remained of his career carving stone Celtic crosses.

Ruskin's disappointment with many aspects of the design and construction of the museum was almost inevitable as, in the end, it had – like almost every other effort to produce a truly medieval style of architecture in industrial Victorian Britain – come up against the hard reality of contemporary building procurement and technology. While the Pre-Raphaelites could evoke a mythical age of chivalry, Arthurian integrity and joyful labour in their paintings, their contemporaries in the architectural profession were constrained by very real budgets, building contractors who had little interest in the happiness of their workers, and clients who continued to want their buildings finished as soon as possible so that they could occupy them. Ruskin's followers therefore found themselves constantly attempting to put his theories into practice with varying degrees of success, and consequently with varying levels of enthusiasm and commitment, ranging from being true believers to intellectually curious agnostics.

Those who shared his religious and aesthetic convictions included: the rather brilliant William Butterfield (1814–1900), who had been encouraged by Ruskin to develop a richer brick polychromatic style (largely in lieu of architectural sculpture) and who was the darling of the Ecclesiologists – refusing on principle to build for Catholics (or participate in architectural competitions); the equally talented George Edmund Street (1824–81), who through sheer industry would go on to build much more, including one of the most important public buildings in the Gothic style, namely the Royal Courts of Justice of 1867–82 (see p.49); the less successful, but equally interesting and largely self-taught, Edward William Godwin (1833–86), whose Northampton Town Hall we shall go on to consider shortly; and the highly imaginative William Burges (1827–81) who was perhaps closest to the Pre-Raphaelites as an artist, and shared their quest for a medieval nirvana. But the contribution of these architects to the British Victorian building stock was utterly dwarfed by the two giants of the latter part of the 19th century, George Gilbert Scott (1811–78) and Alfred Waterhouse (1830–1905), whom H.S. Goodhart-Rendel rather cruelly described as 'the leader(s) of the architectural traders',[21] and whose work we shall return to later.

Continuing with the investigation of Ruskin's impact on the development of architectural sculpture, Northampton Town Hall (1861–4) offers another valiant attempt to realise his True Principles – indeed Godwin himself claimed that his design was entirely founded on *The Stones of Venice*.[22] Godwin is yet another fascinating Victorian architect who would go on to develop an interest in all things Japanese, becoming the artist-architect *par excellence* of the Aesthetic Movement, which he founded with his friends, the painter James McNeill Whistler and the playwright Oscar Wilde (as well as being the lover of actress Ellen Terry), but in the early 1860s, we find him still in sackcloth and ashes in Northampton.

Though his Town Hall now appears to be the type of asymmetrical composition of which Ruskin would have wholeheartedly approved, as the result of the addition of a corner tower in 1892, Godwin's original building (like the Oxford Museum) was actually symmetrical, with a central arcaded three-bay entrance loggia below a traditional town hall balcony with clock tower above, behind which lay his suitably medieval Great Hall (fig.14). The ground floor offers an implied arcade with lancet windows, plate tracery and carved tympana within each arch, while above, the first floor has double lancet windows divided by columns supporting sculptures of the medieval kings of England, saints and a single queen – *Victoria* – beneath stone canopies, with the main entrance flanked by female figures representing truth and justice. While the statues dominate the facade, with their period garb offering a suitably Arthurian vibe, it is the quantity and quality of the supporting

14   Edward Godwin's Gothic Revival Northampton Town Hall, 1861–4

15   Part of the extensive architectural sculpture of Northampton Town Hall by Richard Boulton of Birmingham

16   One of the many medieval scenes on the Town Hall's column capitals

architectural sculpture which is the highlight of the building and which represents one of the finest and certainly the most complete programmes of decorative stone sculpture of any building within the entire Gothic Revival.

Every column capital is intricately carved with an extraordinary variety of individual compositions in which natural foliage encloses dioramas presenting scenes from either local history, in the case of the ground floor arcade, or from the lives of the kings in the capitals which support their aedicular frames. Each of the ground floor tympana have outstanding, deeply modelled reliefs of historical scenes from Northamptonshire's Middle Ages, while the deep cills to the ground floor windows are carved with the coats of arms of local families; and all this is in addition to sharply cut cinquefoils, trefoils, decorated string courses, carved brackets, a pierced balustrade and the masses of foliage and fauna which decorate the bands to the lancet windows, all of which is set against a background of banded polychromatic sandstone (fig.15). Perhaps most impressive of all, is that, despite the almost overwhelming quantity of decoration, Godwin's composition is so finely judged that his smooth ashlar base provides both the perfect foil to the extensive carving and successfully introduces something of the 'Savageness' which his guide Ruskin had prescribed.

The stone carving is all the work of one sculptor and his team, Richard Lockwood Boulton (1832–1905), with whom Godwin had worked previously and whom he had nominated to the noble burghers of Northampton. When one councillor suggested that they should instead seek a local sculptor, Godwin stood firm, stating not only that Boulton could be relied upon to execute his drawings more favourably than any other, but also that he had educated the man himself including the study of Ruskin's writings. Boulton, like so many fine architectural sculptors, was the son of a stonemason and worked for many years with his elder brother, William, before moving to Birmingham where he established his own stone yard. Richard Lockwood Boulton & Sons eventually employed no less than four of his sons, adding wood carving and ornamental brasswork to their skills which they applied to numerous Gothic

Revival churches throughout central England. While Boulton's naturalistic foliage is consistent with the work of the O'Shea brothers in Oxford, his treatment at Northampton differs markedly. The O'Sheas' carving is precise, entirely accurate and life-like, whereas Boulton's work (almost certainly as directed by Godwin) is purposely naïve and rather stylised, thus contributing to and supporting the medieval architecture. While it is essentially archaic in its nature, crucially, it was, as Ruskin demanded, entirely original work – not merely copied from the past, but living, breathing, new Gothic work, executed by a skilled independent craftsman (fig.16).

Another contemporary Goth – who happened to be a close friend of Godwin, and who similarly built relatively little but contributed hugely to the development of Victorian architectural sculpture – was the rather eccentric and highly creative William Burges (1827–88) who designed not only architecture, but also sculpture, metalwork, jewellery, furniture and stained glass. Burges did not share Street and Butterfield's religious convictions, nor, despite his numerous writings, was he a prophet like Pugin or Ruskin, but he was both a serious scholar of medieval architecture (who travelled throughout Europe and beyond, drawing, measuring and recording every aspect of the Gothic architecture that he saw) and perhaps the most romantic of all the Goths, whose architecture walked a fine line between accurate historicism and idealised fantasy. His first significant commission was Saint Fin Barre's Cathedral (1863–79) in Cork (one of his very few competition successes) and here he produced designs for an astonishing 1,260 sculptures including 32 gargoyles, each with the heads of mythical beasts which were executed by the sculptor Thomas Nicholls. Burges provided sketches for each sculpture from which Nicholls developed plaster models and these were then carved in stone in situ by a band of extremely skilled local stonemasons. The tympanum over the main entrance, which depicted a scene from the book of Revelation with the divine in the upper register and the mortals below, is an exceptional design, with the Victorian critic Charles Eastlake suggesting that 'no finer examples of decorative sculpture have been produced during the Revival'.[23] Perhaps the most interesting aspect of the tympana is the modelling of the three central angels, whose sweeping robes and long, sounding horns show the influence of the Pre-Raphaelites and almost anticipate the graceful (occasionally almost ghostly) style of the late 19th-century symbolists such as George Frampton and Alfred Gilbert.

Nicholls had first assisted Burges on his commission for the refurbishment of Gayhurst House in Buckinghamshire (1858–72) and by then he was already well established as an architectural sculptor (or 'artisan-sculptor' as the *Art Journal* described him on 1 June 1862) in and around London from his stone yard (soon to become studio) in Lambeth. He had exhibited several fine reliefs at the International Exhibition of 1862 in London – almost certainly part of Burges's restoration of Waltham Abbey – while the *Hampshire Telegraph and Sussex Chronicle*, 3 December 1853, recorded that he 'had been much employed in the neighbourhood of late' and that his stone carving at Redhill Church had been 'admirably executed'.[24] Meanwhile their edition of 8 September 1855 commends the carving of his new gargoyles on St Olave's Church in Chichester. His meeting with Burges in Buckinghamshire, however, represented a turning point in his career and the two formed an artistic partnership which lasted until Burges's early death at 53 in 1881, after which Nicholls completed numerous then unfinished commissions including the animal wall at Cardiff Castle.

Shortly after the start of the construction of the cathedral in 1868, Burges also started work for a new client who was to become his patron for the remainder of his career. This was John Patrick Crichton-Stuart, the 3rd Marquess of Bute, whose family wealth derived from the coal mines and docks of South Wales which had made him (reputedly) the richest man in the world. It was to be the combination of the Marquess's patronage, Burges's almost unlimited imagination and Nicholls's craft

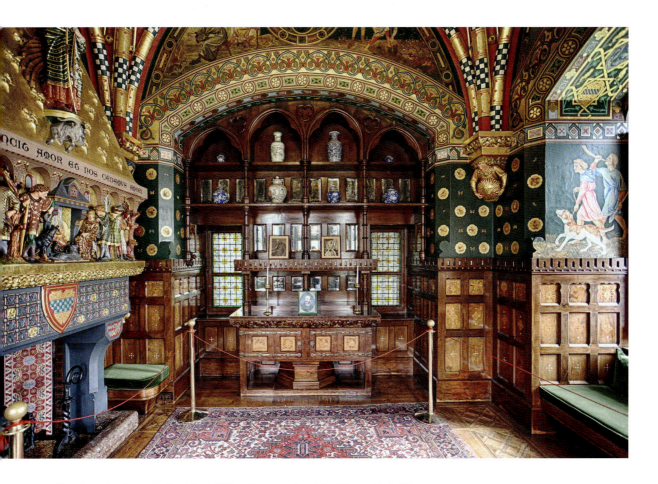

17   The sheer visual assault of architect William Burges and sculptor Thomas Nicholls's Cardiff Castle's Summer Smoking Room of 1868–90

that would produce some of the most remarkable interiors of the High Victorian period in Cardiff Castle (1868–90) and Castell Coch (1875–91). Despite a reputed income of around £300,000 a year, the Marquess was no dilettante. He had shocked English society by his conversion to Roman Catholicism (being confirmed by Pope Pius IX himself, at the age of 20), and he was well educated and scholarly, with an inquisitive mind, continuing his study of religion throughout his life as well as developing further interests in medievalism, the occult, linguistics and, of course, architecture, which offered him the possibility of reflecting the full range of his passions in a single work of art.

Like so many members of the Victorian upper middle and upper classes who owed their astonishing wealth to industry and trade, Lord Bute wished his own life to be as far removed from contemporary circumstances as possible, his religious convictions drawing him towards the same idealistic vision of medieval life which had already inspired the Pre-Raphaelites, Pugin and Ruskin. He had inherited his title and Cardiff Castle shortly before his first birthday, and by his coming of age in 1868 he was determined that, with Burges's help, it should be transformed into his own private, romantic medieval fantasy (fig.17). The first element to be completed was the soaring Clock Tower (a reworking of the tower from Burges's unsuccessful competition entry for the Royal Courts of Justice) – the first, and highest, of the four new towers which Burges would add, it still dominates the castle buildings and grounds and was the only one of Burges's new buildings to have been embellished externally with eight sculptures of the planets resting on pedestals carved with signs of the zodiac. The tower formed a suite of bachelor's rooms, comprising a bedroom, a servant's room and the Summer and Winter Smoking Rooms. Internally, the rooms were sumptuously decorated with gildings, carvings, mosaics and murals, many allegorical in style, depicting the seasons, myths and fables. The Summer Smoking Room which sat at the very top of the tower was a double-height space with an internal balcony that, through an unbroken band of windows, gave views of the sea to the south (which carried the Marquess's coal off to foreign lands) and the mountains to the north (from whence it was mined).

This is perhaps the most original of all the rooms within the castle which Burges created, with the combination of painted decoration, carved forms and the complexity of the space itself providing an almost overpowering immersion in his vision of the past (which was described by at least one critic as 'an onslaught').[25] Its theme is *The Universe* with the ornamentation culminating in a painted dome, where the stars and constellations appear above the sun, represented by a golden chandelier. The floor is made of coloured encaustic tiles, while the wall tiles are brightly painted with legends of the zodiac (by Frederick Smallfield), but it is Burges's and Nicholls's great carved stone chimneypiece which dominates the room and which is its dramatic highlight – swooping down from the balcony, it is surmounted by the winged figure of *Love* above a frieze carved with summer courting couples in high relief.

As the rest of the castle was restored, work progressed along the existing 18th-century range including the construction of the Guest Tower, the astonishing multi-vaulted Arab Room (inspired by Burges's visit to Constantinople, fig.18), the Chaucer Room, the Nursery, the Library, the Banqueting Hall, bedrooms for both Lord and Lady Bute and a new boundary wall to the castle complex, topped with nine animal sculptures. Nicholls was employed throughout and with Burges's imagination unconstrained (as a result of Bute's enthusiastic

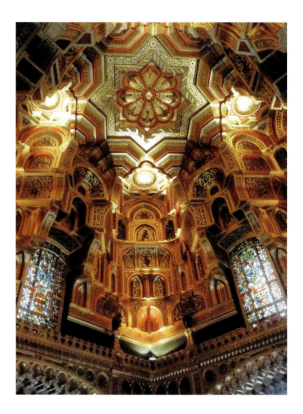

18   The Moorish fantasy of the Arab Room in Cardiff Castle

support and astonishing wealth), he largely avoided any kind of carved detail which involved more than a few repetitions, meaning both that Nicholls (and his considerable team of carvers) must rarely have been bored and as a result produced sculpture of a particular vitality. Unusually, much of the sculpture was also coloured and thus even more fully integrated into Burges's overall scheme of decoration, with the resulting effect that none of the spaces in Cardiff have even a hint of the gloom of much Gothic Victoriana – indeed such is the freshness and optimistic brightness of much of Bute and Burges's merry-making that it has a distinctly modern feel which almost heralds Scandinavian National Romanticism. The contrast with Burges's and Nicholls's collaboration in Cork could not be much greater, as in the cathedral the multitude of sculpted apostles, angels, wise virgins and craftsmen, while medieval in style, maintain a grounding in realism. However, in the castle, the figures, birds, animals and castellated details all have a naïve, almost cartoon-like quality, which draws on the sketchbooks of 13th-century Villard de Honnecourt, with whom we know Burges was fascinated. The contrast, too, with the highly accurate naturalistic sculptures in the Oxford Museum (and the creative freedom which the O'Sheas were awarded there) is extreme.

No sculptor could have undertaken this vast quantity of work alone and we know that Nicholls (though definitely personally responsible for the carving of the chimneypieces including the five statues over the chimneypiece in the Library), was assisted by a number of talented local sculptors and masons including the young William Goscombe John (1860–1952), the prominent late-Victorian Welsh sculptor who would later become a member of the New Sculpture Movement. Goscombe John helpfully left an account of the execution process, confirming that while a number of masons transferred from the site of Cork Cathedral to Cardiff, it was in Nicholls's studio in London 'where all the models for the sculpture at the Castle were made and afterwards sent down to Cardiff to be carried out in situ by skilled carvers sent down from London'.[26] Just three years after construction started on the restoration of Cardiff Castle, Lord Bute commissioned Burges to also restore the nearby Castell Coch, a ruined Norman tower house, and Nicholls and his team were again employed to provide a fairy-tale summer residence for his lordship. While the rugged cylindrical towers of its exterior here have a certain defensive menace, the interiors echo Cardiff Castle in their richness and pictorial romanticism with Burges's new suite of Hall, Drawing Room and Lord and Lady Bute's bedrooms being considered amongst his best work. Charles Handley-Read, one of the first to study and promote Burges's work, perhaps summed him up best: 'that whereas Burges's buildings are not infrequently flawed by imperfections, while certainly as an architect he is obviously surpassed by a number of his contemporaries, his decorations occupy a position of special eminence, if not supremacy'.[27] Certainly, his collaboration with Thomas Nicholls produced what are amongst the most outstanding examples of interior architectural sculpture of the Gothic Revival.

One of those contemporaries who surpassed Burges architecturally (and indeed most other competitors) was George Gilbert Scott. Scott is a deliciously Victorian character. The son of a vicar, he built a very successful practice during the 1830s and 1840s by specialising in workhouses, orphanages and lunatic asylums, before establishing himself as the 'go-to' architect for both new Gothic Revival churches, which he designed throughout the country on an industrial scale (church building itself having been given new impetus by the rapid expansion of the towns and cities, the Catholic Emancipation Act of 1829 and the new missionary zeal of the resuscitated Anglican church), as well as numerous church and cathedral renovations, including Ely, Durham, Salisbury and Exeter.[28] Unlike Butterfield, whom Ruskin had encouraged into experimenting with polychromatic brickwork in lieu of sculpture, Scott both encouraged sculptors to contribute to the decoration of his buildings and incorporated extensive architectural sculpture in all his work. While certainly lacking something of Ruskin's missionary zeal and often departing from his *True Principles*, he was nevertheless a committed Goth, sharing with Ruskin, to quote him, a 'religious horror of all styles of pagan origin'.[29] He certainly did as much as Charles Barry to popularise the style amongst the public, both through the scale of his output (almost a thousand buildings, designed, restored or altered), the scale of many of his commissions, and the quality of his best work (as well as being, as Goodhart-Rendel suggested, a consummate Victorian businessman).

As noted in Chapter 1, Scott developed a close working relationship with the firm of Farmer and Brindley early in his career and recommended them consistently to his clients throughout the 1850s, 1860s and 1870s as he continued with his ecclesiastical work and went on to add major public

19 A late Victorian stone carver's workshop

buildings to his burgeoning portfolio. William Farmer (1825–79) and William Brindley (1832–1919) had established their firm of architectural sculptors and ornamentalists on Westminster Bridge Road in Lambeth, London from where they dominated the trade for many years, providing stone and wood carving, sculpted figures, terracotta work and church furnishings while also running a very profitable sideline importing and selling marble (fig.19). They also worked extensively for Alfred Waterhouse (on over a hundred of his buildings), but it was Scott who was their 'most notable and prolific patron'.[30]

Farmer and Brindley led their team, as talented sculptors themselves, and employed and trained a substantial team of carvers and apprentices to support them on their various and numerous projects throughout the UK, with several notable sculptors serving their apprenticeship with them. These included John William Kitson (1846–88), who became one of the foremost architectural sculptors in the United States; also Harry Bates (1850–99), who commenced work with them in 1869, and Charles John Allen (1862–1956), who stayed with them for over ten years. Bates and Allen were later to contribute significantly to the New Sculpture Movement. Their workshops and yards in Lambeth were extensive and the vast majority of their sculpture was either produced there and delivered to site as required to maintain progress on building construction, or modelled there for local carving. The firm developed a close relationship with the nearby Lambeth School of Art (later the South London Technical School of Art), which many of their apprentices attended. While in many ways it was typical of the art schools and colleges throughout Britain at the time, providing an entry-level drawing and sculptural education for aspiring architectural sculptors – with Fine Art sculptors often commencing their education here too, but progressing on to the Royal Academy School or even the École des Beaux-Arts in Paris – its role in the development of British architectural sculpture in the second half of the 19th century cannot be underestimated. In turn, the School was also linked to Doulton & Company's large and successful pottery works, which had moved to Lambeth High Street in 1826. With the appointment of John Charles Lewis Sparkes (1833–1907) to the staff at Lambeth in 1857, the bond between the School, Doulton's pottery and Farmer and Brindley's studio was strengthened and much developed, to the benefit of all three, with Sparkes later recalling that: 'The manufacturers came without hesitation to the technical school who would not go near an art school. The head carvers of the district come to the men and lecture on their work and in fact it has been, as I hope it would be, a proper and much wanted development of the art school.'[31] Such was Lambeth's reputation for training in sculpture in particular that students who had already studied at regional schools would often transfer to Lambeth prior to progressing to the Royal Academy School; and such was Sparkes's reputation as a teacher of art that he was later appointed as the first Principal of the new National Art Training School in 1881.

By the 1860s, Gilbert Scott's practice 'had by now grown to a size at which contemporaries marvelled, and his familiarity with much of what his office was producing was of the sketchiest nature',[32] but we certainly know that there were three key projects from this period which were designed by his own hand in every aspect, and which represent the best of his work with Farmer and Brindley, namely the Albert Memorial in Kensington Gardens, the Foreign Office building in Whitehall and his magnificent Midland Grand Hotel at St Pancras Station.

The Memorial was, and is, the largest and most significant monument ever to be erected in Britain and, funded entirely by public subscription, was a tribute to Prince Albert which reflected both his considerable achievements and the nation's, and particularly Victoria's, great sense of loss (fig.20). Scott's design of 1863 took the form of an enormous Gothic baldachin – or ciborium as he described it – which framed a colossal, seated statue of the Prince, holding a copy of the catalogue of the Great Exhibition (modelled by John Henry Foley). Scott's sources were the 13th- and 14th-century Gothic Scaliger tombs in Verona and the more recent Gothic monument to his namesake Sir Walter Scott in Edinburgh, by George Meikle Kemp of 20 years earlier. He developed his detailed designs through a series of working drawings and a large model (made by Farmer and Brindley) to which Henry Hugh Armstead (who had overall responsibility for the coordination of the figurative sculptures), added the sculptural groups, for the Queen's final personal approval.[33]

Around Albert's statue, outside the four piers of his sheltering canopy, were various allegorical groups representing *Agriculture*, *Commerce*, *Engineering* and *Manufacturing*, with the four continents, complete with natives and appropriate wildlife (bison for the Americas, elephant for India, camel for Asia, etc.), framing the entire composition, between which steps cascaded out into Hyde Park on all sides (fig.21). These groups were executed by 11 sculptors, with most of the leading lights of the period involved, including John Bell, Henry Weekes, William Calder Marshall and Thomas Thorneycroft – this was, after all, Fine Art, rather than architectural sculpture, and with the direct link to the Queen, they represented the most prestigious of commissions. The base of the monument on which Prince Albert's statue sits is ringed with a continuous Frieze of Parnassus in which the Arts are depicted in 169 figures, by Henry Hugh Armstead (south and east) and John Birnie Philip (west and north), with the Sciences represented on the corner pillars (by Birnie Philip), while above, around the spire, are the four Cardinal Virtues (by James Redfern) below four golden angels, with the entire composition topped off with a richly decorated golden Christian cross. In addition to the sculpture, there was hardly a surface of Scott's architecture which escaped decoration, with mosaics in each of the four great external gables (representing the

20   One of the great symbols of the Victorian age – George Gilbert Scott's Gothic Revival Albert Memorial of 1863–75

21   Sculptor John Henry Foley's *Asia* with sculptor Henry Weekes's *Manufactures* in the background

Arts once more), a dedicatory legend around the four sides and a delightful starlit sky above Albert within the canopy itself, all by Clayton and Bell (whose stained-glass windows graced numerous Gothic Revival churches throughout what was then the empire). No doubt under the influence of Ruskin once more, their sources were the ancient mosaics of Venice, and indeed most of them were cast by Salviati's workshop in Murano.

Construction started in 1864, with Farmer and Brindley providing decorative surrounds to the mosaic panels, acanthus-scrolled bases and perpendicular Gothic canopies to the statues, spiral columns, lions with scrolls, Gothic tracery within the spire, the four attenuated pinnacles that frame the gables above the canopy and the gargoyles which drain it. The golden cross atop Scott's spire was finally installed in June 1868 and the scaffolding struck in 1871, but it would be many years until the vast number of sculptures were completed, with Foley's bronze of Prince Albert not finally installed until 1876, two years after his death,

with his pupil G.F. Teniswood overseeing the final casting and gilding. Overall, the monument was an extraordinary artistic achievement, with Scott not only producing one of the key edifices of the Gothic Revival but also orchestrating the integration of architecture, architectural sculpture and figurative sculpture in a single work of art. Art historian Charles Handley-Read described it as: 'ambitious, skilfully designed and built with the full gloss of a highly developed professionalism; it is an accurately judged memorial to the Consort and it sums up many elements in the High Victorian ethos – but it is both slightly brash and slightly vulgar'.[34, 35]

For Scott, it was a hugely prestigious commission which earned him a knighthood, and following his initial appointment and the publication of his design, it led to a deluge of work for his practice throughout the 1850s and 1860s. Despite initially losing the architectural competition for the new Foreign Office building in Whitehall, such was his reputation by then, that he was directly awarded the commission nevertheless and proceeded to develop a Gothic design for these important government buildings. Unfortunately for Scott, shortly before construction was due to commence, Lord Derby's Whig government fell and he was succeeded as Prime Minister by Lord Palmerston who detested the Gothic style and insisted that Scott now design a Classical building, if he wished to retain the commission. As Scott himself recalled in his biography *Recollections*, Palmerston: 'told me in a jaunty way that he could have nothing to do with this Gothic style, and that though he did not want to disturb my appointment, he must insist on my making a design in the Italian style, which he felt sure I could do quite as well as the other'.[36] Faced with the loss of such a prestigious public project, Scott relented and (much to the disgust of true believers which included several of his assistants who moved on principle to George Edmund Street's office) produced the Italianate design which survives today. Construction started in 1861 and concluded in 1868, by which time work was well underway on the Albert Memorial, and Scott engaged Farmer and Brindley along with John Birnie Philip and Henry Hugh Armstead (all of whom were then contributing to the Memorial) to provide the sculpture on the Foreign Office.

While Farmer and Brindley (notably their Harry Hems, 1842–1916) carried out the general architectural sculpture including the capitals, running friezes and minor tympana, Armstead and Philip produced allegorical scenes for the spandrels of the ground-floor arched windows. These included *Prudence*, *Valour*, *Government* and *The Continents* by Armstead and *Law*, *Art*, *Manufacture*, *Commerce*, *Science*, *Agriculture* and *Literature* by Birnie Philip. Armstead also executed reliefs representing *Justice*, *Fortitude*, *Truth* and *Obedience* over the main entrance, statues of the various colonial secretaries in niches in the upper storeys and medallion portraits of *Queen Elizabeth*, *Drake*, *Livingstone*, *Wilberforce*, *Cooke* and *Franklin* within further tympana. The spandrel sculptures are all in appropriately Classical garb and supported by winged angels, while *The Continents* have strong echoes of the Albert Memorial sculptures on the same themes, with *Africa*, for example, represented by a muscular, bare-breasted native against a background of a palm tree and a hippopotamus (fig.22). These are by far the best of the bunch – sharply carved, strong, fresh and vigorous (one might almost say Modern) – and make Philip's work look safe and academic. Despite the damage to Scott's reputation as a leading Goth, one has to marvel at his virtuosity in producing a Classical building of this standard. His initial Gothic design was not entirely lost, however, and he was able to use many of the details which he had already developed for the Government Offices on his grandest work of all – the new Midland Hotel (1865–74).

The Midland Railway Company announced its arrival in London in 1865 by holding an architectural competition for a new terminus which was to include a grand station hotel that would establish the company's brand in the capital city. While Scott's starting point was his unsuccessful Gothic Foreign Office design, he took great personal interest in the design of the hotel and, despite the vast workload of his practice:

> designed St Pancras with his own hand and with loving care; he disposed the towers and *flèches*, he drew out the elevations and thoughtfully related the openings in the walls, and then he applied the riches of 50 sketch-books to ornament the construction, inside and out, with eclectic 14th-century Gothic detail according to his stated philosophy. The result is a building which, had it been his only major work, would have placed him at once among the first half-dozen of Victorian architects (fig.23).[37]

From a distinctly Venetian portico on the Euston Road, Scott's building sweeps up to the great Gothic arch which originally provided the main entrance to the station. Above, a series of arches and balconies with Lombard friezes and bartizans step up to the top of the pinnacle-clad tower and from here the main bulk of the hotel shoots off to the east

22   The Foreign Office building of 1861–8 which Prime Minister Lord Palmerston instructed Gothic architect George Gilbert Scott to design in the Classical style

23   George Gilbert Scott's Midland (now St Pancras) Hotel in London of 1865–74

(completely screening civil engineer William Henry Barlow's glass and cast-iron train shed) where it concludes in a mighty clock tower which, on its completion, made it, briefly, the tallest building in Europe. It is a vibrant composition in which the essentially vertical proportions of the Gothic are finely balanced with the broad horizontals of continuous balconies and a richly bracketed parapet. While Ruskin would have approved of the exterior, the interior was a thoroughly modern Victorian building, with a cast-iron frame, concrete floors, fireproofing, elevators (called 'ascending chambers' at the time), flushing toilets, electric lighting and Britain's first revolving door, along with an interior decoration scheme that included extensive gold-leaf gilding, hand-painted wall patterns and heraldic murals, silk carpets and a spectacular double staircase, thus elevating it to a position as the most luxurious and expensive hotel in London.

Scott himself confirmed that he:

> designed windows suited to all positions, and of all varieties of size, form and grouping; doorways, cornices, parapets, and imaginary combinations of all these, carefully studying to make them all thoroughly practical, and suited to this class of building. I did not aim at making my style 'Italian Gothic;' my ideas ran much more upon the French, to which for some years I had devoted my chief study. I did however, aim at gathering a few hints of Italy, such as the pillar-mullion, the use of differently coloured materials, and of inlaying.[38]

In his memoirs he openly admitted that he had 'had a vast deal of bad carving done for me, it is true, some of it detestable. This has been mainly owing to the extent of my business, which has been always too much for my capacity of attending to it . . . Nevertheless where my real influence has been brought to bear, the results have been very different.'[39] He goes on to explain that in the stone carving at the hotel he 'urged the adoption of a bolder style, using natural foliage in a great degree, but attempting to get something of the boldness of the best conventional types. I think that this has been admirably attained by Mr Brindley.'[40]

Brindley and his team of nine stone carvers executed the gargoyles, capitals, head-stops, brackets and tracery in a combination of Ancaster and Ketton limestone and Mansfield red sandstone under Scott's exacting supervision (fig.24). In addition to his 50 sketchbooks, Scott had also by then amassed a considerable collection of medieval stone carvings from his travels around Europe which he made

24   London-based Farmer and Brindley produced the architectural sculpture on the Midland Hotel and on most of George Gilbert Scott's other major buildings

available to Brindley and his team, with several kept on site as benchmarks for particular sculptural elements – there were to be no Ruskinian creative contributions from the sculptors here; their role was to execute Scott's design down to the minutest detail.

Any lingering doubts that Gothic could be applied just as successfully to public buildings as to ecclesiastical were triumphantly swept aside by the hotel's exuberant design with which no-one was more delighted than Scott himself, writing that: 'It is often spoken of to me as the finest building in London; my own belief is that it is possibly *too good* for its purpose.'[41] He completed many more churches and public buildings, including the new Glasgow University (1864–70) in a similar style to the hotel, but 'with the addition of certain Scottish features'[42] – but none were to equal his achievement on behalf of the Midland Railway Company.

By the 1860s, Scott was far from alone in designing complex secular buildings for which there was no medieval precedent in the Gothic style. In 1867, proposals were submitted by 11 architects, including Scott and Alfred Waterhouse, for the design of the new Law Courts on the Strand, but to Scott's particular embarrassment it was his former assistant – who was 13 years his junior and whose professional integrity was now much more highly regarded, one George Edmund Street (1824–81) – whose design was selected to proceed to construction (despite the assessors proposing that Charles Barry once more carry out the planning for the successful architect – to which Scott successfully led the protests). Like so many Goths, Street was mainly an ecclesiastical architect and had never designed a large civic building before, but his proposals attracted the judges as a result of their simplicity and minimal Gothic detail: 'He had learned from Butterfield the art of elimination; he too could build boldly in brick, could leave plain surfaces tellingly alone, could do without crockets and trefoils.'[43] Construction was much delayed as a result of a site to the south of the Strand suddenly coming into contention and by the time that the first spade entered the ground in 1870, Street's competition-winning design had undergone a complete transformation (including the adoption of many of the best features of the unsuccessful competition entries), but nevertheless, with the exception of the main entrance with its screen, the gable to the Great Hall behind and *flèche* above, it continued to show a remarkable degree of restraint in comparison to most contemporary Gothic buildings of any significance, with rich detail used sparingly in contrast to great planes of smooth ashlar walling (fig.25).

Like Scott in his best work, there was no room for invention or any creative contribution from the stone carvers and indeed his lead assistant (Augustus W. Tanner) at the time marvelled at Street's ferocious industry in producing all the details for the masonry: 'on one occasion ... he covered fourteen sheets of double elephant paper with a mass of beautifully drawn full-size mason's mouldings, with in addition, on nearly every sheet, explanatory portions of the building ... All the details were written in and referenced complete, and for all practical purposes might have been given to the builder at once.'[44] Street produced 'a treasury of novel and beautiful details',[45] but he had no intention of relying on the building contractor to carry out his sculpture and went to considerable lengths to ensure that almost all the stone carving was omitted from the principal contract and was awarded instead to the firm of Earp and Hobbs Limited of London and Manchester, with whom Street had already worked on most of his Gothic churches, in which they had provided carved capitals, bosses, tracery, pulpits, fonts, reredos and much other decorative work.

Thomas Earp (1828–93) was born in Nottingham and studied at the School of Art there before travelling to London where, while working for building contractor George Myers, he contributed to several of Pugin's projects, before establishing his own business and yard in Lambeth. He entered into partnership with another architectural sculptor, Edwin Hobbs, in 1864, after which they opened premises in Manchester, which became Hobbs's

25 George Edmund Street's Gothic Revival Royal Courts of Justice on the Strand, 1873–82

domain. By 1873, when construction of the Law Courts commenced, Earp had established his reputation within the city, with perhaps his most famous work being the Queen Eleanor Memorial Cross at Charing Cross, having been completed in 1865. Fortunately, the Law Courts project was overseen by the Government's Office of Public Works, and thus, extensive records of every aspect of the project were retained. They provide a fascinating insight into the production of architectural sculpture during this period, including Earp's contemporary rates for stone carving which he submitted to Street, prior to being engaged. 'Ordinary carvers', Earp reported, 'were paid at least 1s per hour . . . while the foliage and animal carvers might receive 1s 6d'.[46] Figure carvers and sculptors, the aristocrats of the trade, could earn between 1s 6d and 2s, or even more. Earp also recommended the full-time services of a smith or at least a boy to continually sharpen the carvers' tools. The total estimated cost for the carving was £20,000, with an allowance of an additional £533 for the scaffolding (as Street had requested that most of the work be carried out in situ in the hope of reducing costs). Earp employed 20 carvers under the supervision of a foreman and, as Street expected of him, often also carved himself (fig.26). The carving consisted of 40 armorial shields, four free-standing gable figures (including

49

26 Sculptor Thomas Earp's extensive architectural sculpture on the Law Courts contrasted with the sheer planes of ashlar of architect George Street's architecture

Moses holding the tablets of the law, *Christ*, *King Alfred the Great* and *King Solomon*) and a few smaller figures who were also related to the purpose of the building. The shields, which were placed between the windows of the top floor, bore the coats of arms of the contemporary leaders of the legal profession including the then Lord Chancellor and Lord Chief Justice, while others included relevant virtues such as *Concordia*, *Prudentia* and *Rhetorica* as well as portraits of Street himself and the main contractor, Henry Bull. The remainder of the carving was predominantly floral decoration in the stiff leaf style of the early 13th century with the odd touch of humour, such as the decoration around the Judges' main entrance being a series of squabbling cats and dogs. With the long delay in commencing construction, the scale of the building complex and the quantity of decorative work, completion was not achieved until 1882, a year after Street's death, by which time the new building was described as 'a magnificent mausoleum to the Gothic Revival'.[47]

And so we come to the other giant of Victorian Gothic architecture who, along with Scott, dominated the architectural profession during the latter part of the 19th century – Alfred Waterhouse (1830–1905). Almost 20 years younger than Scott, Waterhouse began to eclipse him during the 1870s with the construction of three of the most substantial architectural commissions of the Victorian age – the immense Eaton Hall in Cheshire (1869–83) for the Duke of Westminster (almost entirely demolished in the 1960s),

Manchester Town Hall (1868–78) and the Natural History Museum in London (1873–81). Having established his reputation as an efficient planner of public buildings with the Manchester Assize Courts of 1859–65 (see above at p.32), he moved from Manchester to London in the year of its completion with the hope of next securing the commission for the Royal Courts of Justice. As we have seen, it was Street who was successful, but Waterhouse stayed on in the capital and eventually founded what was to become the largest (and most profitable) architectural practice in the country. To a quite remarkable portfolio of public buildings, which included town halls in Knutsford, Bedford, Reading, Hove, Rochdale and Alloa as well as Manchester, he added numerous rambling country houses, university buildings for both Oxford and Cambridge, hospitals, banks and churches throughout the country, hotels (including the Metropole in Brighton of 1888–9) and several very fine offices for the Prudential Assurance Company in London, Nottingham, Newcastle and Edinburgh.

While a committed Goth in his youth – described as 'an eager imbiber of the writings of Pugin, Scott and, above all, Ruskin'[48] – his zeal faded as his practice grew. While Eaton Hall, Manchester Town Hall and the Natural History Museum were amongst the most important Gothic Revival projects of the entire movement, by the late 1860s Waterhouse was experimenting in French Renaissance architecture, with both Strangeways Prison in Manchester (1866–8) and the Great North Western Hotel in Liverpool of 1868–71 already having much of the Loire about them.

After working with the O'Shea brothers on Manchester Assize Courts, his move to London saw him become yet another successful architectural client of Messrs Farmer and Brindley, and having developed an effective working relationship with them – like Scott before him – he used them almost exclusively on his projects throughout the country from the start of the 1870s. They were responsible for almost the entire programme of sculpture on Manchester Town Hall (with two relief roundels depicting the local trades of weaving and spinning attributed to Thomas Woolner), including both decorative details and, it must be said, some particularly fine statuary of the type normally reserved for Fine Artists. Waterhouse saw the sculpture here as an integral part of his Gothic design, offering both a further connection with the Middle Ages and another layer of meaning to the building, and he provided niches for statuary on all sides of the building, with a particular focus on the Albert Square elevation and the tower on the Princes Street corner. His proposals to the Council as to appropriate historical figures for the statuary included Elizabeth I, Charles I, Roger de Poitiers, Thomas de Gresley, Thomas de la Warre and Humphrey Chetham, but the Council's Building Committee took a much more radical and distinctly republican view, rejecting several of Waterhouse's proposals, including Charles I, and instead selecting a number of local figures including Henry, First Duke of Lancaster, Thomas de Gresley and John Bradford, replacing King Charles I with Charles Worsley (who had taken part in the Long Parliament and fought against the King), and just to ram the point home, they also commissioned a statue of Cromwell from Matthew Noble (1817–76) for a site outside the Cathedral (with Queen Victoria exacting her revenge by refusing to open the completed building).

The contrast between Farmer and Brimley's work here and the intentionally naïve work of Richard Boulton at Northampton, which was designed to look as if it had actually been carved in the 14th century, could not be greater. Here all the sculpture has a particularly sharp contemporary feel, with excellent drapery including lace collars, fur trimming and chain mail, with Henry of Lancaster in particular looking ferocious as he sweeps back his cloak to reveal his drawn sword. In fact, all those commemorated look entirely natural within their niches, rather than constrained by them, with toes gripping the edges of the hexagonal bases and arms, and drapery extending beyond the

27 Farmer and Brindley's Humphrey Chetham and Henry, Duke of Lancaster on Alfred Waterhouse's Manchester Town Hall

confines of the stone slots (fig.27). When it came to architectural decoration, like the best of Scott's work, this was drawn in some detail by Waterhouse and his assistants and executed to a high standard by Farmer and Brindley's stone carvers. The themes are distinctly Ruskinian with great variety and little repetition amongst the 13th-century curling fern capitals, ivy brackets, griffin gargoyles and bosses composed of various interlocking beasts. It may not quite equal the extreme naturalism of the O'Shea brothers' carving in Oxford, but considering that it is the combined work of the country's largest and busiest architectural practice and the country's largest and busiest stone carving company, the results are hugely impressive.

The bulk of Waterhouse's other work was carried out in brick with stone dressings; indeed, as far as his public clients in particular were concerned, his efficient planning, organisational ability and economical methods of construction were at least as important as the quality of his architectural expression. But importantly for the continuing development of architectural sculpture, Waterhouse was also an innovator, using both cast terracotta for much of his later architectural sculpture and eventually faience as well, after its development by Burmantofts Pottery, from 1879 onwards. Much to Ruskin's horror, by the latter half of the 19th century, there were numerous companies offering the mass-production of architectural detail in terracotta, with a Mr M.H. Blanchard of Lambeth, for example, advertising to the 'Nobility, Gentry, Architects, and Builders' that his factory could provide: 'Groups, statues, friezes, capitals, panelling, pinnacles, finials, terminals, Tudor, and other chimney shafts, balustrading, fountains, fonts, tazzas, vases, coats of arms, devices, and every description of architectural ornament, at prices in many instances nearly half the cost of stone.'[49] Waterhouse shared Ruskin's aim of making Gothic a living, continually developing style rather than a revival simply based on reproduction, but in Waterhouse's view, this meant embracing new techniques and methods of construction including the use of iron, steel and terracotta. The principal attraction and reason for the increasing use of terracotta was its ability to stay much cleaner than stone in the increasingly toxic atmosphere of Britain's cities, in which all buildings were slowly turned black as a result of every home, office and factory being heated by coal fires. Terracotta also had the additional benefits of being factory-produced, which provided a consistent quality, being extremely durable and not therefore subject to spalling or discolouration, and – most attractive of all for Victorian building clients – being, as Mr Blanchard had noted, much less expensive to produce than individually carved stones. While many architects strongly disapproved of the very idea of architectural sculpture being 'mass-produced' in this way, there were many more architects and sculptors who, like Waterhouse, valued the accuracy of this process in which a finished terracotta sculptural element could be cast directly from the sculptor's clay model, rather than being subject to the vagaries of an intermediate stone carver's skills and interpretation. As Benedict Read noted:

> it was not just that it was cheap, kept its bright colour, and that its moulds could be reused as a precise visual discipline (these reasons have been cited in its favour); but that the whole nature of its manufacture and its hesitancy between the status of fine and applied art fitted in more naturally (even when figurative) into a subsidiary role along with other media (such as mosaic and majolica) in a total, integrated decorative philosophy.[50]

The £186,000 surplus from the Great Exhibition had been allocated to improving science and art education in Britain and most of it was spent in South Kensington in London where Prince Albert envisaged the creation of a new cultural and educational campus (jokingly referred to at the time as 'Albertopolis'). The first element of this to be completed was the Museum of Manufactures (now part of the V&A), which opened its doors to the public in 1857, followed shortly after by the (now lost) Royal Horticultural Society Gardens (in which sculpture figured prominently) which then covered 22 acres, opening in 1861. After 12 years of painful development (involving numerous sites, various political interventions and an ever-decreasing budget) in 1873 construction work finally started on the next major element of the plan, namely Alfred Waterhouse's Natural History Museum (1873–81).

To our eyes, the broad symmetrical facade of Waterhouse's building, with its central entrance below the tower, looks the very essence of traditional architecture, but in the 1870s it represented almost as radical a development in terms of building construction as Paxton's glass and iron Great Exhibition buildings had been two decades before. For the first time in England (and very possibly the world), in lieu of loadbearing masonry, he erected a steel, reinforced concrete and cast-iron structure which, rather than having occasional ceramic decoration within brickwork or other masonry, was clad entirely in terracotta panels. Despite the use of this new technology, there was no lack of richness or depth in his design and he proved it to be quite capable of being used to produce a very fine Romanesque building, which successfully harked back to its morally acceptable, pre-Gothic roots. Perhaps surprisingly, considering its industrial nature, the firing process gave his terracotta, in his own words, 'beautiful tints of which we might avail ourselves if we chose boldly to use them'.[51] But even the intrinsic beauty and economic advantages of using terracotta were overshadowed by the opportunity that it gave Waterhouse to provide an abundance of architectural sculpture at little additional cost, with the griffin sentries on his parapets and his great arched entrance offering just a flavour of the delights within.

As in the Oxford Museum, the richly decorated, top-lit, Central Hall is the architectural highlight of the institution, with here, once more, the steel frame exposed and echoing the rib cages of the exhibits below, but now with the addition of two grand axial staircases which lead its many visitors to the arcaded upper levels of the building (fig.28). All the decoration was carefully designed to reflect the building's purpose and to supplement the teaching, with Sir Richard Owen, the museum's first director, working closely with Waterhouse

28 The Central Hall of Alfred Waterhouse's Natural History Museum of 1873–80

on the selection of suitable birds, beasts, fish and fauna as subject matter. Waterhouse himself drew every element of architectural sculpture in the building and while one might imagine that these might take the form of fairly basic sketches from which a sculptor might work, here they are beautifully detailed and rendered drawings (many of which survive) showing precisely what he required in each case. These were then modelled in clay in three dimensions by Edouard Romain Dujardin (1829–85), a Frenchman who by then was a senior member of Farmer and Brindley's team. From these, plaster of Paris moulds were created which in turn, were then provided to Messrs Gibbs and Canning Limited of Tamworth, who were responsible for the provision of all the terracotta for the building (fig.29).

As one would expect in a scientific establishment, the ornamentation was divided into several classes – to the west, zoological, decorated with extant specimens, while to the east, geological, decorated with extinct ones. While the plants in the main hall are from around the world, those in the north hall are native to Britain.[52] Many of the most elaborate figures, such as the major roundel reliefs in the arched arcade of the main hall, were only cast once, but most of the minor ones were much repeated around the building, thus making best use of the

ONE TRUE CHRISTIAN STYLE

29   Sculptor Edouard Romain Dujardin's terracotta monkeys climb into the vaults of Waterhouse's Central Hall

30   Terracotta, incorporating sculpture of various natural forms, plants, birds and animals, is used throughout the interiors and on the exterior of Waterhouse's Natural History Museum

manufacturing process. These include the flora, fauna and birds which embellish the column capitals as well as numerous interlocking arches and spandrels throughout the building, the marine life between rippling tiles on the bases of the columns in the front galleries, and the delightful tribes of monkeys who inhabit the arches of the main hall, injecting some unexpected humour into this most august of Victorian institutions (fig.30). Waterhouse also provided drawings for the ceramic tile work, the mosaic floors and the stained-glass windows. All in all, it was something of a Victorian *Gesamtkunstwerk* which the contemporary *Builder* magazine found to be 'a remarkable work, eminently suited to its intended purpose, and presenting, in the interior especially, unusual architectural interest both of ensemble and detail, and forming a very fine illustration of what can be done with terracotta as a material for architectural embellishment on a great scale'.[53]

It was both Waterhouse's finest work and a fitting commentary on the state of the Gothic Revival by the end of the 1870s. While its Romanesque style, the subjects of its decoration and the honest expression of its structure would have delighted Ruskin, its framed and clad construction, its use of cast-iron and concrete, and its mass-produced sculpture would have appalled him in equal measure. To that extent, the Natural History Museum was particularly symbolic of the Victorian age and perfectly expressive of the fundamental conflict which underscored Ruskin's medievalist philosophy which was what, in the end, resulted in the Gothic Revival finally running out of steam.

3
ET IN ARCADIA EGO

To describe 19th-century Classical architecture as a competing 'Revival' is actually something of a misrepresentation as the golden thread of Classicism had simply continued unbroken while the Goths crusaded. Since its introduction to England with the completion of Inigo Jones's (1573–1652) Palladian Queen's House in Greenwich (1616–35), Classicism had not only survived but prospered, providing the country with much of its greatest 17th- and 18th-century architecture, which included many of its most important public buildings and one of the world's finest collections of large country houses. Jones was followed by Christopher Wren (1632–1723) and he by the masters of English Baroque, John Vanbrugh (1664–1726) and Nicholas Hawksmoor (1661–1736), who in turn were succeeded by the elegant restraint of Robert Adam (1728–92) and William Chambers (1723–96) before John Nash (1752–1835) transformed much of London with his grand Neo-Classical terraces, and of course, these outstanding architects were accompanied by a vast supporting cast who brought Classical architecture to the burgeoning regional cities and provincial towns.

Classicism was sustained throughout this period by the upper classes of British society, for whom it had come to represent the very peak of human achievement and intellectual development, with a Classical education in the languages, mythology, architecture and literature of ancient Greece and Rome being regarded as the only suitable education for a gentleman. From the 1660s onward, this was further reinforced by the necessity for a Grand Tour of the Classical sites, which were then being excavated, as well as Italian Renaissance and Palladian architecture, with an extensive itinerary quickly becoming something of a rite of passage for the nobility and wealthy landed gentry. This fashion continued well into the 19th century with the historian Edward Gibbon suggesting that: 'According to the law of custom, and perhaps of reason, foreign travel completes the education of an English gentleman.'[1] Many of these young men developed a passion for the archaeological investigation of the relics of the ancient civilisations, often funding excavations and publishing details of their finds, with the Earl of Burlington (1694–1753) the most prominent and influential advocate of Palladianism, eventually designing his own villa, Chiswick House (1725–), in partnership with William Kent (1684–1748).

By the start of the 19th century, such a tour was similarly expected of any self-respecting (and suitably wealthy) aspiring young Classical architect with Charles Cockerell, for example (as noted previously), spending over seven years travelling and studying in Greece. Inspired first by the literature of the country and then by his first sight of the Elgin Marbles – which he thought 'so *True to Nature & so full of Life and Movement* that one might almost suppose they were cast from *living models*'[2] – he dedicated himself to raising British architecture up to the level of that of the ancient Greeks. Interestingly, like Ruskin, he too had no interest in simple Revivalism, stating that: 'if our new buildings are to be something more than servile and lifeless copies (which too many of them are), we must dispassionately study *all the acknowledged masterpieces of the past*, absorb the ideas embodied in them, & then with *our own needs and methods* in mind, develop those which are capable of being developed, & abandon those which are not',[3] and thus (in a similar way to the proponents of the Gothic Revival), he saw Classical architecture as offering a fresh vision of an ancient style that was alive, relevant and dynamic.

By the 1840s and 1850s, Cockerell had produced a series of magnificent public buildings, culminating in St George's Hall in Liverpool (1840–54, fig.6) with Harvey Lonsdale Elmes (1813–47), the Fitzwilliam Museum in Cambridge (1837–47) with Elias George Basevi (1794–1845) and the Ashmolean Museum in Oxford (1841–5). These buildings were typical of the new Greco-Roman phase of Classical architecture. John Nash's United Services Club of 1828 on Pall Mall was joined by Decimus Burton's Athenaeum Club on the other side of Waterloo Place in 1830 (complete with a fine gilt statue of *Athene* by Edward Hodges Baily (1788–1867), between tripod lamps atop its entrance portico, fig.31), and followed soon after, further along the same London street, by Charles Barry's Travellers' Club (1829–31) and – the finest of them all – his Reform Club (1837–41), thus establishing a new Italian Renaissance 'palazzo' style of city-centre building which would soon be adopted throughout the country to provide further clubs, banks, town houses, offices and warehouses which offered a fashionable new archetype with flattering social connotations. While the focus of the British Empire's political and social power remained in London, by 1852 its wealth had become much more widely distributed around the country and found its expression in a great wave of new Classical architecture in the regional cities.

Cuthbert Broderick (1822–1905) produced his greatest work and one of the most important public buildings of the High Victorian period with Leeds Town Hall (1853–9). With a considerable debt to St George's Hall in Liverpool, he provided this manufacturing town (Leeds did not achieve city status until 1893) with a new municipal complex which included law courts, a council chamber,

31   Decimus Burton's Athenaeum Club, Waterloo Place, London (1830)

council offices and a grand civic hall, once more fronted by a giant Corinthian colonnade but here below a crushing clock tower which rose from a further square Corinthian colonnade, to a decidedly French domed cupola (all designed to put nearby competitor Bradford well and truly in its place) (fig.32). As befitted such a prestigious building, the architectural sculpture was extensive and the Rawden Hill millstone grit sandstone into which it was carved has ensured its survival largely intact.

With one or two exceptions, the modelling and carving was a family affair, led by local master mason Robert Mawer (1807–54). Born in Nidderdale, 30 miles north of Leeds, he served his seven-year apprenticeship while assisting with work on nearby Ripon Cathedral, eventually rising to a partnership with Hugh Collitt and George Hope in Collit and Company Stonemasons in Leeds. In 1842 he

32 Cuthbert Broderick's Leeds Town Hall (1853–9) was designed to reflect and assert the town's new-found status

established his own yard and sculpture studio at 7 Oxford Place in Leeds, and most unusually was assisted there by his wife, stonemason Catherine Mawer (1803–77), her nephew, William Ingle (1828–70), apprentices Matthew Taylor (1837–89) and Benjamin Payler (1841–1907), and their son, Charles Mawer (1839–1903). Interestingly, prior to starting work on the Town Hall, most of their work had been on Gothic buildings including St Peter's Church in Leeds (Leeds Minster, 1837–41) and St George's Hall in Bradford (1849–53).

For the Town Hall, Ingle was responsible for the general architectural sculpture (assisted on this occasion by one Thomas Whiteley, as well as his regular assistants), including the extensive rusticated and vermiculated base, and he personally carved a number of the keystones, while Catherine was responsible for the excellent capitals of the mighty Corinthian columns and pilasters, the parapet and vases, and much of the detail on the tower and ventilation turrets (most of which was carved on site). The keystones were divided between sheep heads, as symbols of the local wool trade, the heads of various individuals connected with the project and – to provide suitably flattering company for them – a series of Greek gods, with impressive moustaches, flowing beards and helmets (with most of these actually modelled on other contemporary citizens of the city, with various clues as to their identity included in the details) (fig.33). It was while working on these sculptures that Robert Mawer died in November 1854, with many of the outstanding keystones being completed by Catherine. He is himself commemorated in two of the heads, identifiable by a feather in his cap to represent this, his greatest achievement, and a crown, to signify his role as the leader of the carvers, while the Mayor of Leeds and Cuthbert Broderick also feature (with architect Broderick modestly standing in for Zeus). It was a massive undertaking for the Mawer team and one on which they acquitted themselves well, with the general architectural detail being sharp and clear and the figurative work boldly modelled in the Classical tradition.

When it came to the arched tympanum above the main entrance, however, the Council was not content to employ a local firm and sought to further enhance the city's reputation by employing the architectural sculptor who had led the work on the Houses of Parliament and who, at that very moment, was engaged by no less a person than Prince Albert – in other words, none other than our friend John Thomas. Thomas provided them with an exultation of their city with a central crowned female figure, as Miss Leeds, with laurel wreath and distaff, supported by four further robed allegorical figures representing manufacturing, the arts and sciences. From the left, *Manufacture* holds a bale of cloth, a mallet, an anvil cog and pincers; *Music* and *Poetry* hold a lyre and a horn; *Fine Arts*, a palette and bust of Minerva; and *Science*, a compass and globe (fig.34). Twin owls, the symbols of the city, sit on pedestals on either side of the central figure, and she is further supported by minor sculptures of *Pan* and *Athena*. The entire arch is framed with rich sculpted panels and two small boys on either side of the entrance doors, with rams draped around their shoulders, acknowledge the local wool trade once more. While the panels form an integral part of Thomas's overall design for the entrance, it has been suggested that they were

33 One of sculptor Catherine Mawer's many keystones, in this case a self-portrait of one of the 19th century's few female architectural sculptors

34 Sculptor John Thomas's side panels and tympanum to the main entrance

also carved by Catherine Mawer. This is entirely possible as it was quite normal for a lead sculptor to model detailed elements of their composition in clay for others to transfer into the final stone carving. Bearing in mind Thomas's contemporary workload, he may even have executed no more than the overall design in two dimensions himself, although it has to be said that the intricacy of carving of much of the door surround, particularly the details of the swirling foliage around the youths, is much finer and more delicate than the other architectural sculpture around the building. Consequently, the design and execution of Thomas's contribution, in its complexity and almost excessive detail, is in complete contrast to the Mawers' work, which was carried out under Broderick's direct control and shares the same restraint and rather stern boldness of his architecture.

As to Thomas's goddesses of *Manufacturing*, *The Arts* and *Sciences* in the tympanum, they are here particularly frumpy, formulaic and unnatural, with drapery which, with the exception of the hint of a breast on *Manufacturing* (perhaps to spare the blushes of his clients), obscures almost every element of their anatomy. He was certainly capable of producing better Classical work (such as his excellent pediment group for the Great Hallway of Euston Station of 1849), so I think we must conclude that the drop in quality of his contribution here was as a result of his prodigious workload and the remote location, rather than the overstretching of his talent. Though Thomas was hardly a Fine Art sculptor, his doorway in Leeds provides an excellent example of a prominent sculptor wishing to assert his own art, rather than merely contributing to a prominent architect's overall vision, and it stands in some contrast to, say, Waterhouse's entrance to the Natural History Museum, where he worked hand-in-hand with Farmer and Brindley.

The remarkable Catherine Mawer – whom I have discovered is the only female Victorian architectural sculptor from a stonemasonry background (there were a number of contemporary female Fine Art sculptors such as Susan Durant (1827–73) and Mary Thorneycroft (1814–95) – retained control of her late husband's stone yard and formed a very successful new partnership with William Ingle which allowed them to dominate the Yorkshire region throughout the 1860s, providing architectural sculpture to the Albert Memorial in Queensbury (1863), the Wool Exchange in Bradford (1864–7), the Commercial Bank in Bradford (1867–8) and numerous Gothic churches including the Church of St Peter in Hunslet Moor (1866–8) and St Clement's in Leeds of the same dates.[4]

Rather than leaving our rather romantic, rags to royalty, sculptor John Thomas on something of a low note, let us consider what is surely his most impressive Classical work – the former West of England and South Wales District Bank in Bristol (1854–8) (now the Harbour Hotel), on which he collaborated very successfully with local architects William Bruce Gingell (1819–99) and Thomas Royse Lysaght (1827–90) to produce one of the finest, and certainly the most richly decorated, Victorian Classical urban palazzo buildings in the country (fig.35). Gingell and Lysaght's Venetian Cinquecento design was based on Jacopo Sansovino's 16th-century Library of St Mark, but here, with Thomas's assistance, it almost drips in a profusion of decorative sculpture, with every spandrel, keystone, rusticated block, arched window reveal, bracket, frieze and cornice the subject of an intensity of carved detail that has rarely been equalled. Importantly, however, the architects and sculptor have here worked hand-in-hand to produce a wholly integrated and entirely convincing work of art. The depth of the facade, particularly on the piano nobile, is quite astonishing with a grand Ionic order between each of the arched Venetian windows framed by double, swagged Ionic columns, with the spandrels graced by reclining female allegorical figures armed with the usual litany of sheaves of corn, sickles, books, palettes, pincers, supported by a host of cherubic offspring, flanked on either side by alternating boat's bows and brackets with garlands of fruit. On the ground floor the spandrels of the ribbed and decorated arched windows are graced by male figures (with globes, mallets, lyres,

35   The former West of England and South Wales District Bank in Bristol of 1854–8 by local architects William Bruce Gingell and Thomas Royse Lysaght

36 The astonishing richness, depth and exuberance of sculptor John Thomas's sculpture on the bank

sheep, picks, anchors, butter churns, wreaths, and so on) on either side of generously bearded mythical head keystones, whose flowing locks consist of fruit, seashells, leaves and seaweed, with the odd garland or cob of corn (fig.36). To top all this off, the frieze below the richly bracketed parapet offers a further generation of putti, industrially plying their various trades between scrolled cartouches above each Ionic capital. Despite being in many ways utterly over the top, Thomas and the architects have somehow managed to carry it off, both as a result of their use of cool white Portland stone throughout (which offers as much light as shadow), and the consistently high quality of the carving. Credit for its beautifully sharp execution has to go to what must have been a substantial team of local craftsmen who worked under Thomas's direction (who, we must remember, was still also supervising the execution of all the architectural detail on the Palace of Westminster), thus providing regional Bristol with a bank building of considerable panache which, had it been located instead in the mighty capital of the British Empire itself, would still have stood head and shoulders above the competition.

For the West of England Bank, the messages sent through the building's architecture and supporting sculpture were crystal clear – not only offering the most discerning of local customers a natural repository for their funds, but also celebrating Bristol's unique maritime, agricultural and industrial heritage (as reflected in their customer base), while acknowledging the importance of the arts and sciences to the cultural life of the city. It was an ebullient (and extremely expensive) display of self-confidence and ambition, which was matched by the rapid expansion of the bank's business during the next decade, which, unfortunately, was quickly followed by its collapse in 1878, which had a glacial effect on the city's economy for many years after. Similar (and perhaps rather more cost-effective) palazzos of banking were replicated throughout the other regional towns and cities, with Liverpool boasting the former Alliance Bank in Castle Street of 1860–62 (architects Lucy and Littler) and the former Liverpool Union Bank in Brunswick Street of 1870 (both with generous domed banking halls); and for Manchester, what was originally the headquarters of the Bury Banking Company (now Barclays) in Bury of 1868 (architects Blackwell and Son and Booth), which is graced with quite exceptional sculpture by Manchester's Joseph Bonehill (1830–90). The Bristol bank is also almost exactly contemporary with Manchester's Free Trade Hall by Edward Walters (1808–72) which was constructed between 1853 and 1856 and shares both a similar Lombardo-Venetian architectural source and further sculpture by the indefatigable Mr Thomas, in this case with nine relief panels depicting *Free Trade*, *The Arts*, *Industry*, *Commerce*, *Asia*, *Europe*, *Africa*, *America* and *Australia* (which preceded John Foley's similarly themed, though rather more ambitious, efforts on the Albert Memorial by several years). Compared with his carving in Bristol these are relatively restrained compositions, with the female figures breaking into three dimensions while their various symbolic accessories are largely in relief. Again, as in Bristol, given his other contemporary work, it must only have been possible for Thomas to direct local stone carvers in this work, but nevertheless it represents another very successful artistic collaboration.

In London itself, perhaps the best example of the type was the National Provincial Bank of England on Bishopsgate (now the National Westminster Bank and known as 'Gibson Hall') of 1864–5 by architect John Gibson (1817–92). He had trained under Charles Barry (contributing significantly to the detailed design of the Palace of Westminster) and had a similarly flexible approach to architectural style, completing numerous churches in the Gothic style and bank buildings, in which he rather specialised, in the Classical. His first effort in Glasgow, the National Bank of Scotland on Queen Street of 1847, had been so successful that he was appointed architect to the bank for all its future work and soon attracted further banking clients throughout the length and breadth of the country. The Glasgow bank is something of a little gem, with architectural sculpture by – would you believe it? – John Thomas once again, with his principal contribution being a free-standing royal coat of arms on the attic above the central bay, supported by a lion and unicorn, which in turn are flanked by female figures representing *Peace* and *Plenty*. Interestingly, the building, rather than being demolished, was moved, stone by stone, to Langside Avenue in 1902–3, with the city engineer remodelling the interior to create what is now Langside Public Halls.

In Bishopsgate, what Gibson produced was an extraordinary temple to commerce – one of the few bank buildings which comes close to Gingell and Lysaght's bank in Bristol in terms of its ebullient plasticity and the depth of modelling of its facades. Unlike the Bristol bank, it is simply a banking hall without offices above and thus has a grand Corinthian order spanning from a semi-basement to its parapet. The principal architectural sculpture comprises relief panels between the column capitals above the arched windows to the banking hall and, free-standing, at attic level above each of the columns as single figures, except on either side of the main entrance where the columns are doubled and the sculptures become modest groups. The parapet statuary was executed by two sculptors – Felix Martin Miller (1819–1908), who was Master of Modelling at the

South Kensington schools for many years, and Henry Wayte Bursill (1833–71), who would go on to produce much of the sculpture on the Holborn Viaduct. Miller modelled one group and two single figures (which were modelled by Miller and carved by James Underwood), while Bursill undertook three groups and one single figure (which he and Underwood carved together). The figures and groups represent the regions of Britain, its cities and industries, with *Wales*, for example, featuring *Saint David* standing at its centre with sword raised, flanked by a seated bard with a harp and a miner with a lamp and pickaxe, all of whom are clothed in Classical garb (reflecting the style of the architecture). The single figures, who are all female, carry various objects to confirm their role – such as *London*, who holds a shield with the coat of arms of the city in one hand and a key in the other. Individually, they are fairly unremarkable in terms of the quality of the modelling, but they certainly play their part in the overall composition of the building (though what is becoming ubiquitous contemporary netting makes close scrutiny almost impossible). The relief panels above the ground floor windows by John Hancock (1825–69) are quite different, both in terms of style and quality (fig.37). Hancock had been introduced to the Pre-Raphaelites by Thomas Woolner and, though never admitted to the inner group (largely due to Rossetti having developed a particular dislike for him), was much influenced by them. His panels, which include *The Arts*, *Commerce*, *Science*, *Manufactures*, *Agriculture* and *Navigation*, have an almost mechanical precision that, though carved in stone, appear almost to have the subtlety of bronze. These are all dominated by a central, winged, female figure who is flanked by groups of men and boys who portray the subject of each panel. The treatment of their hair and angel's wings, and their somewhat eery, pensive gazes into the middle distance, give all the figures more than a hint of the influence of Pre-Raphaelite painting, albeit that they are clothed in Classical, rather than medieval, garb.

Gibson later went on to consistently use architectural sculptor Charles Henry Mabey (1836–1912) on much of his future work, including the Neo-Classical Todmorden Town Hall in Yorkshire (1871–5), where Mabey provided a particularly fine pediment frieze. When an extension was required to the bank in 1878, with two further bays being added to the building, it was Mabey to whom he turned again to provide two further statues and panels. Mabey, who had a studio in London at Storey's Gate, ran a very successful business as an architectural modeller and decorator, and regularly advertised to draw the attention of 'architects and others to an extensive stock of new designs for buildings in all styles . . . Figure and architectural modelling and carving . . . ceiling flowers, cornice enrichment, capitals, trusses, enriched panels, chimneypieces, etc, Reredos, pulpits, fonts, tombs, monuments . . .'.[5] But to dismiss him as an ambitious stonemason would be a gross injustice as his work here, particularly on the two new panels, is quite outstanding and, in the context of the history of British architectural sculpture, extremely important (fig.38). His panels portray *Mining* and *Shipbuilding* with what would have been a quite astonishing level of realism in 1878. The figures are now in contemporary dress and their compositions are almost abstract, alive with movement and dynamism, and quite brilliantly capture the raw energy that was being poured into both industries throughout the country at that time. In this respect, it is not too much of a stretch to suggest that they anticipated elements of the later New Sculpture Movement. Overall, the architectural composition of panels which together form a frieze, combined with the shift from allegorical subjects to the portrayal of real life, certainly appear to have anticipated the architectural sculpture on John Belcher's later, highly influential, Institute of Chartered Accountants' Hall of 1893.

37   John Hancock's relief panel *Commerce* above the main entrance of John Gibson's National Provincial Bank of England (1864–5)

38   Charles Mabey's dynamic composition *Shipbuilding* (1878) on the later extension

Such conspicuous commercial self-promotion, even within a Classical framework, had by now departed considerably from Cockerell and the other Greek Revivalists' aim of drawing upon the grace and dignity of antique works to restore British architecture to the heights from which, they perceived, it had fallen. But further north in Britain, in the Calvinist land of the Scots – whose own capital city, which had been the base for the Scottish Enlightenment, was now dubbed 'The Athens of the North' – there lingered a taste for something more severe.

In 1822, Scottish landscape painter Hugh William Williams (1773–1829) had exhibited his paintings of Athens alongside views of Edinburgh, thus identifying the physical parallels between the two cities: both lying on flat plains and sharing a rocky eruption at their centre (the Acropolis and the castle) and a nearby port (Piraeus and Leith). The following year, Charles Cockerell had collaborated with local Classical architect William Playfair (1790–1857) to design the National Monument of Scotland as an exact replica of the Parthenon on Calton Hill above the centre of the city (as a memorial to Scottish soldiers who had died in the Napoleonic Wars). Construction had started in 1826 but funds soon ran out and the project was abandoned in 1829, leaving just the portico and thus what subsequently appeared to be a ruined Greek temple atop its own Scottish acropolis. William Playfair had more success below where he was commissioned to design the National Gallery of Scotland in 1850 to complement his earlier, adjacent, Royal Scottish Academy building of 1822–6, thus providing the city with two Greek temples as a new symbolic centre with the arts at its very core (fig.39). Playfair had used the Doric order for the Royal Academy building but switched to Ionic for the National Gallery. It is, however, Ionic of the most correct and severe style, with double hexastyle porticos to east and west and tetrastyle to the north and south, with architectural sculpture limited to the column capitals, balustrades, acroteria and antefixa, with even the tympana left utterly plain. Completed in 1859, it is one of the purest examples of the Greek Revival in Britain, and while Playfair successfully

39   The Royal Scottish Academy of 1822–6 by William Playfair stands in the very heart of Edinburgh – 'The Athens of the North'

adapted the style to serve new purposes, it still fell rather short of the living, breathing rejuvenation of ancient architecture to which Cockerell had aspired. For something more vigorous, we need to travel some 40 miles or so due west to what was then the industrial powerhouse of Scotland, a city that was fast outstripping Edinburgh in terms of enterprise, innovation and consequently wealth – Victorian Glasgow.

By the 1860s, Scotland was one of the wealthiest countries in the world and while Edinburgh remained its official and cultural capital city, Glasgow was the vast coal-fuelled machine which was now driving the country's economy. Its population had overtaken Edinburgh in 1851 and, at 450,000, was considerably larger than both Manchester and Birmingham, and thus second only to mighty London, the capital of the empire. Its early trade in cotton and tobacco with the United States had been superseded by iron and steel manufacturing, engineering and shipbuilding, with its products exported to almost every corner of the expanding British Empire.

Here, too, there were numerous architects providing Neo-Classical buildings for their clients (as well as Gothic and Scottish Baronial buildings, if required) and the city already boasted several Athenian edifices – including, for example, Archibald Elliot Jnr's Royal Bank of Scotland on Exchange Square of 1827 and John Burnet Snr's powerful Elgin Place Congregational Church of 1856 – and it was a style which would continue to be deployed in the city throughout the remainder of the 19th century. But amidst what was a considerable and growing pool of local talent which had sprung up in response to the city's increasing wealth, there practised perhaps the most daringly original and accomplished of all the Victorian Classicists – Alexander 'Greek' Thomson (1817–75). Much less well known today than he ought to be (largely as he practised in Glasgow, rather than London), in his day he was well enough known to have Professor Thomas Roger Smith (1830–1903; President of the Architectural Association, 1860–61) refer to him as the 'one living architect of genius' in a lecture to the Society of Arts in London in 1865.[6]

As a committed Classicist, Thomson held strong views on Ruskin's writings, as he explained in one of his lectures:

There is no writer on Art half as well known as Mr Ruskin, no one more eloquent or more amiable, no one who has said more good and true things about Art, who has a more loving regard for the beauties of Nature, no one who can so readily, so pleasantly, and so instructively translate what he sees in Nature and Art into plain language so that all men may read and thereby become sharers with him in those pure and noble pleasures which his sensitive and exquisitely refined mind seems to imbibe from all the springs of truth. And yet I know no one who has done more to mislead the public mind in matters of Art than he.[7]

Thomson, like his fellow Classicists, regarded it as, 'a matter of fact that the Greeks, who carried mental culture to a much higher degree than any other people, devoted their best energies to the study of aesthetics and to the development of the aesthetic faculty'[8] whereas Gothic 'is not associated with learning in any way'.[9] But just as Ruskin shunned the exact reproduction of medieval Gothic architecture, so Thomson believed that 'the best way for us to imitate the Greeks is rather to follow their example than copy their work'.[10]

Born in a cottage in Balfron, near Glasgow, Thomson's father died when he was just seven, followed by his mother when he was 13, so there was never any question of a Grand Tour of the Antiquities in which he might have witnessed Greek architecture at first hand. During his architectural pupillage (arranged by a successful elder brother) his knowledge of Classical architecture was learned from contemporary publications, works of Classical architecture in Scotland and the publication of the works of French and German contemporary Classicists including Karl Friedrich Schinkel (1781–1841), whose works significantly influenced Thomson's. Taking the temples and monuments of ancient Greece merely as a starting point, Thomson produced architecture of striking boldness and originality in which Classical elements were combined in picturesque compositions of interpenetrating forms, of which his two (largely) surviving Glasgow churches provide excellent examples. In his Caledonia Road Church of 1856 he combined a great Classical portico, raised on a massive plinth like some ancient ruin, with a magnificent yet rather severe square tower dominating the galleried two-storey nave below. The St Vincent Street Church of 1859 enjoys a much more dramatic site which slopes steeply in both directions, and he has extracted every ounce of possible drama from it with another asymmetrical, full-blooded and yet superbly judged composition. Here, rather than simply a portico, we have a complete temple, raised on a further, massive, masonry plinth and accompanied by a further campanile of quite extraordinary inventiveness, as Andor Gomme and David Walker described in their *Architecture of Glasgow*:

> This begins as a plain tower, square in section, near the top of which is, on each side, a large T-shaped opening, in the horizontal part of which are inset two Egyptianesque caryatids in the form of sideway-facing busts which support the lintel [fig.40]. Above this the tower has four small, slightly bulging corner turrets which end in pinnacles. Between the pinnacles is a cylindrical drum flattened on four sides with a recurrence of the pylon motif used at the ends of the aisles enclosing a completely black opening. The drum is topped with a cylindrical peristyle which has columns in the shape of fat corn-shocks or shaving brushes. Finally the dome is like a long drawn-out policeman's helmet with a kind of sugar castor at the top, for which the inspiration appears to be Hindu.[11]

It is an exuberant architectural eruption that is all the more remarkable as it forms a totally convincing element within what is otherwise a rather severe composition of plain ashlar and minimal decoration.

40   The extraordinary tower of Alexander Thomson's St Vincent Street Church of 1857–9 with sculpture by John Mossman

Thomson's radical reinventions extended throughout almost every element of his buildings, with every detail of his designs drawing on Classical precedents but reworked in new and original ways. Much of his decoration, for example, was incised into the stone rather than in relief and stripped to its bare essentials – the simplest of running 'Greek key' patterns, circular discs, rows of acroteria, his cyclopean rustication – all executed with an almost machine-like precision, giving the impression that the buildings had been carved from solid blocks rather than constructed; and yet there is somehow also a lightness of touch which provides vitality too. In many of his houses he placed the window frames and glass behind stone mullions to give the impression of an open colonnade while he devised his own orders, drawing on Egyptian architecture as well as Greek, and often stripping column capitals and pediments to their most elemental form. His often rather severe exteriors gave way to interiors of colour, warmth and richness which bear comparison with William Burges's Gothic fantasies in Wales (indeed Burges recommended that his students at the Architectural Association study Thomson's work); and despite completing a vast portfolio which also included offices, terraces, tenements and warehouses, his standards rarely dropped, nor did his creativity falter.

In his architectural sculpture he relied on one man and his team throughout his career – the sculptor John Mossman (1817–90). It was an artistic partnership which began soon after Thomson established his practice and which developed throughout it, allowing him both to continue to experiment in stone and to execute his architecture with a sympathetic fellow artist. Mossman and his sons completely dominated the art of sculpture in Glasgow throughout most of the 19th century, working not only as Fine Art sculptors of busts, medals, statues and many of the magnificent tombs in Glasgow's Necropolis, but also as architectural sculptors. Mossman was one of the founders of the Glasgow School of Art in 1853, where he taught throughout his career; along with Thomson he was both a founder member and later President of the Glasgow Architectural Society and a founder member of the Glasgow Institute of the Fine Arts. His family were descendants of James Mossman, who had been goldsmith to Mary, Queen of Scots, and his father William trained as a sculptor in London under Francis Chantrey (1781–1841), the leading British sculptor of the Regency era. He moved to Leith in 1821, where he established a firm of monumental sculptors, before relocating to Glasgow in 1828. His three sons, John, George (1823–63) and William (1824–84), all trained under him as sculptors and inherited his firm in 1853, renaming it J., G. & W. Mossman, which it remained until 1857, when William Jnr left to establish his own studio. All three had also trained in London: George at the Royal Academy School; William under Baron Marochetti, William Behnes and John Thomas (for whom he worked on the Houses of Parliament); and John, who also trained with Baron Marochetti and later William Allan at the Royal Scottish Academy. But it was to be John who was the finest sculptor and who had the most successful career, supported by his partner George (also a good friend of Thomson), with both often collaborating with their brother William on major commissions.

John established his reputation in the city with his (now demolished) Peter Lawrence Memorial in the Necropolis and continued as the most important maker of statues of his generation – these included James Lumsden (1840), Robert Peel (1853) and David Livingstone (1875), as well as busts of the Duke of Hamilton (1863), Henry Glassford Bell (1874) and Sir Michael Shaw-Stewart (1880). With most architects Mossman was engaged to embellish their work, but with Thomson he was instrumental in realising his architectural vision which demanded absolute precision and exact replication of his details in addition to the production of the rather exotic sculpture which adorned his churches.

Thomson's incised carving in particular required greater coordination than relief carving where blocks were left proud and rough for later carving once they had been positioned. This 'chip-carving', as it was known, within perfectly smooth planes of ashlar, was fundamental to Thomson's architecture. In several extreme examples, such as in the lower side entrance to St Vincent Street Church, Thomson and Mossman produced what appeared to be a portico, complete with the capitals of four supporting columns, that convincingly gives the appearance of having been carved out of the solid stone mass of the church's massive plinth, like some half-completed archaeological excavation (fig.41). On Ellisland, Thomson's villa of 1871, Mossman produced eccentric Egyptian lotus flower columns on either side of the main entrance which stop short of the beam which they apparently support, while the stone window mullions rise, half-wall and half-column, to capitals of entirely original design; while on his (sadly lost) Queens Park Church of 1869, Mossman produced layer after layer of overlapping stone motifs and planes below its richly decorated, pierced Hindu dome. Thomson designed Mossman's own studio in 1856 (also now lost) which architect Thomas Gildard (1822–95) described in 1888: 'In quality of composition, if not also of detail, I do not know if, in any of his subsequent works, he has surpassed it.'[12] In many ways, this was the ultimate expression of their artistic collaboration which allowed Thomson to fully express his remarkable creativity as the most original of all the 19th-century Classicists. Mossman's final tribute was a marble bust of Alexander Thomson, commissioned two years after his death in 1875, which remains on display in the Glasgow Art Galleries and Museum.

J. & G. Mossman continued successfully throughout the remainder of the century, with John providing the architectural sculpture on two of the great John James Burnet's early buildings before his death in 1890 – Burnet's first major commission, The Institute of Fine Arts on Sauchiehall Street (1878–9, demolished 1967), and the first phase of the Clyde Navigation Trust building on the Broomielaw. For the Institute of Fine Arts building he produced two fine figurative friezes below a crowning statue of *Minerva* flanked by griffins, while for the Clyde Navigation Trust building he produced a bold allegorical pediment centred on *Father Clyde*, below *Poseidon* in a boat pulled by two rearing sea horses, with the nautical theme continuing below in the form of two ships' prows, complete with chains, anchors and ropes with Poseidon's trident as a bowsprit, above the side entrance arches (fig.42). The young Burnet was particularly fortunate to work with Mossman at the height of his powers and it proved to be just the first

41   The side entrance of the church which appears to have been excavated from a solid block of stone by John Mossman

of many successful sculptural collaborations for this architect. Brother William Jnr's skills were equally sought after and he worked throughout the city providing a considerable amount of fine architectural sculpture, such as the locally well-known herculean *Atlantes*, who support a great entrance door canopy on their shoulders and provide a base for two draped allegorical female figures displaying the shield of the Bank of Scotland at its city-centre branch on the corner of George Square and St Vincent Place, with fellow sculptor John Tweed (1869–1933) describing them in 1872 as 'exceedingly striking' in his guide to Glasgow of the same year.[13]

Despite the Mossman family's reputation, undoubted skill and domination of their art within the city, when it came to the most significant subjects for civic commemoration, as in Leeds, the city fathers would nevertheless invariably still commission the best Fine Art sculptors from London; thus while the city's most important public space, George Square, includes two statues by John Mossman (*Robert Peel* and *Thomas Campbell*), it also has three by Baron Marochetti (plus *The Duke of Wellington* nearby), as well as further statues by Flaxman, Chantrey and Foley, and (in my opinion) the finest of them all: *William Ewart Gladstone* by William Hamo Thorneycroft (1850–1925 – of whom we shall hear more later); and this pattern of patronage was fairly consistently replicated throughout all the other regional cities.

British society was undergoing immense change and it was the increasingly wealthy middle class who were now in the ascendancy. It was their companies which were commissioning the factories, docks, railway stations, offices, theatres, hotels and apartment blocks; and, through their increasing involvement in politics and public life (as a result of the Great Reform Act of 1832 and further extensions of the franchise in 1867), it was they who were now also regularly becoming the clients of architects and sculptors engaged on the design of town halls, schools, universities, professional institutions, museums and art galleries; and for the first time, they also began to commemorate themselves

42   John Mossman's outstanding sculpture on John James Burnet's Clyde Navigation Trust building of 1883–6

in public statuary. In 1871, the councillors and aldermen of what was then Birmingham Town Council held an architectural competition for the design of their new town hall (the Council House). Much to their disappointment, they received only 29 entries for what they regarded as the town's most significant civic building; and what is more, those entries were almost entirely from small local practices. Nevertheless, this allowed them to indulge in their own minor 'Battle of the Styles', with the selection committee soon deadlocked between the Gothic design of Martin & Chamberlain and Yeoville Thomason's Classical offering. The dispute was not resolved until 1874 when a majority was finally secured to proceed with Thomason's palatial Corinthian design, and the firm of Richard

Lockwood Boulton & Sons, which had yards in Birmingham and London, was soon selected to undertake the architectural sculpture.

Thomason had decided that the arch over the main entrance should have a mosaic in lieu of sculpture (which was executed by Salviati Burke and Company of Venice), but the five pediments which terminate the wings and central advanced section of the building were all graced with allegorical sculpture by Boulton & Sons. Interestingly, Boulton's work here is entirely within the Classical tradition and therefore in complete contrast to the naïve medieval sculpture that he had so brilliantly carved just ten years earlier on Northampton Town Hall for his former patron and instructor, and Goth, Edward Godwin. The four outlying pediments are curved, and within their deeply coffered arches are groups representing *Manufacture*, *the Union of the Arts and Sciences*, *Literature* and *Commerce* (thus echoing the themes of the Salviati mosaic, as well as almost every other Victorian bank and town hall). Interestingly, all the sculptures are carved in the round in three dimensions, rather than in relief (as in the lost pediment grouping on St George's Hall in Liverpool and its precedent on the Panthéon in Paris); and while the allegorical figures are consistently clad in Classical drapery (in the style of Liverpool and Paris), interestingly, the workmen who are included along with various machine cogs, rifles, anvils and pottery to represent the town's many trades are in contemporary dress (and thus treated as little more than additional tools themselves). The central triangular pediment offers a further symbolic microcosm of late Victorian society, with *Britannia* in Classical garb with her arms outstretched, here representing the nation (rather than Queen Victoria), flanked by two suited industrialists (who clearly regarded themselves as being responsible for the creation of *Britannia's* wealth and new position as global top-dog). Outside them, standing back and crouching within the angled corners, are four bare-armed and aproned members of the working class, surrounded once more by the flotsam and jetsam of the town's manufacturing trades; and just in case anyone has missed the central meaning of all this, *Britannia* is holding two laurel leaf crowns above the industrialists' heads (fig.43).

In the Bolton Town Hall of 1866–73 by Leeds architect William Hill (1827–89) assisted by Bolton's own George Woodhouse (1829–83), the building is dominated by another great clock tower as in Leeds, and, despite the recorded objections of various economy-minded councillors, the building is richly decorated. Indeed when it came to the principal sculpture for the triangular tympanum of the main portico, they wanted nothing but the best, inviting E.G. Papworth, J. Birnie Philip, W.D. Keyworth Jnr, Burstall and Taylor, and William Calder Marshall to compete for the commission (fig.44). Calder Marshall (who was then working on his sculpture of *Agriculture* for the Albert Memorial) was selected and produced yet another allegorical grouping in Classical attire, but this time centred on a larger than life-size crowned female figure representing *Bolton*, her hand resting on a shield. She is supported by the usual cast of young women and cherubs representing *Manufacturing* and *Commerce*, surrounded by yet more tools of trades. Sculpted in white Portland stone and completed in three dimensions, it is one of the most successful Classical pediment groups of the period, not least because of the contrast between the white Portland stone of the sculpture and the blonde sandstone of its architectural backdrop, thus allowing the excellent detail to be unusually well appreciated from ground level.

These Classical expressions of civic pride, self-congratulation and inter-regional one-upmanship reached their zenith, however, with the construction of Glasgow's sumptuous City Chambers between 1880 and 1888. Competition-winning architect William

43   Boulton & Sons' distinctly Republican pediment group on Yeoville Thomason's Birmingham Council House of 1874–9

44   William Calder Marshall cleverly employed contrasting stone for his pediment figures on Bolton's Town Hall of 1866–73

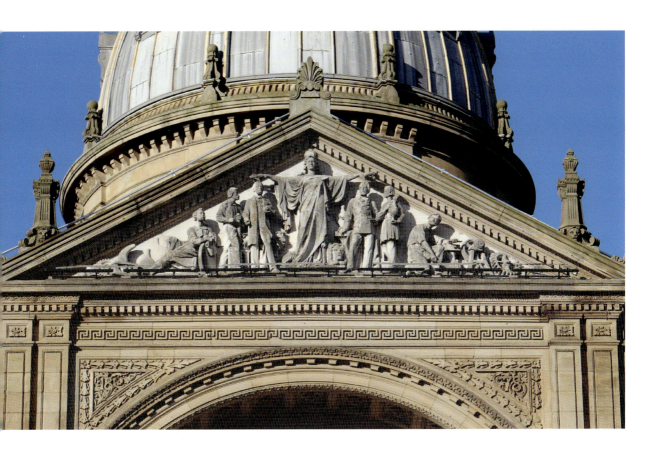

Young's (1843–1900) design follows the same basic parti as Leeds and Bolton. A tall, rusticated central tower, here balanced by domed wings and a strong central pedimented main entrance section, with its own smaller flanking cupolas, together successfully address the city's central George Square (fig.45). Inside, every surface of the vast central staircase hall, is clad in either marble, terracotta or mosaic and displays a lavishness previously unparalleled outside London, thus expressing this northern industrial city's new-found wealth. As one might anticipate, the architectural sculpture was extensive and, fortunately, the process of its creation was well recorded.

The contractor for all the building's masonry was Morrison & Mason, who employed 230 stonecutters at their yard in the city – 80 of whom were employed on architectural sculptural detail on the City Chambers such as the carving of column capitals, domes, balustrades and aedicules. They were the first firm of masons in Glasgow, and one of the first in Britain, to introduce machine technology for working stone, thus allowing the main structure of the building to be assembled largely from fully worked blocks, while much of the architectural sculpture was carried out on site. This was created by a further band of both individual sculptors and further companies, including our friends Farmer and Brindley from London and J. & G. Mossman from Glasgow, all of whom were appointed on the recommendation of the architect. Despite the abundance of sculpture it was, very accurately, felt to be 'both restrained and coherently conceived. Free-standing statues and panels in bas-relief provide a pattern of visual accents at various key points in the structure, as well as a narrative expression of the building's cultural and historical purpose.'[14] Architect William Young took great care to ensure that all the sculpture was appropriately proportioned, insisting that each piece was first modelled full-size in clay, before being cast in plaster and coloured to match the stone, and finally hoisted into place for him to then view from street level; and

45   The pediment and tower of architect William Young's Glasgow City Chambers of 1880–88, with frieze relief by George Lawson

46   A panel of George Lawson's frieze above the main entrance representing *Knowledge*

it was only after he had approved what was proposed in its setting, that it was finally carved in stone.

George Anderson Lawson (1832–1904), a Scottish sculptor who had established his studio in London, was selected to undertake both the principal tympanum and a lower allegorical frieze above the main central entrances (on which he was assisted by locals John Tweed and James Alexander Ewing, 1842–1900) (fig.46). The frieze is centred on the Glasgow coat of arms flanked by reclining female figures, with beautifully composed side panels in which contemporarily clad figures (who are emblematic of the sciences and the arts), stand or lean, in entirely relaxed, natural and life-like poses, either conversing amongst themselves or staring down at the citizens entering the building below. His tympanum, far from featuring the distinctly Republican *Britannia* of Birmingham, celebrates the Golden Jubilee of Queen Victoria in 1887 and is centred on a raised, seated figure of the Queen, on either side of which is a veritable scrum of supporting figures representing the countries of the empire, who are there to pay her suitable homage. Unfortunately, it is all rather cluttered and one cannot help but wonder if poor Lawson (who had after all excelled himself below) was presented with an ever-increasing and, in the end, ridiculous quantity of characters to accommodate, by his committee of clients.

The 22 second-floor window spandrels to the building's principal spaces are by John Mossman and depict the city's various trades, and he also produced free-standing allegorical statues depicting *The Arts* high above George Street, as well as two excellent pairs of caryatid figures in the George Square entrance loggia. The third-floor balustrade of the George Square elevation is adorned with eight (rather hefty) free-standing allegorical figures by Edinburgh sculptor John Rhind (1828–92) representing *Harmony*, *History*, *Prosperity*, and so on, all in voluminous Classical garb. It is known that Charles Grasby (1834–1910), Edward Good and James Harrison MacKinnon (1866–1954) also made contributions (fig.47). In all, it represented one of the most complex and extensive programmes of architectural sculpture ever carried out in Britain and one of the most successful of the Victorian period.

In addition to their involvement in public life, the newly wealthy middle class were now also commissioning town houses and rather grand country houses of their own, and while their entry into the highest levels of the nobility remained largely barred to them through birth, the lower levels were accessible through either outstanding achievement, extraordinary wealth, marriage or simply the suitable education of their sons along with one or two generations of distance from 'trade'. As we have seen, the regional cities which they dominated were constantly growing larger and more prosperous, while a long and painful depression in British agriculture which started in the early 1870s both detrimentally affected the income of many of the upper class and land-owning gentry (with the exception of those who had discovered coal beneath their estates) and speeded the flight of the working class from the countryside to even more appalling living conditions in the booming industrial conurbations. By the 1880s, the middle class were regularly appearing in public statuary and their ranks soon began to outnumber the nobility, national statesmen and military heroes, with only the Empress of India herself holding her own (with Waterhouse's Manchester Town Hall containing perhaps the largest collection of these 'local worthies', mostly executed by local sculptors William Theed, 1804–1901, and Matthew Noble, 1818–76). This provided a very substantial increase in the number of potential commissions for sculptors throughout the country and offered opportunities to many sculptors who might otherwise have struggled to find their own work, resulting in a significant reduction in the quality of much regional work, with many badly executed statues quickly becoming local laughing stocks. Sadly, there are many examples of particularly poor work, with Bolton in Lancashire, for example, suffering both Thomas Rawcliffe's unrecognisable *Benjamin Disraeli* and J. William Bowden's *John Fielding* within a few hundred yards of each other in Queen's Park.[15]

While most of the civic and commercial buildings which the middle class were now commissioning were still being produced in stone with copious carving, the revolutionary technology which Joseph Paxton had developed in conservatories and glasshouses – and used to such dramatic effect in the Crystal Palace – continued to be developed and applied to an increasing range of building types.

47 One of John Rhind's allegorical figures representing *Wisdom*

48   Peter Ellis's revolutionary cast-iron and glass Oriel Chambers in Liverpool of 1864–5

These included the great wrought-iron train sheds in London and the regional cities, cast-iron framed factory buildings throughout the country, and in one or two locations they even made an appearance in city centres, such as in Gardener's Warehouse in Glasgow of 1855–6 by John Baird (1799–1859, with whom Thomson had served his pupillage) with its exposed cast-iron facades, and in Peter Ellis's (1805–84) Oriel Chambers in Liverpool of 1864–5, which employed a complete cast-iron structural frame beneath a veneer of stone cladding and included the world's first paternoster lift which Ellis himself had invented (fig.48). For most Victorians, however, these experiments were rather shocking and while they could accept and indeed marvel at the elegant spans of their train sheds, these largely glazed, iron-framed city-centre buildings which were devoid of almost any form of decorative embellishment were just too radical a departure from tradition. Indeed the criticism of Ellis's building was so severe that it compromised his career, with *The Builder* of 20 January 1866 describing Oriel Chambers as a 'large agglomeration of protruding plate glass bubbles' and a 'vast abortion' lacking any aesthetic qualities – which was fairly extreme language for the time. These buildings did, however, represent an entirely new aesthetic, but it was one that would have to wait until after the Second World War in the 20th century to achieve any level of public acceptability.

Ruskin – still active, influential and increasingly political – was, as we might expect, appalled by these developments. His *Unto This Last* was published in

1860 and he followed up with *Fors Clavera* from 1871 onwards, which took the form of a series of letters to British workmen on social issues of the day. He thus successfully attracted a new generation of architects to his moral crusade including George Street's former senior assistant, Phillip Webb (1831–1915), who had designed The Red House for William Morris in 1859, now widely regarded as the first building of the Arts and Crafts Movement. With its asymmetrical plan and elevations, windows positioned to suit the needs of the spaces within (rather than conforming to any external pattern), use of simple materials and almost total lack of any decoration, it offered Morris and his new wife a rural idyll and an escape from London, which he described at the time as 'the spreading sore'.[16] It was an architecture which was purged of all the pretensions of Victorian society, which valued simplicity, truth to materials, the honest expression of structure, and crucially from our perspective, a focus on craftsmanship over almost all applied art. It appealed particularly to a relatively small, wealthy middle-class avant-garde who (having generated their wealth from the industrial revolution) were now liberated from work, free of the rigid formality of the upper classes and the snobbery of the lower middle classes, and found themselves able to live out their puritan fantasies in the wealthiest country in the world. Small country houses were central to this movement and Morris, despite his avowed Socialism and commitment to handicrafts, manufactured everything to furnish them, from stained glass and furniture to wallpaper and fabrics. Irresistibly attractive as many of these houses were, it was only towards the end of the century (as we shall see) that the movement made any significant contribution to commercial or civic architecture, and with it, to the history of architectural sculpture.

The majority of the middle class desired their architecture to be a little less of a moral crusade and more of a stylish backdrop to their increasingly comfortable way of life. Tastes were therefore changing and broadening as the later decades of the century progressed, and while the thread of Classicism continued unbroken and Gothic remained the preferred style for ecclesiastic and much public architecture, many sought something lighter and more congenial with neither sanctimony nor spartan restraint. It was to be two further assistants from George Street's office who would most successfully respond to these emerging trends – namely, Richard Norman Shaw (1831–1912) and William Eden Nesfield (1835–88). Both men (like Webb before) had been drawn to the quality of Street's architecture and to his wholehearted commitment to the Gothic cause, and they commenced their own partnership in 1863 as enthusiastic Goths; but within a few years, their architecture became much freer and they drew on both French and English vernacular sources and particularly England's great Elizabethan country houses for their inspiration. Shaw produced his magnificent, and rather sumptuous, 'Old English' Cragside in Northumberland of 1869–82 for the industrialist William Armstrong, while Nesfield produced something approaching a French chateau in Kimnel Park (1871–4) for Hugh Hughes, a copper mine owner. Together, their town houses were soon identified as Queen Anne, with decoration limited largely to main entrance door surrounds, the odd newel post and occasional Suffolk pargetting and strapwork. Their contemporary Ernest George (1839–1922) broadened the range of sources even further, bringing back sketches from his tours of northern Europe and applying Dutch gables and details from Flemish guild halls to his townhouses in Chelsea and Knightsbridge, such as 39 Harrington Gardens (1882–3) for the dramatist W.S. Gilbert, and several vast, rambling country houses, such as Rousdon House in Devon (1870) for Sir Henry Peek (of Peek Freans biscuit-making fame).

However, these changes would be nothing compared to the radical developments which would soon transform British architecture and sculpture during the last two decades of the century, leading to an exceptional level of integration between these arts and heralding one of the richest periods for the production of architectural sculpture in the history of Great Britain.

4
HARMONY ATTAINED

In the late 1870s and early 1880s, from a series of sparks in Paris and London came an explosion of creativity, which, fuelled by the wealth of the British Empire, united the country's best architects and sculptors in a new shared pursuit of artistic excellence, leading the Pre-Raphaelite painter John Everett Millais to suggest that:

> So fine is some of the work our modern sculptors have given to us, that I firmly believe that were it dug up from under the oyster shells in Rome or out of Athenian sands, with the cachet of partial dismemberment about it, all Europe would straightway fall into ecstasy, and give forth the plaintive wail 'We can do nothing like that now!'[1]

The source of this new artistic movement, which was soon to be christened 'New Sculpture', is the subject of some controversy, with Benedict Read identifying the arrival in Britain of the French sculptor and teacher Aimé-Jules Dalou (1838–1902) along with the work of the painter sculptors George Frederic Watts (1817–1904) and Frederic Leighton (1830–96) being the primary influences, while Susan Beattie, in her authoritative book on the New Sculpture Movement, identifies the (very limited) work of English sculptor Alfred Stevens (1817–75) and principally his major work – the bronze groups on his monument to the Duke of Wellington in St Paul's Cathedral to which he had devoted most of his career – as the movement's primary catalyst. There can be little doubt that they all contributed to varying degrees with the attribution of exclusive rights, merely academic.

Aimé-Jules Dalou – one of the finest French sculptors of the late 19th century, who had been a pupil of the great French sculptor Jean-Baptiste Carpeaux (1827–65) – was implicated in the failed Paris Commune of 1871 and exiled, arriving in London in July of that year. He exhibited several portrait busts in clay at the Royal Academy the following summer and such was the reaction to his work that he was appointed to teach at both the National Art Training School (which later became the Royal College of Art) and the South London School of Technical Art (SLSTA – the latest incarnation of our old friend, the hugely important Lambeth School of Art). Through his teaching, he introduced his British students to a new language of sculpture in which a subtler and more intricate detailing of surfaces brought a new realism to the replication of the human form in particular. This, combined with the reintroduction of the 'lost-wax' (*cire-perdue*) method of casting from the Continent (in which the sculpture was finely modelled in wax and then simply melted out of the mould), gave the bronzes which emerged from this process an exceptional richness of texture and thus a dramatic new vitality.

At the same time, there also emerged a number of painter sculptors who used sculpture to explore their subjects in three dimensions prior to painting, including both George Watts and Frederic Leighton (later Lord Leighton). Leighton had produced a small plaster sketch of a figure which was seen and admired by Dalou, who encouraged him to execute the work full-size. Leighton engaged the young sculptor Thomas Brock (1847–1922), who had trained with John Foley, to assist him and provide technical support. The product of this collaboration, which was first exhibited at the Royal Academy in 1877, was *Athlete Wrestling with a Python*, which is generally acknowledged to be the first example of 'New Sculpture' (fig.49).[2] Benedict Read compared Leighton's *Athlete* to John Bell's *The Eagle Slayer* (p.15), as a man similar in muscular action, yet what he identified in Leighton's sculpture was: 'the way in which it treated the human form, rendering in a naturalistic and fairly detailed way the musculature of a figure in action, achieving this by careful and detailed modelling directly in the variegated surface of the bronze'.[3] It makes *The Eagle Slayer*, which itself seemed so powerful and realistic just a few decades earlier, appear smooth, stylised and something of an idealised portrait, rather than a replication of an actual human figure. It was this striving for realism, achieved through fine surface texture and dramatic expression, which was to be the hallmark of the movement, and while bronze remained the preferred medium for most sculptors, many experimented in mixed media and soon also began to attempt to achieve a similar level of energy and vigour in stone.

As to the influence of the enigmatic Alfred Stevens, Susan Beattie saw much of what appeared to be the entirely original treatment in Leighton's *Athlete* in several of the elements of Stevens's Wellington Monument, such as the bronze 'Truth, [who] with infinitely more subtle, understated power, braces her limbs in combat with Falsehood, a serpentine monster with a human torso',[4] and suggests that had the contemporary critic Edmund Gosse not attributed the iconoclastic role to Leighton's *Athlete* in his seminal essay under the title 'The New Sculpture' in the *Art Journal* in 1894, Stevens's much more significant role would not have been overlooked by posterity. Considering both sculptures, it is hard to disagree with Beattie, but the reality is that with Stevens's tomb incomplete at the time of his death in 1875, and at the time occupying a small side chapel in St Paul's Cathedral (it was not moved to its current more prominent position until 1892), its contemporary influence was inevitably limited. In contrast, Leighton's *Athlete* was exhibited in London and Paris, being awarded a gold medal at the Paris International Exhibition of 1878, and Leighton was elected President of the Royal Academy that year which brought New Sculpture to the fore in the teaching there. It soon also led to a number of its practitioners being elected as associates including Joseph Boehm (1878), Charles Birch (1880), Hamo Thorneycroft (1881), Thomas Brock (1883), Alfred Gilbert (1887), Edward Ford (1888), Harry Bates (1892) and George Frampton (1894). By the mid-1880s New Sculpture dominated submissions to the Academy and brought a whole new set of attitudes, ideas, subject matter and aesthetic conventions which would soon be applied to architectural sculpture, as well as continuing in the statuary through which the new movement had developed.

As we have seen, architectural sculpture spanned the broad divide between the two arts, and while some architectural sculptors such as John Thomas, Thomas Nicholls or John Mossman often strayed into

49 Frederic Leighton, *Athlete Wrestling with a Python* (1877), regarded by many as the first key work of the New Sculpture Movement

the area of Fine Art sculpture in their commemorative statues or allegorical compositions, this was almost exclusively one-way traffic, with Fine Art sculptors such as Baron Marochetti, John Bell or John Foley only working with architects in the provision of free-standing sculpture, such as Bell and Foley's contribution to Gilbert Scott's Albert Memorial. On occasion, as we have seen, the likes of William Calder Marshall (who also contributed to the Albert Memorial) were very occasionally brought in to add a sprinkle of stardust to a civic building, such as on Bolton's Town Hall, but these were really the few exceptions that more or less proved the rule. But in the 1880s, while the New Sculpture Movement was fast gaining momentum, a further and initially quite separate, radical shift took place which had an enormous impact on the world of architectural sculpture, with, in 1884, the founding in London of the Art Workers' Guild.

In the early 1880s, the architectural profession itself was in a state of turmoil, divided between those members of the Royal Institute of British Architects who wished to see architecture established as a registered profession along with law and medicine, with a central professional body setting and maintaining standards, and those who saw architecture as one of the arts to be passed on from master to pupil as in time immemorial. Richard Norman Shaw led 'the architect as artist' camp and encouraged his assistants to foster friendships, not with their fellow professionals, but with their fellow artists, stating that:

> In France, Architects, Painters and Sculptors were trained together in one common school of the Arts (*the École des Beaux-Arts*). If Architecture in England was missing its way, it was for the young men to bring her back from professionalism. The Architects of this generation must make the future for themselves and knock at the door of Art until they were admitted.[5]

A number of assistants from Shaw's office, including W.R. Lethaby, Ernest Newton and E.S. Prior, therefore arranged a meeting with a number of their artistic contemporaries at 8pm on Tuesday 8 January 1884 at the Charing Cross Hotel to discuss the establishment of a society which should consist of 'Handicraftsmen and Designers in the Arts'. Their aim was no less than to reunite the Arts as they perceived that they had operated prior to the Renaissance – as a new Ruskinian Medieval Guild. John Belcher, the architect (1841–1913), chaired that first meeting and it was attended by 16 aspiring young architects, two painters (Alfred Parsons and John McLure Hamilton), one designer (Lewis Foreman Day) and two sculptors (Hamo Thorneycroft and George Blackall Simonds, 1843–1929 – an acknowledged expert in lost-wax casting). By the end of the year, the group had a name – The Art Workers' Guild – and 56 members who now included four sculptors, 26 painters, 11 craftsmen and 15 architects, with George Simonds elected as the first Master. In 1888, the products of their collaborations were first exhibited in public under the title of the 'Arts and Crafts Exhibition Society', thus both providing a name for what was to become one of the most internationally admired British artistic movements and also bringing their collective works to the public's attention for the first time.

The most significant aspect of the Guild's beliefs, from the perspective of architectural sculpture, was its concept of artistic unity, and thus crucially, for the first time, it now brought together the very best architects and the very best sculptors of this new generation to contribute as equals to a collective architectural vision – and the British public did not have to wait long to appreciate the impact that this new approach would have. In 1886, architect John Dando Sedding (1838–91) was elected as the second Master of the Guild and was also commissioned that year to design the Church of the Holy and Undivided Trinity with Saint Jude in Sloane Street, London (on which he was ably assisted by Henry Wilson, 1864–1934, who oversaw completion of the building after Sedding's death). Sedding, like Belcher, was a little older than most of the Guild members, had travelled on the Continent with Ruskin and, like Webb and Shaw, had trained in George Street's

50   Sculptor Henry Hugh Armstead's bronze angel lectern in the Church of the Holy and Undivided Trinity, Sloane Street, of 1886–90

51   The chancel gates of the Church of the Holy and Undivided Trinity, Sloane Street, by its architect John Dando Sedding

office, but his membership of both the Guild and the Arts and Crafts Exhibition Society had brought him into contact with the new generation of artists who were his fellow members. His views on architectural sculpture were clear and stated passionately: 'To me it is little short of a scandal that the reredos of St Paul's – one of the costliest pieces of sculpture of the century – should go, as a matter of course, to Messrs Farmer & Brindley, while the successors of Flaxman and Stevens could have done the work right nobly',[6] and Holy Trinity was to give him the opportunity to express these principles for the first time.

Sedding had already developed what might best be described as a Free Gothic or Romanesque style in his quite remarkable Church of Our Most Holy Redeemer in Clerkenwell which was then under construction, and the exterior of Holy Trinity shares the same banded stone and brickwork (which Shaw had made fashionable with his New Scotland Yard building of 1887), but here in an Early English Gothic style, with twin hexagonal towers framing the nave and its large ogee-arched, traceried, clear glass window. One's first impression of the interior of the church is of austerity, and it is only as one begins to explore that we find many of the members of the Guild represented, making the church, in the opinion of John Betjeman, a 'Cathedral of the Arts and Crafts Movement'. Henry Armstead executed the carved roundels in the spandrels of the arcades and the bronze angel lectern (fig.50); the figures in relief along the choir stalls are by Frederick Pomeroy; the cherubim round the shaft of the font are by Alfred Boucher (1850–1934) under Onslow Ford's (1852–1901) direction; a relief beneath the High Altar of *The Entombment* is by Harry Bates; Nelson Dawson crafted much of the metalwork including the gilded strapwork to the organ screen; Sedding himself designed the chancel gates with flanking *Angels* by Frederick Pomeroy (fig.51); Edward Burne-Jones produced much of the stained glass, with the east

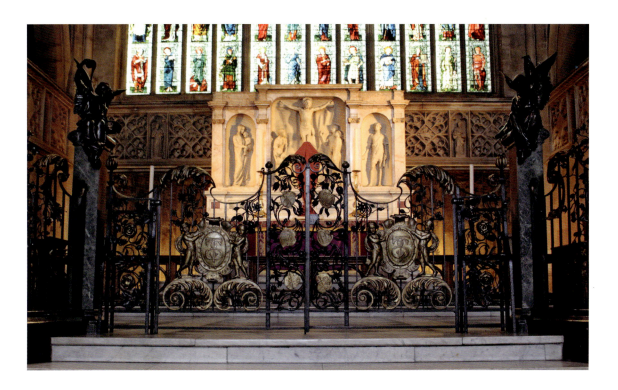

window in particular providing panel after panel of exquisite Pre-Raphaelite saints. Construction commenced in 1888, although sadly Sedding died in 1891, shortly before his church was completed (but that did leave us with a fine bronze memorial to him by Pomeroy). Far from all this work having been left to craftsmen (as Ruskin had dictated), it was carried out under Sedding's direction by some of the finest artists of the period, both providing one of the first examples of the new Arts and Crafts architecture and raising the craft of architectural sculpture to a place amongst the finest of the arts.[7]

As an example of the Guild's ideals, the Church of the Holy Trinity is therefore crucially important, but as far as the evolution of the New Sculpture Movement is concerned, it is really only Harry Bates's altar frontal relief, *The Entombment* (which it was long thought depicted the dead Christ supported by angels, but actually offers the resurrected Christ), which provides the nervous energy in the handling of form and the sensitivity to the particular qualities of bronze that was exhibited in Stevens's work, in a composition that also combines the sensuality and romantic realism of Dalou. Bates soon established himself as a key member of the movement with his dynamic bronze *Hounds in Leash*, which was exhibited at the Royal Academy in 1889, and he went on to undertake numerous architectural commissions, as well as producing a number of allegorical works and public statues including his outstanding equestrian *Lord Roberts* (bronzes of which survive in Glasgow and Calcutta).

Interestingly, and despite Sedding's contempt for them, Bates (and a number of his contemporaries including Charles John Allen, 1862–1956) had served a long apprenticeship as a carver with Farmer and Brindley before, in common with so many of the fine sculptors of his generation (including Frederick Pomeroy, Goscombe John and George Frampton), studying at the South London Technical Art School (under Dalou, Lanteri and Frith). For Harry Bates, this was followed by further study at the Royal Academy, and for many of the leading New Sculptors, this was then followed by a further period of extended study and apprenticeship on the Continent in either Rome (Thorneycroft) or Paris (Thorneycroft, Bates, Goscombe John, Drury and Pomeroy), thus providing a level of artistic education and exposure to the leading European sculptors which had been denied to almost all of their predecessor architectural sculptors who had progressed from craftsman to artist.

While Bates, Onslow Ford and others were engaged on their work on Holy Trinity for Sedding, John Belcher (the architect who had chaired the first meeting of the nascent Guild at the Charing Cross Hotel) engaged Hamo Thorneycroft to assist him with the design and execution of his Institute of Chartered Accountants' building in Moorgate Place in London (1889–93). In terms of its architecture, it could not have proved much more of a contrast to Holy Trinity as it represented a further development of the Renaissance Classical palazzo which had first been seen in Barry's London clubs half a century previously, but with the Chartered Accountants' Hall, Belcher took Victorian Classicism in an entirely new direction which would soon be identified as 'Edwardian Baroque' and, crucially, which established an extensive programme of architectural sculpture, as one of the essential elements of the style.

Even amongst those who had appeared to be the most committed Goths, there had been a significant shift towards Classicism during the 1880s, with Guild member Reginald Blomfield, for example, having written extensively on English Renaissance architecture, and Richard Norman Shaw (in many ways the progenitor of the Guild) having produced 170 Queen's Gate in London, the first 'Wrenaissance' town house. And, with his palatial Bryanston country house in Dorset underway by the end of the decade, he spoke for many of his contemporaries with typically Scottish candour: 'From the date of the Exhibition in 1851 until recently we were all intensely Gothic – and intensely wrong. We were trying to revive a style which was quite unsuited to the present day. Since 1880 however, we have been gradually awakening to the fact.'[8] Belcher (who had inherited his father's London practice and whose education had included two years studying contemporary architecture in Paris) had, like Shaw, started out as a Goth, having produced the (now sadly demolished) Mappin and Webb building in the City of London in 1870 in a Venetian Gothic style of which Ruskin would have whole-heartedly approved; but by the late 1880s (assisted first by Beresford Pite and then John James Joass) his Damascene conversion was complete.

In terms of both the history of British civic architecture and the British architectural sculpture of the next 30 years, it is hard to overemphasise the importance of Belcher's Institute of Chartered Accountants' Hall (fig.52). Almost certainly inspired by the Baroque architecture of Genoa, which he had recently witnessed himself for the first time shortly before starting his design, it was to be an urban palazzo in the grand manner. With its bold, deeply recessed rustication which wraps around its ground floor Tuscan columns, its grand Doric order above, the deeply overhanging cornice, the exquisite scrolled pediment with cartouche above its main entrance, and crucially, its extensive carving and figurative sculpture, it was to provide a particularly suave new imperial architectural language which, in contrast to the Gothic Revival which had sought to project Britain above all as a Christian country, was an unapologetic expression and celebration of Britain's astonishing wealth and power.

William Hamo Thorneycroft led the team of sculptors on the hall, assisted by his principal carver George Hardie, Charles John Allen, a young John Tweed and local sculptor J.E. Taylerson. Thorneycroft had the most blue-blooded of sculptural upbringings, being the son of sculptors Thomas Thorneycroft and Mary Thorneycroft (who was herself the daughter of a sculptor, John Francis). He had studied under his father and Frederic Leighton at the Royal Academy prior to his Continental training in Rome and Paris, returning to win the Royal Academy Gold Medal in 1875, after which he exhibited regularly and was soon winning commissions. His *Mower* of 1884 and *Sower* of 1886, introduced a note of contemporary realism into his

52 Architect John Belcher's hugely influential Chartered Accountants' Hall, 1889–93

work, and it was a theme which he was to express even more powerfully in his architectural sculpture. Thorneycroft and Belcher were well acquainted through long-standing family connections which had been forged by their parents, John Belcher had designed pedestals for Hamo Thorneycroft's father's memorial sculptures, Hamo Thorneycroft had modelled the bronze bust of John Belcher in 1881 which is now in the Royal Academy, and John Belcher had designed a house for Hamo's brother John (and would design another for Hamo, 2A Melbury Road, while work on the Chartered Accountants' Hall was underway).[9]

Under Thorneycroft's direction, his team executed what is read as a continuous frieze above the windows of the piano nobile, but is in fact a series of panels which wrap around the building on the two street elevations (fig.53). As Reginald Blomfield noted at the time, this arrangement of having a frieze at this low level was unconventional, but had the frieze been placed any higher, much of the impact of its excellent detail would have been lost. This demonstrates both Belcher's appreciation of the artistic value of Thorneycroft's contribution to the overall architectural composition and a desire to provide his client (who had initially balked at the cost of the sculpture) with obvious value for their investment – a point he emphasised in a contemporary lecture to the RIBA: 'In this grinding mercenary age, when clients expect so much for their money, such an extravagance as sculpture seems out of the question – a luxury which the mere utilitarian aspect of a building will not allow.' However, he believed that:

> if the sculptor be taken early into consultation he will be able, if he rightly appreciates architectural completeness, to give expression to the purpose and object of the building, to emphasise its character, and animate it with life and beauty. When it thus becomes an integral part of the whole design, clients (whether individuals or committees) are more likely to value its significance and importance. If left to be added later on – if funds permit – and treated as an 'Applied Art' it is sure to be omitted on motives of economy and eventually forgotten.[10]

To further ensure the legibility of the frieze, Thorneycroft modelled many of the figures in clay in his studio (with friends and family members acting

53   One of William Hamo Thorneycroft's frieze panels

as models), taking plaster casts from the clay and then transporting them to the site where he and Belcher could judge their effect from street level, before they were carved in situ in stone.

The three bays to the left of the main entrance represent the *Arts*, *Sciences* and *Crafts*, as depicted by female figures in Classical dress, while all the remaining panels celebrate the heroism of labour, with figures in contemporary dress representing *Education*, *Commerce*, *Manufactures*, *Agriculture*, *Mining* and *Building*, with Belcher, Thorneycroft and George Hardie, Thorneycroft's carver, represented amongst this latter group. Around the corner in Great Swan Alley the panels reflect the empire's global reach, with the *Railways* and *Shipping* covered, along with *India* and *The Colonies*, with each of the panels being centred on a female figure helpfully holding a tablet confirming the theme of the group. (The introduction of plain English texts, rather than what was now perceived as elitist Latin or Greek inscriptions, being a further innovation.) The figures are excellent, generally engaged in conversation, with their contemporary dress particularly well represented here in all its wrinkled, tucked and stretched state, along with the usual tools of the trades. The overall effect of the frieze is utterly convincing and was, even then, hugely admired.

Below the first-floor windows is a further horizontal panel but here blank and divided by a series of caryatids by Harry Bates (see fig.1) (almost certainly inspired by the winged half-figures on the Palazzo Podesta in Genoa, which Belcher had recently admired). Bates was also responsible for the massive carved corbel on the corner of the building, incorporating the arms of the Institute along with two figure brackets which support a pillared oriel above. The dome is surmounted by the blindfolded figure of *Justice* by Thorneycroft, supported by truncated figures representing accountants by her feet (fig.54). All the minor carving is by Farmer and Brindley. Amongst all these riches, it is Bates's carving which Susan Beattie particularly admires: 'Constantly expressive, in their masses and planes, of the blocks from which they are cut, sparing yet precise in detail,

54 Harry Bates's corbel group on the Institute of Chartered Accountants' Hall, London

heroic and yet full of humour and vitality, they are so exquisitely matched to Belcher's building as to become an indispensable part of its meaning and character.'[11] There is a new self-confidence here in this great celebration of the collaborative ideal, which established the essential relationship between sculpture and architecture within Belcher's new English Baroque style, and it is all carried off with a swagger that fully anticipated the Edwardian age.

Almost exactly contemporary with Belcher's Chartered Accountants' Hall are two buildings by architect Aston Webb (1849–1930, along with his partner Edward Ingress Bell, 1837–1914), who went on to occupy a position of architectural dominance during the Edwardian period on a par with Waterhouse and Scott in the Victorian era (for both of whom Webb, incidentally, had himself

55 Harry Bates's *Queen Victoria* above the entrance to architect Aston Webb's Victoria Law Courts in Birmingham of 1887–91

previously worked). These buildings give us a fascinating insight into this period of extraordinary architectural flux around 1890, one being in a heady mix of Gothic, Flemish and Renaissance elements – the Victoria Law Courts in Birmingham (1887–91) – and the other a palatial Classical building (though sporting a Venetian campanile) – the South Kensington (now Victoria and Albert) Museum (1891–1909), with both, though architecturally looking backwards rather than forwards, nevertheless providing extensive opportunities for members of the New Sculpture Movement. That we find Aston Webb working so closely with this group of sculptors is interesting and significant as Webb was neither a member of the Guild nor particularly sympathetic to the concept of the architect as artist, being a staunch supporter of the Royal Institute of Architects who were then promoting architecture as a profession. Nevertheless, even he recognised the vitality and quality of the work of the New Sculptors, though because of his distance from the Guild's ideals, he used them to merely contribute elements within his overall vision, rather than offering them artistic collaboration, as Belcher had.

The Law Courts in Birmingham are the city's finest Victorian building and were the first in the city to be entirely clad in terracotta (as popularised by Waterhouse who led the architectural competition's assessors), with the sculptural programme central to the expression of the ideals of Law and Order to which the building was dedicated. Webb's elevations offer intricate layers of detail in which the wall surface is fragmented to create a picturesque effect of rich, Flemish, Gothic excess. He was assisted in developing his detailed design by the artist and illustrator Walter Crane – friend of Morris, early British Socialist and founder of the Arts and Crafts Exhibition Society – who by 1888 had become the third Master of the Guild.

The great arch of the main entrance swoops up to create an aedicule within which sits the figure of *Queen Victoria* by Harry Bates which is central to the building's symbolism (indeed the Queen laid the foundation stone herself in 1887). She sits, in full ceremonial regalia, holding an orb with a winged Victory and a sceptre, 'seated like a judge and alludes to the certainty of justice to be found in a British court of law. At her feet, this national justice is endorsed by the figure of St George, patron saint of England, who slays the dragon in obvious reference to Good conquering Evil'[12] (fig.55). The spandrels on either side contain further figures representing *Patience*, *Mercy*, *Truth* and *Temperance* – all attributes of Justice – but here not just framed by the architecture but almost captured and held within it by banded terracotta columns which conclude in stylised naturalistic capitals. High above, the great clock face is flanked by reliefs representing *Time* and *Eternity*, below a *Royal Coat of Arms*, with the central gable topped off with a blindfolded *Justice* in Classical garb by W.S. Frith (1850–1924, who had succeeded Dalou as Modelling Master at the South London Art College and was to work with Webb again and again) (fig.56). Each of the further gables have sculpture referring to Birmingham's various trades including *Gunmaking* and *Pottery*, and the sculpture continues within the building in sumptuously ornate arches, extensive tracery and carved canopies to the judges' benches. Overall, it is a superbly coordinated design in which the architectural detail and sculpture are fully integrated within the architect's vision and in which New Sculpture features prominently.

The terracotta in which the sculpture was cast from Bates's and others' models was all produced by Edwards of Ruabon, with almost all of the architectural detail and most of the minor relief sculpture being carried out by Guild member William Aumonier (1869–1943), who had established his workshop of architectural sculptors and wood carvers in New Inn Yard, just off the Tottenham Court Road in London, in 1876. As if to emphasise that all members of the Guild were valued equally, Aumonier, though clearly from the world of masonry and stone carving, was treated as the equal of his more illustrious sculptor 'brothers' and in fact exhibited part of his work on the Victoria Law Courts at the Royal Academy Summer Exhibitions in 1889 and 1890 (though the Academy placed it within the Architecture rooms and not amongst the Sculpture).

Webb's other major work of this period was his design for the South Kensington Museum – a much larger, more illustrious and considerably less successful building. Like most of the South Kensington projects including Waterhouse's own Natural History Museum, it was dogged with delays caused by funding crises and constant changes of

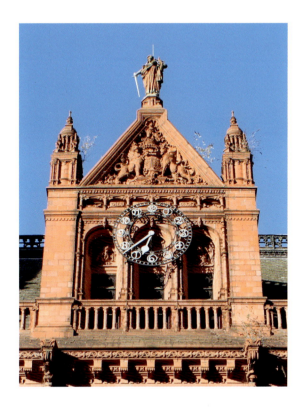

56 A blind-folded *Justice* by W.S. Frith above the *Royal Coat of Arms*

brief, until Queen Victoria finally laid the foundation stone here as well in 1899, although she had died before its completion in 1909 when it was renamed in her and her husband's honour as the 'Victoria and Albert Museum' (fig.57). The architectural sculpture here is stretched rather thinly around the great mass of this building, culminating (as one would expect) around the main entrance where further significant practitioners of the New Sculpture Movement are represented. The principal statues of *Victoria* and *Albert* flanked by *Inspiration* and *Knowledge* are by Alfred Drury, with the spandrel relief compositions of *Truth* and *Beauty* by George Frampton (1860–1928) and statues of *Edward VII* and *Queen Alexandra* by William Goscombe John (1860–1952), above which is something of an architectural wedding cake which concludes in an enormous domed lantern. Beyond the main entrance, the major sculpture is a series of 36 full-size statues between the second-floor windows representing British artists by a variety of contemporary sculptors, but these are very much traditional niche figures, rather than integrated elements of the architecture (fig.58).

Another prominent member of the New Sculpture Movement was Frederick William Pomeroy (1856–1924), yet another student of the South London School of Technical Art, where he trained under both W.S. Frith and Aimé-Jules Dalou and from where he progressed to the Royal Academy, winning the Gold Medal and Travelling Studentship in 1885. This allowed him to study in Rome and under Emmanuel Fremiet and Antonin Mercié in Paris, before returning to London where he collaborated with Frith before seeking his own commissions.

57 The arch and tower above the main entrance to architect Aston Webb's Victoria and Albert Museum of 1899–1909, with spandrel figures by George Frampton and archivolt relief panels by Alfred Drury

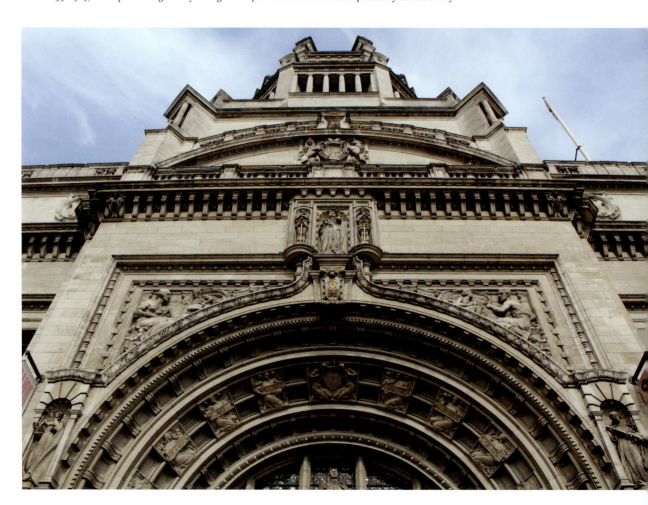

HARMONY ATTAINED

58 Alfred Bertram Pegram's sculpture of fellow sculptor John Flaxman – one of the series of portraits of English painters, sculptors and architects that occupy the first-floor niches

highly regarded); but instead, having come across Pomeroy's work in the London churches of John Dando Sedding, he invited the young sculptor to carry out the architectural sculpture on the Town Hall. Mountford's design for the Town Hall, rather bizarrely for this no-nonsense steel town, took the form of a rather grand Stoke stone, Late French Renaissance Guild Hall, crowned by a massive clock tower which, in reference to the source of the city's wealth, is surmounted by a bronze statue of Vulcan, the master of the forge (by Italian sculptor Mario Raggi, 1821–1907). Despite a rather long and drawn-out local controversy over the expense, Mountford succeeded in persuading the Council both to fund an extensive programme of architectural sculpture and to appoint Pomeroy.

By the time that Pomeroy started work on the commission, he would have already seen Thorneycroft's proposed frieze for the Chartered Accountants' Hall, a panel of which had been exhibited at the Royal Academy in 1891 and by 1892 the final version was well underway on Moorgate Place. It was hardly a surprise, therefore, that Pomeroy proposed two rather similar major friezes for the Town Hall, here just above the ground-floor windows, depicting both *The Arts* and *The Industries of Sheffield* (fig.59). These are in relief and while the figures, who appear in contemporary work clothes along with their tools, are beautifully composed against a background of architecture and machinery, their expressions and poses lack any great vitality, despite their flowing aprons and voluminous garments and

In 1890, London architect Edward William Mountford (1855–1908) was selected to undertake the design of the new Sheffield Town Hall (1890–97) and, with encouragement from the Council, he initially intended to appoint the local (and largely self-taught) sculptor Benjamin Creswick (1853–1946) as his stone carver (whose terracotta frieze on the Cutler's Hall in London of 1887 was

59 One of sculptor Frederick Pomeroy's six relief panels in the entrance hall of Sheffield Town Hall depicting 'Purity'

60 Architect Edward Mountford's Sheffield Town Hall of 1890–97 with sculptures of *Thor* and *Vulcan* below *Queen Victoria* by Frederick Pomeroy

thus they serve more to evoke the drudgery of most industrial work, rather than its invigorating impact on the local economy and community. There are also a number of statues in niches around the exterior of the building, including *Peace*, *War*, *Justice* and *Queen Victoria*, and several very fine entrance door tympana with cartouches enclosing the city's coat of arms, supported by *Thor* and *Vulcan* (fig.60). The sculpture continues inside with a number of allegorical themes presented in the entrance hall such as *Brotherhood*, *Patriotism*, *Fortitude* and *Affection* with explanatory legends, and the spandrels to the arches of the main stairwell have reliefs of various local historical myths and legends such as the *Slaying of the Wharncliffe Dragon*. Overall, though the sculpture is perhaps better coordinated than integrated, it is yet another impressive late-Victorian public building and marks the production of a very extensive sculptural programme by its relatively young sculptor and the establishment of yet another enduring architect/sculptor partnership, with the two working together again and again throughout Mountford's very successful career.

With due credit to Thorneycroft for his pioneering role on the Institute of Chartered Accountants' Hall (and to Pomeroy, Frith, Allen, Tweed and Goscombe John), it was to be Harry Bates along with Alfred Drury and George Frampton who were to make the most significant contributions to architectural sculpture during the next decade or two, and whose architectural sculptures would achieve the highest standards in terms of technique, originality and in the extraordinary emotional charge with which their mature work was imbued. Frampton was to prove the most influential of all the architectural sculptors and, having trained initially in an architect's office, he above all the others showed a particular sympathy for the aims of his architectural collaborators. After the South London Technical Art School, the Royal Academy and Paris, he developed his unique 'symbolist style, which combines dreamlike and suggestive qualities with a draughtsmanly perfection'.[13] In particular, he was a master of the low relief, in which, more than any other medium, he believed: 'lay the possibility of reconciling intricacy and understatement, sculpture's illusion of reality and painting's colour and line, and of securing that mysterious, elusive harmony of the sensual and the austere'.[14] Fascinated by the sensuality of the French and Austrian Symbolists and the painters and sculptors of the Florentine Renaissance, he described himself in 1897 as 'an art worker and not the more restricted title of sculptor'.[15]

Of course, architectural sculpture was just one aspect of the output of the New Sculpture Movement and in many ways, inevitably by its very nature, it imposed a constraint upon the 'art workers' involved and the opportunities to develop a shared artistic vision were much fewer than those in which they simply made a sculptural contribution within the architect's overall design. In their own work they were free to fully express themselves and, in particular, return to the use of their preferred bronze. Indeed, there were a number of leading sculptors of the new school who were involved in next to no architectural sculpture at all, including the hugely successful Joseph Edgar Boehm (1834–90), who inherited many of Baron Marochetti's techniques of undercutting and deeply modelling bronze to provide even greater contrasts between light and shade; and perhaps the finest of all late Victorian sculptors, Alfred Gilbert (1854–1934), whose bronzes of *Perseus Arming* (1882) and *Icarus* (1884) were hugely influential within the movement and whose sole contribution to architectural sculpture – a series of reliefs in Daly's Theatre in London – were demolished with the building in 1938. Both Gilbert and Frampton also began to experiment in mixed media, with Gilbert combining bronze and marble in one of his greatest works, the hauntingly beautiful *Monument to the Duke of Clarence* in Windsor Castle of 1892–9, and Frampton in his statues of *Dame Alice Owen* (1897) and *Lamia* (1899).[16] In both architecture and sculpture, Britain was at long last finally attracting interest from Continental Europe rather than constantly being one step behind.

While architects and sculptors in the regional cities were excluded from direct involvement in the teaching of the London art schools, several soon joined the Guild and the new artistic innovations of London's architects and sculptors were also extensively covered in contemporary publications. By the 1890s almost any new sculpture of significance was reviewed in the *Art Journal*, which was founded in 1839, and the same went for new architecture, with *The Builder* having been founded in 1843. By the end of the decade, however, these stalwarts of the arts scene were being challenged by *The Studio* – which began publication in 1893 – to promote the work of the Guild, and Britain's leading architectural magazine, the *Architectural Review*, first went to print in 1896, riding the wave of this sudden upswing in national creativity. Regional artists also contributed to and attended the Royal Academy's Summer Exhibition and many of them had worked as assistants or been educated in London, Paris or Rome. The Glasgow architect John James Burnet, for example, was educated at the École des Beaux-Arts in Paris during the 1870s, first exhibited at the Royal Academy in 1882 and had a network of friendships with fellow artists throughout Britain, the Continent and the USA through his education at the École; and so, despite his apparent remoteness from the action in London, he was following events closely, as his own work in Scotland from the 1890s showed clearly. Burnet became one of his country's most successful architects, eventually moving to

London after winning the competition to extend the British Museum, but it was his work from this period in Glasgow that represented his greatest artistic achievement, as well as making a substantial contribution to the national contemporary scene.

By the start of the 1890s, Burnet had already completed his Clyde Navigation Trust building (with John Mossman) when he embarked on a series of red sandstone buildings in the centre of Glasgow that established the 'Glasgow Free Style' which would dominate the city's architecture until the start of the First World War. The first of these was Charing Cross Mansions (1889–91), an enormous five-storey apartment building that spanned an entire block of the city. Its scale would have challenged most architects but in Burnet's hands, it simply swept around the street corner from Sauchiehall Street into St George's Road and continued on to a great corner drum, which acted as a hinge to turn the wall plane into Renfrew Street (fig.61). Its steeply pitched roofs, chimneys and dormer windows owed something to Paris, but below this level Burnet

61   William Birnie Rhind's *St Mungo* and *Night and Day* which frame the mighty corner clock on John James Burnet's Charing Cross Mansions of 1889–91

brought something of what was then Glasgow's swaggering commercial confidence to the details. While rich, sharp architectural carving abounds, the main sculptural programme is focused on the central bays of the curving facade. At its base is one of Burnet's trademark broken, segmental pediments enclosing Glasgow's coat of arms on an elaborate cartouche incorporating a circular band inscribed 'Let Glasgow Flourish', surmounted by *St Mungo*, Glasgow's patron saint. Putti rest on either side of the broken pediment, above which standing female figures representing *Spring* and *Autumn* frame a marble panel with the bearded head of *Father Time* below a great clock, which sits below a further stone arch, surmounted by two further female figures representing *Industry* and *Commerce*. We have now reached the stone balcony of the attic floor, which is here solid and inscribed 'Charing Cross Mansions' below a further broken pediment, within which two standing naked youths support a scrolled shield with the powerful vertical thrust continuing with a hexagonal tower concluding in a domed lantern. Having lost John Mossman, Burnet had turned to Edinburgh sculptor William Birnie Rhind (1853–1933) for assistance and the two would work again on several occasions, including Burnet's Professional & Civil Service Supply Association building (1903–7) on George Street in Edinburgh, with Rhind himself making a number of further significant contributions to architectural sculpture, most notably on the National Portrait Gallery (1898) and the Scotsman building (1900), also in Edinburgh.

The second of Burnet's buildings from this period is his extension to The Athenaeum on Buchanan Street in Glasgow (1891–3) in which the sculpture is remarkably restrained and yet superbly integrated within the overall architectural composition. Here, Burnet provides a rocketing verticality within an asymmetrical composition of great bay windows to the left and a stair and lift tower to the right. The bay is topped with a pair of *Muses* on octagonal piers below a statue of *Pallas Athena* contained within an aedicule below a concluding split pediment with pylon (almost certainly derived from Shaw's

62 John James Burnet's architecture approached perfection in the Savings Bank Hall of 1894–9 on which he collaborated with sculptor George Frampton

recently completed New Scotland Yard). With the exception of a couple of rather mannerist attenuated putti above the entrance door, the sculpture is fairly conservative, but well executed on this occasion by William Kellock Brown (1856–1934). Like Birnie Rhind he worked mainly in Scotland, combining architectural sculpture with monumental sculpture and teaching at the Glasgow School of Art from 1888 to 1898. Much influenced by Frampton, he completed numerous architectural sculpture commissions in Glasgow, including four allegorical Pre-Raphaelite maidens on the Castle Chambers of 1898–1902, and an extensive programme of sculpture on the Hutchesontown District Library of 1904–6, including *St Mungo with Female Figures*.

The final building, and best of the three was Burnet's Baroque palazzo – the new banking hall for the Glasgow Savings Bank in Ingram Street (1894–9) (fig.62). It was connected to a much larger bank building (designed by his father, John Burnet Snr) which contained the usual supporting office accommodation, allowing John Jnr to focus entirely on form and space in his banking hall. Despite its scale, this is one of Glasgow's finest pieces of architecture in which it becomes impossible to draw any boundary between the architecture and the sculpture. On Ingram Street, great, split, pedimented windows light the hall, containing cartouches, whereas to the side streets, crouching *Atlantes* support the split ends and frame female figures who represent the rather stern Scottish virtues of *Industry*, *Commerce and Frugality*. The main entrance, however, is the sculptural tour de force of the building with great Doric columns holding back the rusticated wall plane to allow a route through, while within, Corinthian columns once more support crouching *Atlantes*, here framing an aedicule containing a stone *St Mungo* between twisted columns, with both his crozier and undergarment gilded. He is flanked by two further female figures representing *Industry* (who is spinning cloth) and *Agriculture* (picking fruit from a tree). Burnet's proportions never miss a beat, from the stonework details to the subtle treatment of the building's corners and the dome to the banking hall. It is a superbly confident work of art that, with assistance from an excellent sculptor, is carried off with gusto.

The sculptor here is George Frampton, with much of the carving executed by local man William Shirreffs (1846–1902), but interestingly, *St Mungo* (which was carved by Frampton in London) is the only element to be gilded, reflecting his interest in mixed media. The metalwork here is outstanding too with the main entrance gates by Longden & Co. of London who also provided an exquisite letterbox decorated with oak leaves and a bell push entwined with mistletoe, while the railings are by the Glasgow firm of George Adam & Son. The division of labour here very much reflected the mix of local and London expertise within the regional cities with clients prepared to push the boat out on occasion to engage the very best artists, even if for only one or two key elements of their new buildings. Burnet's suggestion of Frampton reflected his awareness of the latest developments in London, while for Frampton it proved to be an introduction to Glasgow where, during the next few years, he would be engaged on what was to be the most significant public building project outside London of this period.

Such was the success of the first Glasgow International Exhibition of 1888 that it made a profit of £46,000, a sum which was doubled by public subscription, with the aim of providing a new School of Art, Concert Hall, Art Gallery and Museum for the city. A site was provided for the building by the City Council in Kelvingrove Park in the west of the city, but by 1892, the cost estimates for the cultural complex had so increased that it was decided to proceed with simply the Art Gallery and Museum (with Charles Rennie Mackintosh later providing his famous School of Art in the centre of the city). An architectural competition was held, which was judged by Alfred Waterhouse alone, and on his recommendation (and to the disgust of the many local architects who had entered, including John Burnet) the commission was awarded to John William Simpson of London (1858–1933), ably assisted by Edmund John Milner Allen (1859–1912), reigniting the bitter hostilities which had surrounded Englishman George Gilbert Scott's appointment to design the new Glasgow University buildings a quarter of a century earlier.

Simpson's Baroque design was described as 'an astylar composition on severely classical lines, but with free Renaissance treatment in detail'[17] to which I would add only that its insistent verticals which culminate in its various towers and attenuated domes give the building complex a distinctly uplifting presence (fig.63). Had it been executed in white Portland stone rather than in Glasgow's then fashionable red sandstone, it would not have looked out of place in South Kensington where, with its rich and well-balanced composition and razor-sharp architectural detail, it would certainly have been regarded as far superior to Aston Webb's V&A. It was always intended that, as a palace of art itself, it should be the subject of an extensive sculptural programme, and Waterhouse's own encouragement to the city, by letter, to invest in sculpture as well as architecture clearly carried weight with the Council:

in France this association of the two arts, and the prominent place given to sculpture are still the fashion, unhappily in this country it is very unusual to employ sculptors of the first class on architectural work, and our buildings suffer lamentably from this cause. Glasgow has now an opportunity of reviving the practice, and, I believe, if she does so she will never repent it.[18]

Simpson never had any doubt as to whom he wished to see appointed as master sculptor to oversee the programme and to execute its most important elements. All his reports to the Council were framed to lead to the increasingly inevitable appointment of George Frampton. Having already upset the local architects, the Council now appointed the Englishman Frampton, thus creating a similar level of disgust amongst the local sculptors including William Shirreffs (Frampton's assistant on the Savings Bank), who suggested that Simpson and the Council had clearly 'not made a very careful examination of the Architectural Sculpture of the public buildings of Glasgow, or they would have seen they could compare favourably with any similar work in the United Kingdom'.[19] As a sop to this sentiment, the Council decided that a competition would be held for the commissions for a number of the planned external allegorical figures and, following the submission of clay maquettes by the aspiring sculptors, Simpson and Frampton gave the lion's share of this work too to a number of other London sculptors, which of course, simply further fanned the flames of local resentment. Further, Simpson's initial estimate of £5,000 for the entire sculptural programme was immediately blown out of the water by Frampton who, shortly after his appointment, demanded £9,000 for his fee alone. This resulted in a prolonged delay in the execution of the sculpture which actually saw much of the building completed, along with its minor architectural sculpture, by Glasgow stonemasons Peter McKissock and Sons, with vast areas left 'boasted' (that is to say, protruding in the rough) for future carving on site.

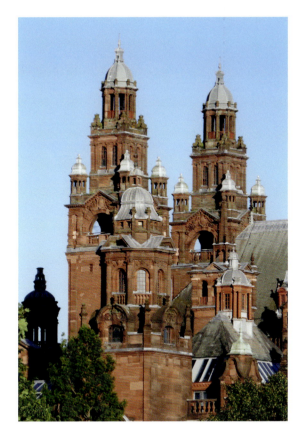

63 The red sandstone towers of John Simpson's Kelvingrove Art Gallery and Museum of 1892–1900

An overall budget was eventually approved and work commenced on the extensive programme of allegorical statuary around the building, with the larger than life-size bronze of a seated *St Mungo as the Patron of Art and Music* by Frampton in the arch of the main entrance, being the highlight (fig.64). This is no mere reworking of his statue on the Savings Bank Hall, but a major and significant work within the New Sculpture Movement. The detail of the saint's vestments is quite extraordinary, with various motifs in relief including the tree, bell and fish from Glasgow's coat of arms, with the weight of a great embroidered cloak depicted in contrast to the lace finery of his gown. Seated at his feet, and

64   George Frampton's magnificent bronze *St Mungo* with supporters at the main entrance to the Art Gallery and Museum

65   George Frampton, *Pheidias* – one of a trio of Greek artists masks above the attic windows on the entrance porch

unusually with their backs to him like bookends, are two female figures representing *The Arts*, one engrossed in a book while the other concentrates on a portative organ, again with excellent drapery and beautifully sculpted hair – their feminine sensuality a foil to St Mungo's monasticism and sanctity.

In the arches above St Mungo are three pairs of spandrels in which further tributes are paid to the city and its arts and industries, with *The Industries of Glasgow at the Court of Mercury* and *Love Teaching Harmony to the Arts* occupying the arches of the east and west returns. But it is the sculptures in either spandrel of the main arch which grab the viewers' attention, where once more Frampton modelled, and Shirreffs carved, two excellent groups of figures in relief – *The Empire Salutes Glasgow.* These quintets of female musicians in medieval dress with their long, rather Nordic, horns (which neatly fill the acute angle of the spandrels) are clearly a reworking of his silver bas-relief panel *Music* of 1895–6 (which, Susan Beattie suggests, may have been based on Luca della Robbia's trumpeter in Florence Cathedral), but their effect here is to provide rather a haunting proclamatory host above the saint's head and, combined with *The Arts* flanking the saint below, a further hint of sensuality (which was much criticised at the time). While their present condition is poor, the partial erosion of several of the maidens' heads has simply added a further ghostly dimension to this ethereal gathering. Frampton and Shirreffs also produced the masks of the *Great Trio of Greek Art* on the parapet, high above (fig.65).

Each of the corner pavilions has seated statues on a range of themes, and it was these sculptures which had been the subject of the competition with Francis Derwent Wood (1871–1926), who had also studied under Lanteri in London and was then teaching at Glasgow School of Art, having been selected to provide four – *Music, Architecture, Sculpture* and *Painting* – which are the most interesting of this category. Like Frampton's female musicians, these are slightly abstract rather than natural, and with more than a hint of Art Nouveau. The other statues in this group were by Aristide Fabbrucci (1859–1921) and Edward George Bramwell (1865–1944) from London, with Glasgow represented by Johan Keller (1863–1944) and Edinburgh by William Birnie Rhind, whose brooding, muscular *Science*, is the best of this group (fig.66). Each of these sculptures was accompanied by a shield in the pediment below with a carved title in English (as we first saw on the Chartered Accountants' Hall), once again allowing those who had not benefitted from a Classical education to fully appreciate the sculptural themes.

66   Sculptor William Birnie Rhind's *Science* on the west pavilion

Beyond these major pieces, the architectural carving was extensive and, if somewhat conservative in its design, beautifully executed in soft red Dumfries sandstone. This included *Scottish Counties* which took the form of much scrolled and foliated coats of arms in the semi-circular tympana to each of the main ground-floor windows, which were themselves divided by pilasters with shield capitals on which were carved artists' names, with all of these carved (under Frampton's direction) by local artists – a young William Reid Dick (1878–1961), James Harrison Mackinnon (1866–1954), William Shirreffs, James Charles Young (1839–1923) and William Vickers (1851–1922). The interior of the building also enjoyed extensive carving which included *Crests of the Glasgow Trades* and *World Composers* around the Central Hall, two particularly well designed and executed compositions – the coats of arms of Glasgow's trade organisations, *The Trades House* and *The Merchants House* – by the north porch, and on the second floor, above the southern entrance, a large relief with the combined coats of arms of Glasgow and the British Empire, with a central shield bearing the legend 'Let Glasgow Flourish' once more. All this work was carved by local architectural sculptors, wood carvers and plasterers R.A. McGillvray & Ferris, and finally, the East and West Courts were decorated with cartouches with the names of *Figures of Scottish History*. If Scotland's artists had been under-represented in the major artistic appointments, this had at least been partially offset for the visitor by the overwhelming nationalism of the sculptural programme, and in the end its extraordinary scale did create a number of local opportunities.

In terms of the comparative quality of the work of this large group of contemporary sculptors, Frampton more than justified his appointment as their principal, with his *St Mungo* and his female musicians and supporters confirming his fascination with European Symbolism, while Derwent Wood's *Music* and other muses reflects his exposure to the coterie of Art Nouveau artists in Glasgow with whom he would have come into contact while teaching at the School of Art. While Charles Rennie Mackintosh has become the most famous member of this group, it was his friends the architects James Salmon Jnr (1873–1924) and John Gaff Gillespie (1870–1926) with whom Derwent Wood collaborated on a number of building designs, including the British Linen Bank in Govan of 1899 and the quite extraordinary and highly original 'Hatrack' at 142–4 St Vincent Street, Glasgow (1899–1902) (fig.67).

On the British Linen Bank building, the architecture is fairly typical Glasgow Free Style but with hints of Art Nouveau in its shallow arches,

67   Architect James Salmon Jnr and sculptor Derwent Wood's 'Hatrack' building on St Vincent Street, Glasgow (1899–1902)

bracketed eaves and complex corner dome, but Derwent Wood's work at ground level has more than a hint of Mackintosh's local 'Spook School', with his sculpture concentrated principally around the corner entrance. Here, a ship's prow (an extremely popular device in shipbuilding Glasgow) emerges in full sail below the corner first-floor oriel window, while seated on the capitals of the columns which flank the entrance are winged zephyrs, who are twisted around to blow wind into the ship's sails through their spiral shells. Modelled by Wood, they were carved by Richard Ferris of McGillvray & Ferris. David Walker, in *Architecture of Glasgow*, describes them as 'tortured angels' and there is certainly something grotesque about them, but they are nevertheless remarkable and powerful sculptures, with their contorted frames exposing life-like bones and taut sinews.

The other building (an office at 142a–4 St Vincent Street), which was locally nicknamed 'The Hatrack' as a result of the curved spikes on its pagoda-like roof, is an astonishing essay in sandstone which appears to stretch the material to its absolute elastic limit, creating a tall, thin, ten-storey building that is much more glass than wall. Working closely with Derwent Wood and McGillvray & Ferris, architect James Salmon Jnr produced a building which is in many ways entirely a work of architectural sculpture, with every element carved specifically for its purpose within the overall composition. There is a consistency and fluency to all the carved detail here – including the sinuous columns with their lotus capitals (first seen over a decade earlier on Arthur Heygate Mackmurdo's (1851–1942) furniture), the rippling stone lines of the first-floor window, the goat-head keystones to the entrance arch and the winged figures to the first-floor corbels – that together represent a level of collaboration between architect and sculptor rarely seen in the city since Thomson and Mossman.

Though it was much admired internationally, in terms of Glasgow's commercial and public architecture, Art Nouveau represented but a minor tributary and its output was largely domestic, it being very rare for a public client to abandon what was now a triumphant Classicism for something more novel. There was, however, one Arts and Crafts architect who successfully broke out of domestic work and into civic architecture around this time – Liverpudlian Charles Harrison Townsend (1851–1928). Townsend joined the Guild in 1888, the year that he established his practice in London (later becoming Master in 1903), and was a friend of both Frampton and Derwent Wood (a fireplace designed by him was executed by Frampton and exhibited at the Arts and Crafts Exhibition of 1896). He is best known for three London buildings which A. Stuart Gray described in his book *Edwardian Architecture* as being 'in a class by themselves' – the Bishopsgate Institute (1894–5), the Whitechapel Art Gallery (1896–1901) and the Horniman Museum (1898–1901).

Perhaps most accurately described as 'Free Style' rather than Art Nouveau or Arts and Crafts, the Bishopsgate Institute has shallow projecting towers capped with cupolas enclosing a boldly arched entrance with glazed screen above below a steeply pitched roof that has more than a little of William Burges about it – all in buff terracotta, with contrasting banding to the hexagonal cupolas. Two delightful horizontal relief bands above the main entrance and the glazed screen above, feature the popular Arts and Crafts motif of the Tree of Life, here with slender trunks and large overlapping leaves laced together by sinuous branches, with the legend 'Bishopsgate Institute' intertwined within the upper band. It is another example of the extraordinary flexibility of the medium of architectural faience which had already figured in both the Gothic and Classical Revivals (fig.68). The Whitechapel Art Gallery is clearly a further development of the Bishopsgate Institute design, with the entrance here bolder and much more deeply sculpted, with the single plane of the entrance elevation extruded to form twin bookend towers once more. It was originally planned that the arch would be surmounted by a mosaic frieze by Walter Crane, but sadly the funding ran out and the decoration on this most restrained of facades is limited to two further bands of stylised tree foliage at the base of each tower.

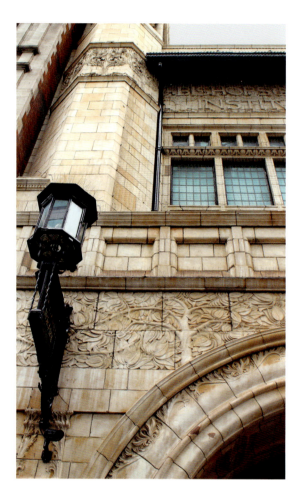

68 The popular Arts and Crafts Tree of Life motif in terracotta on Charles Harrison Townsend's Bishopsgate Institute of 1894-5

Funding was not a problem for the Horniman Museum, being the gift of the extremely wealthy Quaker tea merchant F.J. Horniman. It was designed to house and display his ethnographical and zoological collections. This extremely unusual building, which is organised around the great curved vault of the central gallery, is rather dwarfed by its massive stone tower whose curved sides project as four turrets above the level of the four great circular clock faces (a common philanthropic gesture to those who could not afford their own timepiece), and in turn support a shallow circular stone drum which concludes this rather strange extrusion (fig.69). The front elevation bears a horizontal band of mosaic (as intended for the Art Gallery), but here by brother art worker Robert Anning Bell (1863–1933) representing aspects of human life. Above it is a row of leaf-capped pilasters, flanked by hooded niches with wrought-iron screens which form the capitals to broader pilasters. The Tree of Life is again much in evidence – carved in the pilasters below the niches and around the top of the tower, here by William Aumonier, with Frederick Pomeroy providing a bronze memorial tablet below the mosaic. As Alastair Service noted: 'the street frontage is a rare union of the arts and crafts'.[20]

Compared to the scale and quantity of sculpture on the contemporary Glasgow Art Gallery and Museum, this is modest stuff indeed, and while the restrained ornamentation of the Arts and Crafts Movement was important in preparing the ground for Modernism, it represented a relatively minor tributary in the context of contemporary British architectural sculpture. Indeed, amidst the great flood of major late 19th- and early 20th-century public buildings, one of the few Arts and Crafts buildings to offer a substantial, fully integrated programme of architectural sculpture was in the remodelling of a small public house by Blackfriars Bridge in London.

The Black Friar had been built in 1875, but it was only in the early years of the 20th century that it was completely transformed by architect Herbert Fuller-Clark (1869–1934) and a team of sculptors into what John Betjeman described as 'the most perfect *art nouveau* in London'. Drawing on the 'Black Friar' theme, the sculptors, who included Nathaniel Hitch, Frederick Callcott and the ubiquitous, Farmer and Brindley, provided various carvings of jolly friars – playing musical instruments, dancing, feeding pie to an ass, singing and seated on barrels – along with a series of eight plaques, each with a pair of friars advertising the

69 Architect Charles Harrison Townsend's Horniman Museum (1898–1901) with sculpture by William Aumonier

70　One of Nathaniel Hitch's grotesque reliefs on the Black Friar public house

Champneys's proposal to appoint the more expensive George Frampton was rejected by his client. (It would have been fascinating to see what Frampton would have contributed within this Gothic framework.) Westminster Roman Catholic Cathedral (1895–1903) by John Francis Bentley (1839–1902), offered a masterpiece of Byzantine design (to differentiate it from its more illustrious Anglican neighbour), but largely due to funding strictures, it contained very little architectural sculpture beyond its magnificent arched entrance (by Farmer and Brindley once more) with another fine mosaic by Anning Bell. It had been a long war of attrition, but by the end of the century, Classicism had not only finally triumphed, but was about to flourish once more in one great, final, magnificent hurrah, before the First World War all but emptied the nation's coffers.

John Belcher and Richard Norman Shaw were now the guides (with Ruskin and his moralising now desperately out of fashion) and it would be their ostentatious Baroque style which would come

drinks available within (fig.70). Inside, the theme intensifies, with a number of copper reliefs by Henry Poole depicting friars making wine and beer and enjoying the fruits of their labour, while accompanied by carved monkeys playing musical instruments, against a rather luxurious background of polychromatic polished stone. Pevsner's categorisation of Art Nouveau is pretty accurate as there is little of the asceticism which was central to the Arts and Crafts Movement in this joyous celebration of wine-making and drinking, which was inspired by the Black Friars of London and created by the Brothers of the Guild (fig.71).

By the 1890s, Gothic was all but extinct, with Basil Champneys's (1842–1935) John Rylands Library in Manchester (1890–99) representing one of its final death throes. The extensive sculpture here is by Robert Bridgeman and John Cassidy (1860–1939) after

71　One of Frederick Callcot's fretted copper signs

to represent the new Edwardian age which was about to dawn. Belcher followed up his Chartered Accountants' Hall with his design for Colchester Town Hall (1897–1902) which, like Norman Shaw's New Scotland Yard (1888–90) and Bryanston House in Dorset (1889–94), combined Portland stone with red brick in a design which Nikolaus Pevsner suggested confirmed Belcher as having 'more braggadocio than anyone'.[21] Its symmetrical main facade with seven bays included no less than three pediments, with the two outer arched ones framing a central triangular pediment above the mayor's ornate balcony over the main entrance, whose tympanum was carved with the Borough's coat of arms. The sculpture was by local stonemasons L.J. Watts & Co. and included four allegorical figures who inhabited Belcher's magnificent clock tower – representing *Engineering*, *Military Defence*, *Agriculture* and *Fishery* (a combination which apparently represented Colchester's unique claim to fame) – and six life-size statues of famous locals ranging from *Eudo Dapifer* to *Boudica* within Portland stone niches on the south elevation. One can only assume that Belcher's proposal to have Thorneycroft or Bates engaged as sculptor by the Council cut no ice with the burghers of Colchester, but one has to conclude that their local man, Mr Watts, certainly rose to the occasion.

Town after town and city after city continued to proclaim their wealth in new town hall buildings and the century closed with one which was specifically designed to rival Glasgow in its shameless ostentation. Queen Victoria had awarded city status to Belfast in 1888 in recognition of its rapid expansion, built on linen manufacture, rope-making and shipbuilding, and its city councillors, most of whose families were of Protestant Scottish origin, wished to show their forebears back home just what a success they had made of themselves in Ireland. The jury of the architectural competition for the Town Hall (which was held in 1898) was chaired, yet again, by the 'Great Goth' Alfred Waterhouse, and faced with every entry being a variation on the theme of Belcher's Baroque Classicism, he had no

72   The towers of architect Alfred Brumwell Thomas's grandiose Belfast City Hall (1898–1906)

option but to award the commission to English architect Alfred Brumwell Thomas (1868–1948) who had produced the best of the bunch. Thomas had offered a minor version of St Paul's Cathedral (confirming the resurgence of interest in the early English Classicism of Wren, Jones and Gibb which Reginald Blomfield had done so much to promote through his writings) with an enormous central dome on a two-tier drum, supported by four corner towers, with a central pedimented entrance – but here with a rather suave, welcoming Baroque porte cochère, in lieu of the traditional flight of steps (fig.72). While it is now fashionable to mock these white Baroque Portland stone buildings as overblown and pompous, and to find their expression of the immense power and global reach of the British Empire, if anything, offensive, this is to miss the quality and dignity of the best of it, and while much of the decoration of Brumwell Thomas's Belfast City Hall is excessive, there is still much to savour in the proportions of his architecture, its excellent sculpture and the quite extraordinary level of craftsmanship that is exhibited throughout the building.

The programme of architectural sculpture in Belfast was much more modest than in Glasgow and much of Brumwell Thomas's original programme, including two major equine statues to flank the main entrance, was not carried out. Nevertheless, it does have an excellent pediment tympanum modelled by Frederick Pomeroy (ably assisted by J. Edgar Winter, 1875–1937, a local stone and wood carver) which is centred on *Hibernia* holding a torch, supported by several gods and goddesses including a helmeted *Minerva* (representing the arts and professions), *Hermes* (representing commerce) and *Demeter* with her sheaf of corn (representing agriculture), served by two youths representing *Youth* and *Vitality* whose reduced height forms a transition to the crouching figures who occupy those difficult corners of a triangular tympanum (fig.73). It is notable that this is an entirely Classical composition with neither any hint of contemporary dress, nor tools of local trades, nor explanatory legend. As such, it now appears somewhat old-fashioned when compared to Thorneycroft and Belcher's work at the Chartered Accountants' Hall or even Pomeroy's own work in Sheffield. Nevertheless, the quality of Pomeroy's modelling and Winter's carving, along with the relaxed and quite natural interaction between the figures, brings the group to life and marks it as one of the finest pieces of sculpture in Northern Ireland – quite the equal of Thomas Brock's statue of *Victoria* (1903) upon which it looks down. The now vast resources of Farmer and Brindley (assisted by local masons under their control) once more provided almost all the carved architectural detail both inside and out, including a considerable quantity of minor architectural carving (which is more restrained than on Glasgow's City Chambers – and much the better for it). Brumwell Thomas would go on to become something of a specialist in town halls, completing Plumstead (Woolwich) Town Hall (1906) in Portland stone and red brick (which owes everything to Belcher's Colchester), and later Clacton and East Ham, before the finest of them all, his superb, suave and perfectly proportioned, shimmering white Portland stone Stockport Town Hall of 1905–8.

While the architectural language of Belcher's Chartered Accountants' Hall was now being employed in public buildings throughout the country, strangely, it was not until 1898 that anyone was to attempt another City of London palazzo with a similarly ambitious sculptural programme, and somewhat unexpectedly, it was to be architect Thomas Edward Collcutt (1840–1924) who picked up the baton with his Lloyd's Register of Shipping building in Fenchurch Street in the City of London. By the 1890s, Lloyd's Register of Shipping and its underwriters had achieved global domination in the shipping insurance business and needed a new London headquarters building to appropriately reflect its status. Collcutt was one of those many Victorian architects who, though rarely contributing to the development of architecture, ran a very successful practice following trends set by others. Starting out as a Goth, his architecture quite quickly shifted towards Tudor before morphing into a combination of Early French Renaissance and Byzantine in the vast building which made his name: the colossal Imperial Institute in South Kensington (1887–93) of which only the tower has survived. In 1893, he completed the new headquarters for the Peninsular and Orient Line in a lively Classical style and it was this building which led to his appointment by Lloyd's. With the most generous of budgets and a client who wished to proclaim their wealth, good taste and status, Collcutt abandoned his previous eclectic mix of styles in favour of the now fashionable Baroque, with the bold rustication

73   Frederick Pomeroy's resplendent *Hibernia* with supporters in the pediment of Belfast City Hall

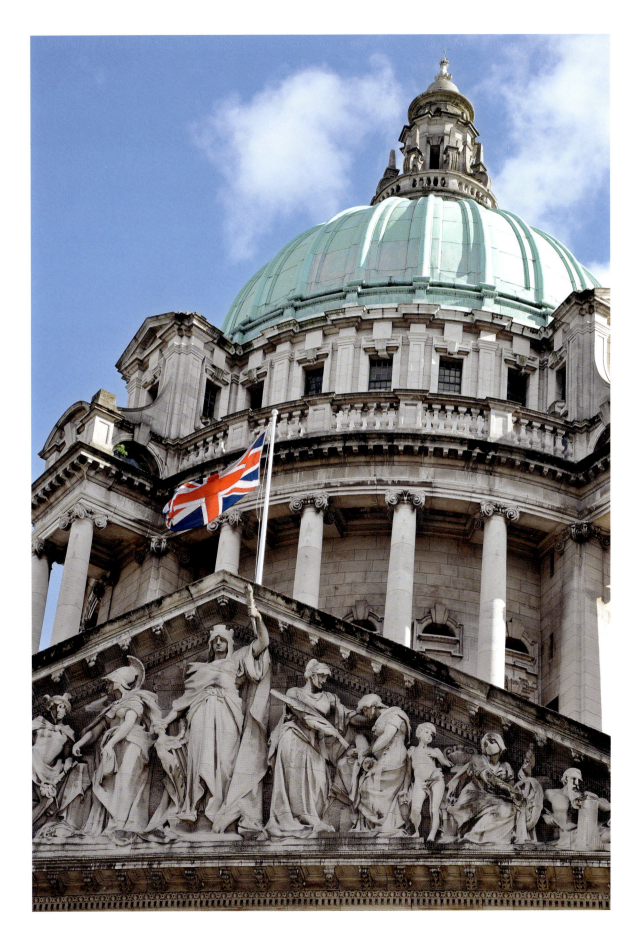

74 Architect Thomas Edward Collcutt's Lloyd's Register of Shipping (1898–1901) echoes the vocabulary of John Belcher's earlier Chartered Accountants' Hall

75 Part of George Frampton's frieze of maidens

which here, not only enveloped the Doric pilasters of the ground floor, but also, as in the Chartered Accountants' Hall, reappeared on the second floor to decorate the deep window reveals (fig.74). The corner is turned in similar style, with Belcher's great corner corbel replicated in two rather slight brackets which support a slim octagonal oriel that projects out at second-floor level where it is transformed into a domed, circular tower. Finally, Belcher's long, running sculptural frieze reappears here below the first-floor balustrade (rather than above the first-floor windows), where it is interrupted by the ground-floor window arches and is then repeated, high above, curving around the corner tower. Collcutt, wishing to further emulate Belcher in the building's sculptural programme, and abandoning poor Walter Smith with whom he had collaborated for many years, instead proposed George Frampton to the directors.

For the carving of the two friezes, Frampton returned to the theme of processional maidens in relief, which he had already developed in the spandrels which framed his *St Mungo* in Glasgow, but here they carry model ships and the tools of the shipbuilding trade, rather than sounding long Nordic horns (fig.75). In the rectangular panels over the side doorways they support naked male figures who hold the tools of navigation, with the globe at their back, and waves and sailing ships laden with fruit at their feet. The maidens, whose gowns are embroidered with the insignia of distant lands, hold various caskets, navigational instruments and one tool – a decorated axe. In the spandrels of the ground-floor windows, the maidens frame the coats of arms of British cities on either side of decorated keystones with the names of the cities on flowing banderoles. On either side of the

76 One of George Frampton's bronze 'modern girls' with ship

main entrance are panels of five maidens, each holding steamships as symbols of the company's long maritime history and connections. On the corner turret and a further half turret on Lloyd's Avenue are groups of six maidens, three in front and three behind, whose heads are all we see. The lower groupings are informal, life-like and quite natural, with one maiden placing her hand on the shoulder of another. Those at high level are more stylised and represent the countries of the world, with a central female figure representing Lloyd's itself, wearing a crown of sails and standing on a ship's prow. The main entrance has a curved stone canopy within which she is replicated, here flanked by a further steamship and a sailing ship. (The excellent carving of the stone is by J.E. Taylorson, 1854–1942, another graduate of the STLTA.) Boldly mixing media, Frampton also provided four jewel-like bronze statuettes of maidens holding further ships who stand, at first almost unnoticed, between the capitals of the ground-floor paired Doric columns (fig.76). Susan Beattie describes them as 'Frampton's modern girls in their richly embroidered medieval gowns', and admires 'their remote and melancholy gaze', which certainly delivers a psychological depth rarely witnessed in architectural sculpture.[22]

In his friezes, Frampton here appears to revel in the possibilities of relief sculpture, and in particular, as in Glasgow, the subtle interplay of low and high relief and the apparent overlapping of plane after plane, within what is in reality a limited depth of carving. There is an obvious interest too in the imagery of the Pre-Raphaelites, the Continental Symbolists such as Gustav Klimt, and even the mythology of the National Romantics in Scandinavia, which is evident not only in the hair and the medieval gowns of the maidens, but also in the symbols with which they are decorated. The architecture is very good, the sculpture outstanding – but in many ways, despite the successful integration of the sculpture within the architectural composition, the two arts are speaking entirely different languages: one about wealth, power, masculinity and the architecture of empires, while the gentle hands and flowing drapery of the other speak of grace, femininity and those attributes traditionally assigned to mothers and maidens. The crisp, fresh white Portland stone again serves both arts, but somehow the shared ideals of Belcher and Thorneycroft are missing here.

The sculptural riches continue within, with an inlaid metal frieze within the marble entrance hall depicting further stirring seafaring scenes, and a remarkable bronze and marble group portraying *The Spirit of Maritime Commerce*, both by Frank Lynn Jenkins (1870–1927), at the head of the stairs, which features *The Spirit* in white Carrera marble with wings of bronze, on a bronze ship, laden with goods and with an imperial lion as its figurehead. The drama of the composition is further heightened by two male spirits who emerge from the bronze waves below the boat, propelling it forward to conquer further distant lands.

Collcutt's architectural setting for all these sculptural jewels may seem a little overwrought and top-heavy compared to Belcher's Chartered Accountants' Hall, but he deserves considerable praise for orchestrating another exceptional artistic collaboration, and particularly for providing Frampton with the opportunity to produce what is surely amongst the finest architectural sculpture in Britain. The quality of his work here was immediately recognised throughout Europe, with the German magazine *Dekorative Kunst* suggesting that it:

> deserves special attention for the magnificence of its general effect and for the enchanting grace of its detailing. When this marvellous work is compared with the conventional, stereotyped sculpture that defaces rather than decorates so many large public buildings today, the difference strikes one as astonishing and leads one to think with longing of the days of the great church-builders when every craftsman was an artist in his own right and put his whole soul into his work and knew nothing of terracotta moulds and stock architectural ornament.[23]

What is more, when one considers that several critics – including Henry Curry Marillier who wrote the review in *Dekorative Kunst* – suggested that Frampton's architectural sculpture on the Lloyd's Register building was actually his finest sculptural work, it confirms the unique status which he had brought to architectural sculpture as an art form.

As both the century and Victoria's long reign drew to a close, Belcher's Baroque style, complete with sculpture, provided the inspiration for the next great wave of British public building throughout the country, right up until the outbreak of the First World War, with Alex Bremner, in his study of Edwardian Baroque architecture, suggesting that it had become 'a manifestation of something residing much deeper in the collective psyche of the British nation'.[24] Almost every architectural competition for any major new building was presented in the style – and indeed, when the competition for the Royal Insurance building in Liverpool was held in 1896 (as with the competition for Belfast City Hall), all the entries were in Belcher's Baroque, with the competition assessor, Richard Norman Shaw, actually selecting the entry of local architect James Francis Doyle (1840–1913) above that of John Belcher himself (with Doyle's effort also cleverly including more than a few elements from Shaw's nearby White Star office). It was constructed complete with an excellent sculpted frieze between the columns at third-floor level by Charles John Allen, who had, of course, also been one of the original carvers on Thorneycroft's frieze on the Chartered Accountants' Hall just a few years previously. Baroque was established as the imperial style, and with the empire at its zenith – its end then inconceivable, with the nation's wealth and self-confidence at an all-time high – there would be no shortage of opportunities for architects and sculptors to celebrate Britain's achievements in sparkling, white Portland stone.

5

THE POWER AND THE GLORY

In the early evening of 22 January 1901, Queen Victoria died peacefully in her sleep at Osborne House on the Isle of Wight, bringing to an end the Victorian age. At the dawn of the new century, Britain thus had a new king, Edward VII, who inherited the throne of what was still the most powerful country in the world. Led by him, the next few years until the outbreak of the First World War would be characterised by a self-confident imperial swagger that found expression in all of the arts, including architecture and sculpture. As historian Simon Heffer has suggested, there developed an 'obsession with show; the importance of the pose; the decline of the spiritual and the rise of the material – all these provided the stuff of the moral, intellectual and industrial decline that made this an age of decadence'.[1]

As we have noted, the Baroque style which typified the 'age of decadence' (soon becoming known as 'Edwardian Baroque') was in fact established with the completion of Belcher's Chartered Accountants' Hall back in 1893, while Edmund Gosse had coined the term 'New Sculpture' in *Art Journal* the following year. Gosse's friend, the painter John Singer Sargent (1856–1925) – who is, perhaps, more than any other artist associated with the Edwardian age – had in fact completed most of his famous society portraits by the time of Victoria's death and would finally close his studio in 1907. So, the principal artistic themes and movements that we associate with the Edwardian age were actually well established by the time of Edward's ascent to the throne, but fuelled by the wealth of the empire, they would mature and flourish throughout his brief reign and on through what has been described as the 'long golden afternoon' which concluded with the outbreak of the First World War in 1914.

The nation's upper and burgeoning middle class now had new and higher expectations of luxury and diversion, creating a nationwide demand for theatres, department stores, hotels, mansion flats, tea rooms, piers and golf courses, while their civic pride and considerable altruism inspired a further wave of public buildings in the form of town halls, museums, galleries and libraries. Continuing technological development offered steel and concrete-framed buildings, and while most were still clad in stone or brick, with the invention of safety elevators they could now be built higher than ever. When the London Coliseum Theatre was built in 1904, 'it contained spacious tea rooms on every tier and between performances five o'clock teas were served by Fuller's. In each tea room was a ticket office and an information bureau where physicians and others expecting urgent telephone calls or telegrams should leave a notification of number of the seat they are occupying, and where telegrams could be bought and dispatched and postage stamps bought', while a 'band in the Terrace Tea Room gave four performances daily'.[2] During the first decade of the new century, London saw the construction of the Imperial Theatre (1901), the Gaiety (1903), the Aldwych (1905) and the Waldorf (1905), and Shaftsbury Avenue alone saw the opening of five new theatres including the Apollo, the Globe and the Queen's. While the capital led in both the luxury and quantity of these palaces of entertainment, the trend was followed throughout the regional cities, with Glasgow, for example, opening the King's and Pavilion Theatres in 1904, the Alhambra in 1910, the Savoy in 1911 and the Metropole in 1913. Gilbert Scott's Midland Hotel, once the capital's finest hotel, became a rather quaint old-fashioned shadow of the Savoy, the Ritz, the Waldorf (with sculptor Emil Fuchs's delightful frieze of joyful putti) and one of Norman Shaw's final projects, his sublime Piccadilly Hotel, which opened in 1908. The world-famous Harrods department store opened in 1905, and included Britain's first 'moving staircase'; Waring and Gillow completed their new building in Oxford Street in 1906; and in 1909, American Henry Selfridge opened the first phase of his enormous new store, designed by American architect Daniel H. Burnham. The national mood was one of 'magniloquent optimism',[3] with Imperialist hero Cecil Rhodes advising his fellow countrymen that, by being British, they had 'won first prize in the lottery of life'.

For the country's sculptors, Victoria's death led to nothing short of a deluge of work to commemorate her life and accomplishments. Public subscriptions for statuary were commenced throughout the entire empire on the news of her death and within a few years almost every New Sculptor was modelling their own version, or versions, of Victoria for reproduction in bronze, or occasionally the now much less fashionable marble.[4] George Frampton provided *Victoria*(s) for St Helens in 1902, Southport in 1903, Manitoba in Canada in 1904, Leeds in 1905 and Newcastle in 1906, and while most of these were in bronze, they were all original commissions rather than simply new castings; William Thorneycroft rather cornered the Indian market with statues in Karachi in 1906, Lucknow in 1908 and Ajodhya in 1908; while Alfred Drury provided a *Victoria* for Portsmouth in 1903, Bradford in 1904 and Wellington, New Zealand in 1905, as well as both Victoria and Albert on the renamed Victoria and Albert Museum in London in 1906. But despite taking pride of place within their various civic settings, these tributes to the former Empress of India were to be nothing when compared to the national monument which was planned for London.

As soon as Victoria's death was announced, a committee was established to consider a suitable monument and within weeks it was agreed both that it should stand at the end of the Mall in front of Buckingham Palace and that Thomas Brock should be appointed as lead sculptor. Originally a pupil of Foley, Brock had been the young sculptor engaged to assist Lord Leighton on the ground-breaking *Athlete Wrestling with a Python* in 1877, and had gone on to study under him as well as Thorneycroft and Gilbert. In the intervening decades he had established himself as one of the leaders of his art, becoming a full member of the Royal Academy in 1891 and going on to found and become the first President of the Society of British Sculptors in 1905. Brock had already produced the seated figure of *Albert* for his Memorial in Hyde Park and also sculptures of Victoria herself to mark both her golden and diamond jubilees. These had been much admired, particularly by the Queen herself, thus establishing him above all other sculptors as the obvious choice to further commemorate her.

An architectural competition was held for the design of the setting for the sculpture and this was won by Aston Webb (thus beating both John Belcher and Ernest George, amongst others). It was by far the most ambitious of all the proposals and included not only a semi-circular colonnade around the statue, but also, at the other end of the Mall, a great triumphal arch which (very subtly) shifted the axis from the Mall to Trafalgar Square. (The refacing of Buckingham Palace in white Portland stone which was eventually carried out by Webb was actually suggested by Thomas Drew, another competitor.) What particularly impressed the committee about Webb's design was that, in addition to his proposed monument and arrangements in front of Buckingham Palace, due to the depth of his proposed triumphal arch at the other end of the Mall, it had the practical benefit of providing additional office accommodation for the Admiralty (thus earning it its name, Admiralty Arch).[5]

As Webb and Brock developed their design, Webb's colonnade was soon lost, replaced by a

77   Architect Aston Webb and sculptor Thomas Brock's Victoria Memorial of 1901-11 with Brock's *Manufacture* with imperial lion

series of gate posts which frame the monument. He further developed his long, low base for the sculpture itself, which was to be divided by steps and decorated with bronzes showing scenes from Victoria's reign (fig.77). Brock's model of the sculpture was presented to the King in 1904 and immediately approved, allowing construction to commence in 1906. While Webb's contribution at this end of the Mall was in the end relatively modest, Brock's statuary was extensive and has long divided opinions. Susan Beattie describes Brock as 'the great plagiarist' and suggests that his Victoria Memorial sculpture is little more than 'an astonishing assemblage of echoes of the monuments of others',[6] while Benedict Read assessed it as: 'one of the supreme achievements of the New Sculpture, redolent throughout with features and reminiscences essential to its whole nature; or of the movement, at least, in its established format, lacking the extremes of finesse of Gilbert's decorative fantasy or Frampton's craftiness'.[7]

Brock's Queen Victoria sits, looking down the Mall, below a gilt winged statue of *Victory*, flanked by further figures representing *Truth* and *Justice*. Facing the palace is a figure of *Motherhood* and, as in Albert's Memorial, around the central group are further groups representing (a tellingly contemporary selection of) *Painting*, *Architecture*, *War* and *Shipbuilding*. At the outer extremities of the structure are bronzes, guarded by imperial lions, offering further interpretations of *Peace*, *Progress*, *Agriculture* and *Manufacture*, and finally, on the surrounding stone gateposts, the dominions and colonies are added to the mix (including *West Africa*, *South Africa* and *Canada* by Alfred Drury and *Australia* by Derwent Wood) (fig.78). While the subjects are familiar, Brock's work is fresh and naturalistic, and while both Read and Beattie agree that it lacks the emotional charge of the best of Gilbert or Frampton (or equally Drury), it is certainly neither stiff nor dull. Victoria (who is double life-sized) is both suitably imperious and yet entirely human, Brock's allegorical figures are evocative of

78   Thomas Brock's gilt bronze *Winged Victory* above his bronze *Naval and Military Power*

solid British stock and his lions are suitably poised, ready to sally forth at the first hint of a threat to the empire. Though in itself marginally more modest than Albert's Memorial in Hyde Park, its position in the heart of the city, combined with the power which Victoria's figure derives from the great axis of the Mall and the backdrop of Buckingham Palace, make this in many ways even more impressive, and such was its impact that it is said (almost certainly apocryphally) that when Brock was presented to the King after its unveiling, the King turned, asked for a sword, and knighted him on the spot.

Webb's contribution to the imperial capital at the other end of the Mall is no less impressive with the grand Ionic order of Admiralty Arch framing its three great archways which are flanked by offices on either side. His intended conclusion of a mighty *Quadriga Driven by Britannia* was unfortunately replaced by additional high-level office accommodation, and such is the scale of this monumental architectural stage-set, that two further fine sculptures by Brock depicting *Navigation* and *Gunnery* on the flanks of the arch at ground level on the Mall side are almost lost (fig.79). Webb's aim in creating this entire piece of urban theatre was an attempt to improve the public spaces and their connections within the heart of the capital which was generally acknowledged as fairly chaotic, particularly in comparison with Haussmann's perfectly planned Paris, and his approach was symptomatic of the developing interest in town and city planning which was then emerging on both sides of the Atlantic (to which we shall return).

While most cities were content to have funded and raised a statue to the late Queen, Liverpool, almost alone outside London, had more ambitious plans. As quick off the mark as London, the Liverpool Queen Victoria Memorial Committee, led by the Lord Mayor, was established on 7 March 1901 and was soon deep in discussions as to a suitable method of paying homage to the late monarch. There was, as usual, no shortage of proposals – a public hall, a children's infirmary and a university were all considered, before it was finally decided to erect a monument that would 'be worthy of Liverpool as the first seaport of the kingdom, and one that posterity could view as erected in the first year of the 20th century, expressive of admiration, esteem, and affection of the greatest of English monarchs, the good Queen Victoria'.[8] A site was selected in the centre of the city (that of the demolished St George's Church) and the subscription fund was launched. In July 1901, the committee invited design proposals from sculptors and architects, shortlisting three teams led by sculptors Robert Lindsay Clarke of Cheltenham, Charles Allen, who had established his studio in Liverpool seven years previously, and Henry Fehr of London, all of whom were requested to produce models of their proposals. After viewing the entries, the committee selected Charles Allen and his local collaborators, architects Simpson, Willink & Thicknesse, on condition that Allen's statue of Victoria arose from her proposed throne to stand proudly within a domed Ionic Portland stone baldachin. As in London (though conceived and completed earlier), four flights of steps climb to a central circular podium on which stands Victoria on a bracketed base. Crowning the dome is the first of the bronze sculptures which populate the memorial

79   Thomas Brock's *Navigation* on one side of Admiralty Arch (1906–11)

80 Charles Allen's Victoria Memorial in Liverpool (1901–2)

in the form of a winged *Fame*, with four small bronze groups above the double Ionic columns of the baldachin, while down nearer ground level between the flights of steps are four further, larger allegorical groups representing (yet again) *Agriculture*, *Industry*, *Education* and *Commerce* (the *Arts*, presumably, not being a high priority amongst Liverpool's councillors) (fig.80). Allen's *Victoria* (which does not come close to the best versions, such as Frampton's *Victoria* in St Helens or Edward Onslow Ford's superb version in Manchester of 1901, in which she sits enveloped in a vast swirling cloak) is rather staid, and the sculptural highlight is the four large bronze allegorical groups. These are all in contemporary dress (while still exhibiting considerable quantities of bare flesh, as in so many previous Classical offerings) in well composed groups on their plinths, complete with scythes, shepherds' crooks, sledgehammers, books and a gyroscope, which appears to have a particularly mesmeric effect upon the group symbolising *Education*. The detail is excellent, with patterned fabrics, leather aprons and workmen's boots beautifully modelled and cast. What unites the entire composition are several flights of circular steps which artfully deal with the changes of ground level across the site and neatly frame the entire edifice.

Beyond this industry immortalising Victoria, there were many further commissions for architectural sculpture, with Edwardian Baroque now dominating almost all major public and commercial architectural commissions and with sculpture established as an essential element of the style. In *Edwardian Architecture*, Alastair Service confirmed the appeal of the architecture of Wren,

Vanbrugh and Hawksmoor 'to English architects, politicians and clients of around 1900. It was a very *English* Classical style and its buildings were of a splendour that seemed appropriate for the centre of a great empire.'[9] For the next decade, the volume of public and private building construction was quite extraordinary as streams of income from across the British Empire flooded back to the mother country. Charles Voysey, Hugh Baillie Scott and Charles Rennie Mackintosh might be successfully providing ascetic Arts and Crafts country houses for their many clients, but when it came to the architecture of Britannia's booming towns and cities, many of these same clients expected nothing less than Portland stone palaces, which became more triumphal and exuberant with every passing year.

Nothing could have more clearly confirmed Edwardian Baroque's journey from radical art to the perfect vehicle for the expression of Britain's imperial values than its adoption for two vast government offices in Whitehall, London. The first, by Scottish architect John Brydon (1840–1901, whom Andrew Saint, incidentally, accords with as much credit for the revival of English Renaissance architecture as Belcher), was the massive block of offices that extend down Great George Street from Parliament Square (currently HM Treasury and HM Revenue and Customs) (fig.81). These were completed after his death by government architect Sir Henry Tanner in 1912. The offices are centred on a grand circular court with two further square courts on either side providing light and air within this extensive office complex (and Saint also sensibly suggests Inigo Jones's early 17th-century Whitehall Palace design as Brydon's inspiration). When it came to the three-dimensional form of the building, however, Brydon owed everything to Wren rather than Jones, with the west towers

81   The portico of architect John Brydon's Government Offices on Great George Street with sculpture by J.R. Mountfield

82 Alfred Drury's sculpture representing *The Horror of War* and *The Dignity of War* on architect William Young's Old War Office (1898–1907)

of St Paul's Cathedral now reworked and looking down upon Parliament Square. The architectural sculpture was in fact extremely limited, consisting mainly of traditional carved heads on keystones and shields in relief between first-floor windows, with the only significant element being the pediment group above the main entrance on Whitehall, which was modelled by J.R. Mountfield. This is centred on an enthroned *Britannia* surrounded by a semi-naked group representing various trades and with a selection of accessories including a large book, a ship and a globe. The style is traditionally Classical, with the male figures so heavily muscled that they almost resemble écorchés.

Further along Whitehall is its more interesting partner – what is now known as the Old War Office of 1898–1906 by William Young, the architect of Glasgow City Chambers, who, like Brydon, also died before the completion of his building, in this case in 1900, with his son Clyde Young and Office of Works architect Sir John Taylor overseeing construction until its completion in 1906. This is a much livelier affair with a bold Ionic colonnade spanning the second and third floors between apparently square pavilions, which neatly solve the problem of obtusely angled streets. The detailing here is much bolder, has real depth and is much enhanced by outstanding sculpture by Alfred Drury.

Here, Drury produced eight groups which surmount the curved aedicules of the corner pavilions, with 'War' – the purpose of the building – as the theme. Despite their height above the street, their double life-size and the quality of Drury's modelling and the carving meant that they lost none of their emotional charge. On Whitehall itself, he offered two mothers, shielding their children within their great cloaks as *The Sorrow of Peace* and *The Winged Messenger of Peace* by the northern tower, and two male figures, *The Horror of War* and *The Dignity of War*, by the southern tower (figs 82 and 83). These were accompanied by *Truth* and *Justice* on Whitehall Place and *Victory* and *Fame* on Horse Guards Avenue. In *The Horror of War*, Drury hardly shrank from his subject, depicting horror on the children's faces, the solemnity of *Truth* and *Justice* and a cloaked skeleton

83 Alfred Drury's *Peace* on the Old War Office

84 Alfred Drury's *Truth* and *Justice* on the Old War Office

with bare skull. Far from being merely subservient sculptural elements within the language of the architecture, these are evocative works of art which are at least the equal of their setting, as Susan Beattie so eloquently described them:

> The War Office Groups illustrate the complete assimilation into their sculptor's personal style of the influences most crucial to his development: Alfred Stevens and the *terribilita* of the Wellington Monument figure groups, the lyrical realism of Dalou, the symbolist images of Frampton (most obviously, in the tree motif on the book held by Justice and the Mysteriarch-like head of Truth), the energy in handling three-dimensional form that Drury had recognised in the work of Bates. It is a measure of his achievement that, in allowing the architectural setting to dictate the general character of his sculptures, Drury has enhanced, rather than subdued their expressive power. Each figure is related to its pair and each group to its seven counterparts by a wholly Baroque balance of mass, gesture and light and shade, maintaining a tragic grandeur that the dark streaking of the pale stonework now serves only to accentuate[10] (fig.84).[11]

To which critic Alfred Baldry added: 'in producing magnificent sculpture he has not forgotten that the object of his effort was to be the completing and enhancing of a piece of well-proportioned and impressive architecture. He has sacrificed none of his own individuality, none of his personal sentiment in his art, and certainly none of his admirable vigour.'[12]

Drury's sculptures here certainly represent one of the architectural highlights of the New Sculpture Movement.[13] They were not the outcome of a long and sympathetic relationship between an architect and a sculptor, nor did they particularly please their client when their cost was revealed to the Office of Works, who stated that the sculptures 'would not have been authorised without further consideration if it had been realised that there would not be a sufficient margin of savings'[14] to pay for them; but on their unveiling, they were instantly regarded as a positive contribution to the public art of the city by both critics and the popular press alike. The War Office, along with so many other Edwardian public buildings, represented an extraordinary marriage between predominantly establishment architects who were focused on meeting their clients' needs and expressing their values, and a sculptor who was intent on evoking a new range and depth of emotion. The most radical architects of this period may have been leading the Arts and Crafts Movement where they worked for a small, wealthy, idealistic upper middle-class elite, but it was the mainstream Edwardian architects and their outstanding sculptors, who truly captured the spirit of the age.

By 1901, John Belcher had swapped his partner Beresford Pite for a Scot, John James Joass (1868–1952) – one of John James Burnet's former pupils – and together the two men won and delivered a series of major commissions. In 1903, they completed Electra House (now part of London Guildhall University) in Moorgate, which was designed as the headquarters of the Eastern Telegraph Company, and once again Belcher invited many of the leading members of the New Sculpture Movement to assist. This was a much larger commission than the Chartered Accountants' Hall and despite the host of fine sculptors involved, the sculpture here plays a very much more secondary role to the architecture in which it is framed. The building is enormous and stands on a granite base of rather bulbous rustication in lieu of the razor-sharp bands in Moorgate Place, with that treatment here reserved for the first floor, where it loses something of its impact. The central section of the building, with its grand arched entrance, is flanked by two floors of offices within an Ionic colonnade, below a modillioned cornice, an attic and dormers. The flanking rusticated towers of the central section extend beyond the cornice, before breaking back to reveal a hexagonal domed tower concluding in a globe, suspended within an armillary sphere. Alexander Stuart Gray described the style as 'ebullience verging on vulgarity',[15] but I almost wish for more depth and modelling as, despite Belcher having thrown everything at it, it remains rather a ponderous beast.

The sculpture (much reduced from the original proposals) is nevertheless profusive, with two fine spandrels to the entrance door arch by Frampton, referred to as *Electricity* and *Engineering* (fig.85). These are surprisingly Classical in style and in some contrast to his rather more ethereal earlier spandrel carvings on both the Lloyd's building and the Glasgow Art Gallery, but by breaking out of their architectural frame (a trick learned from fashionable Japanese prints), they provide a spark of life within Belcher's overall composition. William Goscombe

85   One of George Frampton's spandrel sculptures on Belcher and Joass's Electra House (1901–3)

86   One of Frederick Pomeroy's allegorical panels within the arch of the main entrance of Electra House

without these elements and the planned full frieze at third-floor level, the remaining sculpture appears incidental; and unless the financial constraints became progressively applied during construction, it would surely have made more sense to concentrate the limited quantity of sculpture where it would have made most impact, around the main entrance and on the building's prominent corner.

Belcher and Joass went on to design Mappin & Webb's on Oxford Street, the Royal Insurance Company's offices on St James's Street as well as the astonishing Ashton Memorial in Lancaster (1905–9) (fig.87). Rather disloyally, the Ashton Memorial actually dwarfs both the Victoria and the Albert Memorials and was built by politician and philanthropist, the 1st Baron Ashton (whose family

John provided four of what were meant to be a series of panels representing the various countries of the world (now connected by electronic communication) as a frieze above the main entrance; Alfred Drury modelled five panels depicting putti supporting cartouches bearing the crests of the companies who originally occupied the building; and Frederick Pomeroy sculpted both the globe and armillary sphere that topped the building's dome, as well as several allegorical panels within the entrance arch and the entrance hall which were the only executed portion of a further projected frieze (fig.86). These are all in the same Classical style of Frampton's spandrel figures, and to be frank, most observers would struggle to identify them as New Sculpture, were it not for documentary evidence as to their authorship.

While the building was under construction, the *Builder's Journal and Architectural Record* lamented the loss of the globes with putti originally planned to decorate the building's great cornice, suggesting that 'the ruthless hand of economy has stifled in their birth numerous little boys'[16] – and indeed

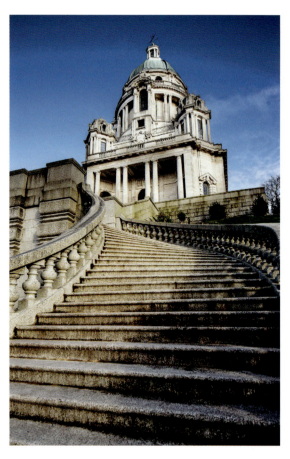

87   Edwardian Baroque at its most ebullient in Belcher and Joass's Ashton Memorial in Lancaster (1905–9)

had made their fortune from the manufacture of oilcloth and linoleum), as a tribute to his second wife after her death. Its elegant colonnaded dome, framed by four smaller cupolas, can be seen from miles around and houses two domed chambers within, one of which has an admirable series of murals by George Murray (1875–1933). The principal sculpture is high above ground level with shields depicting a ship, a railway engine and a reaper below attenuated aedicules. Above these, there are allegorical figures of *Commerce*, *History*, *Art* and *Science* by sculptor Herbert Hampton (1862–1929), a lesser-known graduate of the Lambeth School of Art whose most famous work is the bronze Victoria Memorial of 1906, complete with bronze frieze and guardian lions, in nearby Lancaster.

Framing Dalton Square in Lancaster, in which Hampton's statue stands, is Lancaster Town Hall of 1906–9, also paid for and opened by Lord Ashton. It was designed by architect Edward Mountford (who had previously designed Sheffield Town Hall, p.91) in what was, for the period, an unusually restrained straight Classical style, with a hexastyle Ionic portico facing the square. The pediment sculpture, which was executed in limestone by sculptor Frederick Pomeroy (as we would now expect), contrasts with the darker sandstone of the Town Hall building (as in William Calder Marshall's pediment group on Bolton Town Hall, p.72). It is centred on King Edward VII, who looks down on his mother, here standing below on her plinth in the square. This was just the latest of Mountford and Pomeroy's collaborations which also included their little-known but very interesting Free-Style Liverpool College of Technology of 1900–1902 (now part of Liverpool John Moores University), and was contemporaneous with their work on one of the most important buildings of the Edwardian age, which included what would become Pomeroy's most famous sculpture.

After another limited architectural competition in 1900, Edward Mountford was selected as architect for the new Central Criminal Court – or the 'Old Bailey' as it soon became known (after the street in which it stood). With due debt to

88   Architect Edward Mountford's Central Criminal Court – the Old Bailey (1900–1907)

John Belcher, Mountford's design owed even more to Sir Christopher Wren, with the colonnaded domes, paired columns and gilt finials of Wren's 18th-century Greenwich Hospital replicated in Mountford's proposal. This is no mere copy, however, and the completed building successfully offers both strength and dignity without excess. Few approaching its entrance could doubt the power of the law, to which the building is dedicated (fig.88). The sculpture, rather than being incidental or largely decorative, is brilliantly integrated and (unlike Belcher's Electra House) is concentrated on

89 Frederick Pomeroy's dramatic allegorical group over the main entrance of the Old Bailey, with *The Recording Angel* flanked by *Fortitude* and *Truth*

the main entrance where it has maximum impact and powerfully supports the narrative. Despite his appointment not being announced until 1905, few doubted that Pomeroy would again partner Mountford on what would soon be recognised as their greatest collaborative achievement. The tone was set by the Dean of Westminster who, when invited, selected a quotation from Psalm 72 from the *Book of Common Prayer* – 'defend the children of the poor, and punish the wrong doer' – and this was carved on a stone tablet supported by the twin Ionic columns which framed the main entrance.

The arched doorway itself steps forward from the vermiculated rustication of the ground floor and is framed by two plain banded piers supporting a shallow arch which in turn shelters a pediment containing a cartouche with the arms of the City of London. On top of the arch sits an astonishing allegorical group by Pomeroy which must rank as one of the most powerful architectural sculptures in London. It features *Fortitude*, an unusually strong female figure holding a massive, richly decorated sword, and *Truth*, a bare-breasted female figure who is studying her reflection in a hand mirror. However, it is the central figure, whom Mountford and Pomeroy introduced as *The Recording Angel*, who looks down on all who enter her domain. She holds and reads a scroll which is spread out across her knees, while a great hood covers her head and shoulders, casting her face into constant shadow (fig.89). There can be few who pass beneath her without contemplating that their day of reckoning has come, and wondering too whether or not their names will soon appear on her scroll of the guilty. As in Frampton's and Drury's sculpture, drapery falls gently over the edge of the arch and here the angel's bare feet can be seen resting on a bracket above the city's coat of arms. Even in its day it was criticised as being a rather sinister portrayal of justice, but few can deny the extraordinary potency of Pomeroy's quite remarkable central figure which was almost certainly inspired by Drury's hooded figures on the War Office.

Above the arch is a recessed portico with a frieze by Alfred Turner (1874–1940), yet another graduate of the SLTAS and the Royal Academy Schools, whose work had first come to public notice with the raw realism of his statues of a *Fisherman* and *Fisher Girl* in the Fishmongers' Hall in London (1899–1902). His work here is quite different and though it interprets the Dean of Westminster's selected quotation (right down to the decapitated head of Medusa),

it has a compensating softness, with delicate angels' wings and drapery which swirls around the male and female figures (fig.90). On either side of the recessed portico are two further triangular pediments in which Pomeroy sculpted semi-naked allegorical figures who appear to have taken shelter within the architecture, and who again scrutinise anyone entering the building below, with one, quite naturally (and brilliantly) exposing the sole of her foot which is wrapped around her lower leg.

Fortunately, Pomeroy's work continues within the building, providing further hooded figures beneath the pendentives of Mountford's magnificent dome. Each stands before a throne with her title behind her head, a group of cherubs above, and they are flanked by female supporters whose accessories expound the four virtues – *Justice*, *Mercy*, *Temperance* and *Charity* – which act as something of an antidote to the theme of punishment that is so strongly evoked over

90 Alfred Turner's frieze and inscription above the main entrance of the Old Bailey

91   Henry Thomas Hare's distinctly Jacobean Oxford Town Hall (1891–7)

the main entrance doorway. The interiors are richly decorated in boldly veined marble with mosaic decoration and mural paintings by Gerald Moira (1867–1959) and Sir William Richmond (1842–1921, who had succeeded Ruskin as the Slade Professor of Fine Art at Oxford University), and are probably the finest of any public building of these pre-war years. Pomeroy's most famous sculpture stands high above the courts, on a globe surmounting Mountford's dome – his crowned *Justice* in gilt bronze, her arms outstretched, holding a sword and scales – and, despite the commonly held belief, without her traditional blindfold. Small as she looks from ground level, she is actually 3.65m high and is, in fact, the second version of the sculpture, the first having been rejected as too small, once erected. Sadly, this was to be Mountford and Pomeroy's last collaboration. By the time of the official opening of the courts by King Edward VII in February 1907, Mountford was already in a wheelchair, crippled by arthritis, and he died just a year later, thus bringing to an end one of the most successful and prolific long-term relationships between architect and sculptor of the late 19th and early 20th centuries.

There were, however, many other partnerships of architect and sculptor which operated on a more modest scale and produced fine, minor public buildings in the Baroque. Architect Henry Thomas Hare (1861–1921), for example, worked regularly with sculptor Frederick E.E. Schenck (1849–1908) on several public buildings throughout England from the early 1890s until the time of Schenck's death. Trained initially in Edinburgh and then at the South Kensington Schools, Schenck taught for many years as Modelling Master at the Hanley School of Art in Stoke-on-Trent. In 1888, encouraged by the positive response to his exhibited work at the Royal Academy, he made the move to London, soon meeting Hare who had just won the competition for the new County Offices in Stafford (1890–95). On this they worked together, Schenck producing relief panels of Classical figures for the walls and ceilings of several rooms including the council chamber and the Members' Room (with replicas of four of the panels, *Agriculture*, *Pottery*, *Ironwork* and *Mining*, later being exhibited at the Royal Academy). Their next commission was the somewhat grander Oxford Town Hall and Municipal Offices (1891–7) for which Schenck again provided sculptured panels for the interior (fig.91). Stafford had been in French Renaissance style while Oxford is in something more Jacobean, but by the turn of the century Hare had moved into the new Baroque style consistently and soon mastered it, with Schenck now providing all the modelling both internally and externally on the Municipal Buildings and Public Baths in Shoreditch (1899) and Crewe (1903), and the Central Libraries of Hammersmith (1904/5) and Islington (1905) (fig.92). Their greatest achievement, and Schenck's last major work, is sadly now no more – Ingram House, the headquarters of the United Provident Institution at 196 The Strand (1906, demolished 1961). This included sculpted figures in each of the ground-floor window tympana representing *Justice*, *Truth*, *Temperance*, *Providence*, *Security* and *Industry*, as well as low relief figures between the second-floor windows depicting *Hope*, *Wisdom* and *Peace*, with these themes continuing in the rather sumptuous interior, with murals by Gerald Moira once more.

Meanwhile, in Liverpool, the city's waterfront was being transformed with the construction of what became known as *The Three Graces* (though neither exhibit much Brightness, Joyfulness or Bloom): The Royal Liver building (1908–11) by Walter Aubrey Thomas, with clock towers crowned by the famous *Liver Birds*, carved by German sculptor Carl Bernard Bartels (1866–1955); the Cunard building (the best of the three), headquarters of the shipping line, by William Edward Willink and Philip Coldwell Thicknesse (who had earlier provided the architectural setting for Allen's Victoria Memorial), constructed between 1914 and 1916; and the Port of Liverpool building (the former home of the Mersey Docks and Harbour Board) by Sir Arnold Thornely and F.B. Hobbs, built between 1903 and 1907. But even this collection of grand Edwardian buildings was a modest affair compared with what was then being planned for Cardiff, the capital city of Wales, which was no less than an entirely new civic and cultural quarter for the city, in which sculpture was to play a leading role.

When we last visited Cardiff, it was to explore the medieval fantasy created within Cardiff Castle by the 3rd Marquis of Bute and William Burges – his architectural Merlin. Although the castle's boundary walls contained little more than a few acres, the Marquis's land holdings in the city were extensive including Cathays Park which adjoined the castle. In 1898, he agreed to sell the park's 59 acres to the town council, who were keen to build their own new town hall and to provide further buildings

92   Henry Hare's Islington Library of 1905 in the Edwardian Baroque style, with sculpture by Frederick E.E. Schenck

93 The municipal munificence of Lanchester, Stewart and Rickards's Cardiff City Hall (1899–1906)

for the university and a further series of cultural and civic buildings. In confirming the sale, the Marquis laid down strict conditions as to how the land could be used in future, maintaining that the existing avenues of trees be preserved. The Council held an architectural competition that same year for the first of the new buildings (judged yet again by the now ageing Alfred Waterhouse) which were to provide the new town hall and law courts for the city. Working within the constraints set by the preservation of the trees, Borough Surveyor William Harpur (1853–1917) had already produced a plan for the civic quarter. Inspired by the formal Beaux-Arts town planning theories which had already produced both Haussmann's Paris and L'Enfant's Washington, though on a much more modest scale, his efforts constituted Britain's first (and still finest) planned civic centre. These early attempts to positively plan elements of British towns and cities (such as Aston Webb had already achieved in the Mall) were part of a broader movement which was gaining momentum in Britain inspired by Austrian architect Camillo Sitte's writings on urban design and Ebenezer Howard's development of the concept of planned Garden Cities. Indeed, they represented a further expression of the unification of the arts in which, at their best, interior and exterior civic spaces could be jointly conceived and created.

The architectural competition was won by the newly formed London practice of Lanchester, Stewart and Rickards who were commissioned to design both buildings (with Edwin Alfred Rickards, 1872–1920, the creative driving force).[17] Their language is free-style Baroque once more, but here with more than a hint of the rather more formal Beaux-Arts style. These first two, largely two-storey, white Portland stone civic buildings sit very contentedly within their parkland setting where they are framed by trees of a similar height to their parapets, with just their corner pavilions, towers and domes projecting above the strong horizontal bands of greenery.

The new Town Hall (1899–1906) – which became the City Hall, with Cardiff gaining city status on its official opening – forms the south side of Alexandra Gardens, the main central public space of the complex, but faces away from it, to the south and towards the historic city centre. At right angles to it, occupying the first block of the western series of buildings which flank the Gardens, sits the Law Courts. The City Hall's entrance leads from a low porte cochère through a domed polygonal lobby to a grand entrance hall with double staircase and on to the council chamber, which sets up a cross-axis with the Law Courts (1901–4), marked externally by a tall tower. Both buildings have a rusticated semi-basement with plain ashlar above, with the rustication extending vertically around the main entrances, corner pavilions and bays, the Law Courts having a delightfully elegant, recessed portico served by a broad flight of steps, flanked by bronze dragon lampstands, below two Wren-inspired towers. Both the Law Courts and the City Hall have bays to their corner pavilions on the southern elevations facing the city centre, which form the setting for a series of fine allegorical groups. Of the two buildings, the Law Courts is by far the more elegant design, but there is a certain relaxed munificence about the City Hall which is also rather appealing, not least due to the quantity and quality of its sculpture, which was specifically included as a gift of public art to enhance the lives of the citizens of the city.

In contrast to the procedure adopted for the Glasgow Art Galleries, the appointment of sculptors in Cardiff was one of open public competition in which sculptors were selected from submissions of clay models on relevant themes. Partly as a result of this, rather than selection being based on friendships within the Guild, the result represented something of a changing of the guard in the world of architectural sculpture, with Henry Poole (1873–1928), Paul Raphael Montford (1868–1938) and Donald McGill (–1947) being selected to produce the major allegorical groups and Henry Charles Fehr (1867–1940) the sculpture for the tower. All four had studied at the SLTSA and the Royal Academy Schools, with Poole having been apprenticed to Harry Bates and George Frederic Watts (including assisting Watts on the production of *Physical Energy*), Fehr having been Thomas

THE POWER AND THE GLORY

94 Detail of Henry Poole's *Unity and Patriotism* on Cardiff City Hall

below. Despite Beattie's reservations as to the lack of emotional impact, Poole's group is packed with drama and lively interaction. At its centre is a huge, central, bare-chested, cloaked and crowned king who leans back diagonally to throw a protecting arm around a symbolic figure who represents Welsh womanhood, while staring directly at one of his men who lays his sword in his lap in a pledge of allegiance. On either side of this central group, female supporters beckon others to join the cause, while at the king's feet a sleeping British lion lies peacefully, reminding us that for all the nationalist celebration, Wales remains part of the great British Empire.[19] There is certainly little spirituality or exoticism here, but the messages are clear and the bare physiques of both the men and women and their voluminous drapery are beautifully modelled and carved (fig.94). In complete contrast to the ebullient energy of *Unity and Patriotism* is Poole's sublime *Royal Coat of Arms* above the entrance doors of the Law Courts which reinforces the more understated dignity of this very fine building (fig.95).

Brock's principal assistant, and McGill's work also much influenced by Bates. Despite their debt to the founders of New Sculpture, Susan Beattie detects a departure from the central aim of the movement in the work here in Cardiff and a return to the subservience of the sculptor to the architect, resulting in a distinct shift towards 'rigidly symmetrical or otherwise overtly contrived composition, a return to the stern, rhetorical images of neo-classicism and a stripped, geometrical treatment of form'.[18] There are certainly no wailing banshees as in Drury's Old War Office or sinister *Recording Angels* as on the Old Bailey, but nevertheless, the standard of composition, modelling and carving is consistently high and, as the entire development spanned several decades, it provides a fascinating overview of pre- and post-First World War British sculpture, with Henry Poole's contribution of the major allegorical group *Unity and Patriotism* – the groups of writhing mermen and mermaids above the main entrance to the City Hall and the coat of arms for the Law Courts – perhaps the best of this very good collection (see frontispiece).

Unity and Patriotism crowns one of the four (rather Ritzy) bay windows to the corner pavilions and is complete with an explanatory title panel

Paul Montford produced two further major groups, *Commerce and Industry* and *Music and Poetry*, which topped the bays flanking the avenue between the two buildings, with *Commerce and Industry* centred on an enthroned queen, as a

95 Lanchester, Stewart and Rickards's Cardiff Law Courts (1901–4), with Albert Toft's splendid South African War Memorial (1908) in the foreground

131

companion to Poole's king. As one would anticipate, it is no less lively, with the queen looking out towards the historic city centre, the docks and the sea beyond. She is supported by bare-chested workers and enrobed merchants, along with their usual collection of props such as cogs, ropes, bales of cotton and fruit, and these extend on either side of the group to provide brackets to the top of the pavilion whose blank, panelled sides create a restrained background to the scene (fig.96). Some of this minor carving is a delight, including the barrel, ropes and life-preserver to the side of the queen (and indeed, the helmet, shield and sword beside Poole's king). Montford's two female figures, *Music and Poetry*, front a rather wistful group, while the final group by Donald McGill on the western bay of the Law Courts, entitled *Science and Education*, has two delightful maidens, holding books to represent *Education*, who flank a rather stern *Science* (fig.97). Henry Fehr's contribution is noteworthy – both his stone carvings on the tower representing *The Four Winds* and his rather spiky, wild, bronze Welsh dragon that surmounts the dome of the City Hall.

The interiors of the City Hall are lavish, beautifully proportioned and include both a further excellent coloured mermaid relief frieze by Poole as well as numerous statues by Goscombe John, Pomeroy and others (though *Sir Thomas Picton* has recently been removed on account of his links to slavery). Lanchester, Stewart (who sadly died in 1904, before the completion of these buildings) and Rickards had set a high standard for civic Cardiff and, just as importantly, had again used architectural sculpture as a vehicle to express and communicate civic ideals.

Next to contribute to Cathays Park was the rather interesting architect William Douglas Caroe (1857–1938). He had established a very successful London-based architectural practice with ecclesiastical work at its core, with perhaps his most interesting design being the Offices of the Ecclesiastical and Church Estates in Westminster (1903–5). He generally operated in a sub-Shaw style of red brick with stone dressings. In 1903, the competition was held for the design of the principal building for the University of South Wales and Monmouthshire which was to occupy almost the entire eastern side of Alexandra Park. Caroe might not normally have made the shortlist for such a prestigious commission but had already completed one of the university's first new buildings, the Gothic Revival-style Aberdare Hall in 1895, in red brick and terracotta, and therefore had an existing client relationship. Such was the contemporary popularity of Belcher's Baroque that even Caroe realised that if he wanted to win, then he must attempt it, and in the end, ironically, John Belcher was once more beaten by a fellow competitor who had adopted his own architectural language. Caroe's design is certainly a competent essay in the style (with an additional dash of Jacobean) and sits well behind the avenues of trees which enclose the park. Two pavilions frame a lower pedimented entrance block which contains a shallow, vaulted, rusticated projecting doorway, which Caroe had clearly 'lifted' from Belcher's Chartered Accountants' Hall. Beyond the basics of architectural decoration, all of which is strictly Classical, the architectural sculpture is concentrated around the entrance, with a recessed relief frieze below the pediment and coat

96   Detail of the metalworker and miner on Paul Raphael Montford's *Commerce and Industry*, Cardiff Law Courts (1901–4)

97 Donald McGill's *Science and Education* on Cardiff Law Courts

of arms within it, both by Donald McGill. The higher pavilions have cartouches on their corners, and each has an arched niche with statue.

In 1909, Vincent Harris and Thomas Anderson Moodie won the next architectural competition for the design of the Glamorgan County Council building (1909–12) on a site slightly further along the tree-lined avenue from the Law Courts. It represents something of a rejection of the Baroque and a return to the Beaux-Arts, with its great Corinthian colonnade facing the park whose stylobate is framed by two interesting statues representing *Navigation* and *Mining* by the Scottish architectural sculptor Albert Hemstock Hodge (1875–1918). These were originally intended for the roof of the building where they would have been silhouetted against the sky to greater dramatic effect, but perhaps their contrast with Harris and Moodie's correct Classicism would have been just too great. *Navigation* is the livelier of the two with Amphitrite and Poseidon being dragged through the waves by two sea horses, with their clothes and hair (including Poseidon's long beard) being blown back almost horizontally. *Mining*, though more subdued, is actually a much more powerful (and relevant) piece: a relaxed Minerva (Roman goddess of trade and industry), with arm draped around a companion, gazes out across the park, completely oblivious to three miners on whose faces is etched the achingly hard labour of their industry, and whose taut muscles and bulging veins strain as one offers Minerva a basket of coal while the other two push and drag a heavy steel cart laden with coal behind

98 Albert Hodge's *Mining* outside the Glamorgan County Council building, Cardiff (1909–12)

her. The mythical figures are classic Hodge, but his miners, who look as if they have almost been carved from coal themselves, represent a radical departure (fig.98). Hodge also provided two sculptures, *A Druid* and *A Bard*, on the screen behind the dais in the council chamber, which still survive.

By the time that he completed these statues in 1912, Hodge had already built quite a reputation and was much in demand as an architectural sculptor throughout the country. Initially very much an outsider, he had been born on the Hebridean island of Islay and commenced a pupillage as an architect in Glasgow, before abandoning that profession for sculpture and studying at the Glasgow School of Art. His skill and relationships with the city's architects soon brought him work, and having assisted James Miller (1860–1947) on the second Glasgow International Exhibition of 1901, he went on to work for John James Burnet (1857–1938) on the second phase of the Clyde Navigation Trust building

99 Albert Hodge's magnificent *Demeter Leading a Bull* on the second phase of John James Burnet's Classical Clyde Navigation Trust building (1905)

(1905), sculpting two major mythological groups to flank Burnet's dome – *Demeter Leading a Bull* and another version of *Amphitrite with a Pair of Seahorses* (fig.99). In 1907 he was commissioned to undertake the most ambitious works of his career consisting of two heroic allegorical groups which crowned the corner pavilions of Sir Edwin Cooper's enormous Baroque Guildhall for Kingston upon Hull. Cooper's corner pavilions take on a three-dimensional form as they emerge above the parapets of the building to provide square, cushion-like bases for the free-standing sculptural groups, which are thus viewed against an ever-changing sky which adds further drama to these compositions. The first, entitled *Strength*, is a rather straightforward Britannia, flanked by two powerful (rather Egyptian) supporting lions, while the second, entitled *Maritime Prowess*, is an astonishingly dynamic piece which celebrates the city's long relationship with the sea (fig.100). This is centred on Boadicea in her chariot, reining in her two mighty war horses before directing them onward with her suitably maritime trident (which has much in common with Watts's *Physical Energy*). They are a perfect complement to Cooper's architecture (as is Hodge's *Justice* above the main entrance) and the Guildhall established a further enduring artistic partnership to which we shall return.[20]

Meanwhile back in Cardiff, in 1912, architects Arnold Dunbar Smith and Cecil Brewer won the competition to design the National Museum and Galleries of Wales (1912–27) adjacent to the Town Hall and balancing the Law Courts to the west. Construction started that year but was soon disrupted by the outbreak of the First World War which delayed its completion until 1922, when it finally opened in a much-reduced form. It, too, enjoyed a substantial programme of architectural sculpture overseen by (the now Sir) William Goscombe John. As a result of the delay in construction, this was carried out by yet another generation of British sculptors led by Gilbert Bayes (1872–1953) who modelled the groups *Prehistoric Period* and *Classic Period* for the south elevation,

100   Albert Hodge's swashbuckling *Maritime Prowess* atop architect Edwin Cooper's Hull Guildhall

facing the city. *Medieval Period* and *Modern Period* (fig.101) were produced by Richard Garbe (1876–1957), *Music* was by David Evans (1893–1959), *Art* was sculpted by Bertram Pegram (and the lions around the dome), and a series of groups portraying *Learning*, *Mining* and *Shipping* were by Thomas J. Clapperton (1879–1962). With the exception of Bayes's sculptures, which have something of the severity of the Assyrian sculpture which he so admired, most compare poorly with their neighbouring predecessors, lacking either their scale, impact or clarity of modelling. Bayes is a fascinating sculptor to whom we shall also return later – initially influenced by Frampton, by whom he was sponsored for the Royal Academy School, he also experimented in applied decoration and mixed materials.

101 *Modern Period* by Richard Garbe on the National Museum and Galleries of Wales (1912–27)

In 1911, local architects Percy Thomas (1883–1969) and Ivor Jones won the competition for the Cardiff Technical College building on a site adjacent to the Glamorgan County Council building. With its completion during the war in 1916, standards really began to deteriorate, having little sculpture beyond the now ubiquitous Welsh dragon over the portico. This process of reduction continued with several stripped-down Classical buildings of the 1930s by Thomas and others, before finally reaching its nadir in the massive concrete bunker of Cathay's Park 2 by Alex Gordon and Partners of 1979 that was built to house the Welsh Civil Service. It stares across the park at Lanchester, Stewart and Rickards's urbane City Hall like a rather rude and ill-mannered dinner guest.

Henry Vaughan Lanchester, partly inspired by his work in Cardiff, went on to contribute to the planning of the new imperial capital of New Delhi, as well as providing town plans for parts of Madras and a number of other Indian cities in addition to publishing several books on the subject. He thus established himself as something of an early expert on town planning and became a founder member of the Town Planning Institute which was established in 1914. The more creative legacy, however, from their work in Cardiff was a new artistic partnership between his partner Edwin Rickards and sculptor Henry Poole which would soon bear fruit on Lanchester and Rickards's next enormous commission, the Wesleyan Central Convocation Hall (Methodist Central Hall, 1905–11) in Westminster, which they were awarded in 1905 (fig.102).

Here for the first time, Rickards looked to the Continent rather than to 18th-century England for inspiration. Despite his client being the Wesleyan Methodist Church, this was not to be a place of worship but instead was to provide a 'great service for conferences on religious, educational, scientific, philanthropic and social questions'. Its principal element, therefore, was the vast central meeting hall designed to seat 2,300 participants, below what at the time was the largest free-standing dome in the world (made possible by the building's well-concealed reinforced concrete structure). Rickards's design builds from street level, floor by floor, colonnade by colonnade, stepping inwards and upwards to the crescendo of the great square exterior dome of the hall itself (fig.103). The richness and exuberance of the detailing is quite extraordinary – no simply rusticated base here, but a series of carefully tooled panels which form a base for a giant Ionic order

102 Lanchester and Rickards, Methodist Central Hall (1905–11). The main entrance facade drips with sculpture by Henry Poole

103 No expense was spared in the Methodist Church's attempt to compete with neighbouring Westminster Abbey

which spans the first level, below an attic floor on each of the four corner pavilions, between which, on the level above, are four further recessed colonnades below the base of the dome. Between each of the Ionic capitals are stepped blank panels, topped with crests, shields and helmets, while above the capitals, carved brackets in the form of animal and human heads support the first great dentiled cornice. The main entrance swells forward in a curved bay flanked by great rusticated panels, now with shields between the capitals, and the great arched window which lights the entrance hall is replete with carved decoration, with two central angels supporting swags (fig.104). The entire composition is like Cardiff City Hall on steroids. One is reminded of the opulence of Charles Garnier's Paris Opera House, and in view of his client and their beliefs, impressive as it is, it all seems rather bizarre – until, of course, you realise that this building was designed as a status symbol for Methodism, 100 yards from Westminster Abbey and just around the corner from Bentley's Westminster Roman Catholic Cathedral. Poole modelled and controlled the execution of all this exquisite detail and was responsible for a considerable quantity of the carving himself, but Rickards's drawings of all the sculpture make it clear that, far from this being a shared artistic collaboration, Poole simply executed Rickards's designs in three dimensions in Portland stone.[21]

Of course, there was much more to Edwardian architecture than Baroque public buildings and Arts and Crafts houses. Gothic still remained the preferred style for most small churches, with George Frederick Bodley (1827–1907) designing almost a dozen new Gothic churches between the turn of the century and his death in 1907, as well as providing initial assistance to the young Giles Gilbert Scott (1880–1960), the grandson of Sir George Gilbert Scott,

104   Henry Poole's exquisite sculpture reflects Continental influences

THE POWER AND THE GLORY

105   James Gibson and Frank Skipwith, Middlesex Guildhall (1906–13), main entrance and tower. This building now serves as the Supreme Court of the United Kingdom

who succeeded in winning the competition for the design of the new Liverpool Anglican Cathedral with a Gothic competition entry of 1903. The foundation stone was laid by King Edward VII the following year, although it was not completed until 1978, 18 years after Scott's death.

Finding, like so many councils, that their accommodation was now too small for their growing needs and responsibilities, in 1906 Middlesex County Council appointed James Glen Sivewright Gibson (1861–1951) to design a new Guildhall on a prominent site on Parliament Square, between Westminster Abbey and John Brydon's Treasury building. In deference to the Abbey, Gibson produced an unusual, though not inelegant, stripped-down Gothic building, whose largely unadorned planes of Portland stone provided the perfect foil to an extensive and hugely successful programme of architectural sculpture. It was actually Gibson's partner, Frank Peyton Skipwith (1881–1915), who developed the programme of sculpture and decoration with sculptor Henry Fehr, including an outstanding carved stone frieze which is the sculptural highlight of the building (fig.105). It is located just above the ground-floor windows where it can be fully appreciated by building users and passers-by. It is designed in three sections, with the outer two wrapping around canted bay windows and the central section spanning the main entrance. These sections depict scenes of medieval pageantry from the history of Middlesex – King John and the Barons signing the Magna Carta; Lady Jane Grey accepting the crown at Syon House; Henry III granting a royal charter to Westminster Abbey – with the linear rhythm of their drapery perfectly complementing the architecture (fig.106). It is interrupted on either side of the entrance by two hooded sculptures in niches – one holding a castle and its key, the other a mighty sword – below two further figures who flank the upper arch of the entrance portico, which itself is decorated with a series of carved figures, all of which provides a frame for a great carved Middlesex coat of arms above the doorway. Further allegorical figures occupy Gothic niches – *Architecture*, *Prudence*, *Shipping* and *Justice* on the outer piers supported by seven smaller statues representing *Literature*, *Government*, *Sculpture*, *Britannia*, *Music*,

106   Part of Henry Fehr's outstanding frieze which spans the main entrance of Middlesex Guildhall

107   One of Henry Fehr's angel corbels supporting the balcony on the south side of Middlesex Guildhall

Truth and *Education*. Angel figures act as corbels to the Gothic balcony on the building's south side and crown each ground-floor window, while heraldic bosses with naturalistic carving support the frieze and gargoyles on the tower, whose twisted forms and naturalistic anatomy represent *The Four Winds* (fig.107). The stone carving continues inside in corbels and bosses in the form of heraldic animals and angels, and is complemented here with excellent wood carving on the council chamber benches and elsewhere.

While Fehr's work here may lack the complex layering of, say, Frampton's reliefs on the Lloyds building, nevertheless he achieves an extraordinary rhythm and depth within his coronation groups, as well as portraying real character amongst the soldiers, kings, queens, bishops, pages and rather sinister hooded priests. Overall, it is a triumph in terms of its sculpture and the frieze is perhaps the finest of all from this period. Due credit must also go to Italian refugee, Carlo Domenico Magnoni (1871–1950), Fehr's assistant, who carried out most of the carving under Fehr's direction. The building was opened in 1913, just before the First World War, and used until the abolition of Middlesex County Council in 1965, after which it served as a courthouse before eventually being converted into the Supreme Court in 2009, thus bringing Fehr's magnificent sculpture into a new prominence.

In that same year of 1913, the text of a lecture entitled 'Ornament and Crime' by Austrian architect Adolf Loos (1870–1933) was first published in the French magazine *Les Cahiers d'aujourd'hui.* Loos, like many Continental architects, was a great admirer of the restraint and simplicity of the English Arts and Crafts Movement; he had also spent a number of years in America where he relished both their apparent freedom from what he saw as stifling European tradition and their more relaxed focus on what worked – what was efficient, economical and convenient. His lecture contrasted this very different approach to life with the decadence of the Vienna of the Secessionists (so much admired by Frampton and Gilbert), and like Ruskin before him, he saw architecture as a moral issue, advising his audience to:

Note the forms the countryman employs. They are the essence of the wisdom of our forefathers. But look for the reasons for the forms. If technical progress has made an improvement possible, use it . . . Be truthful. Nature knows only truth. She agrees with iron lattice bridges but rejects bridges with Gothic arches and towers and arrow slits . . . . Truth, be it hundreds of years old, has more to do with us than the lie which walks beside us.

Again, like Ruskin, he had much to say about the role of the working man and expounded his own equally naïve political and economic theories:

> The absence of ornament means shorter working hours and consequently higher wages. The Chinese carver works sixteen hours, the American worker eight. If I pay as much for a smooth box as for a decorated one, the difference in working time belongs to the worker . . . Decorated plates are very dear, while the plain white china from which modern man likes to eat is cheap. One man accumulates savings, the other incurs debts. So it is with whole nations. Woe to the people that lags behind in cultural development![22]

Loos regarded any form of 'applied art' as unhealthy and an unnecessary burden on honest craftsmen, and while lacking Ruskin's Christian zeal, he was certainly the earliest theorist to bring this moralising tone to Modernism. He was just one of the many radical artists of this period whose manifestos now began to be published with increasing regularity. In Italy the Futurists had launched their movement in 1909 and, as their title made clear, they had no interest in the past – they admired speed, technology, cars, aeroplanes, youth, violence and dynamism, and they had views on everything from painting, sculpture and ceramics to industrial design, architecture and politics. While they all differed in terms of their individual obsessions and philosophy, the direction of travel was being steadily set and there was soon little doubt that it would mean 'less' rather than 'more'.

While Britain lacked a new polemicist like Loos, there were several architects and designers who were pursuing a similarly reductivist mode. Charles Henry Holden (1875–1960) had moved to London from his native Bolton in Lancashire in 1897, to work for Charles Robert Ashbee (1863–1942), one of the leaders of the Arts and Crafts Movement, and two years later he moved to the office of Percy Adams, where he soon became Chief Assistant. In 1902, they won the competition for the new Bristol Central Reference Library (assessed by Edward Mountford) with a rather severe, though beautifully proportioned, design in largely unadorned limestone ashlar. Two buttressed gabled pavilions with tall, old-English bay windows (one interrupted at ground floor to allow the main entrance) enclosed a central section in which three arches shelter what appear to be projecting study carrels, above the ground-floor windows (fig.108). The contrast with other contemporary library designs – such as those by Henry Hare in Edwardian Baroque – could not have been much greater and here in Bristol the architectural sculpture was limited to a Bristol coat of arms above the entrance and three tympana within the three central arches. These are by Charles James Pibworth (1878–1958), a local sculptor who had studied at the Royal College of Art (formerly the Kensington Schools) and the Royal Academy. Pibworth is said to have been given free rein to produce his three groups which are focused on

108   One of Charles Pibworth's medieval groups on architect Charles Holden's Bristol Central Reference Library (1902–6)

109   Charles Pibworth's rather meagre sculptural contribution to Charles Holden's Law Society Library (1902–4)

King Alfred, *Saint Bede* and *Chaucer*, and having happily accepted the straitjacket of Holden's shallow arches, he produced very straightforward compositions of standing medieval figures, each flanked by two sitting figures (within those difficult corners). While they make a suitable contrast to Holden's sheer ashlar and the subtle chequerboard stonework in the bay below, they act more as a variation of texture within the overall composition than a work of art of any significance. It leads one to feel that this particular relationship was based on an architect having found a sculptor who would largely do what they were told, and as Holden's architecture became more and more severe, it was to leave poor Pibworth with less and less to do.

Holden's new Library for the Law Society (1902–4), which occupies the corner of Chancery Lane and Carey Street in London, is in the severest form of Classicism – hinted at in the Bristol Library Reading Room – his architecture reduced to almost elemental blocks which step inward and upward (in a fashion which would take hold after the war and be pursued by Lutyens and others), with the merest of elongated Mannerist details (fig.109). Pibworth's role here was reduced to the provision of four small figures who crouch within the ground-floor arches of Holden's rusticated base, and while Alastair Service finds them 'Michelangelesque', Susan Beattie finds Pibworth's meagre contribution 'a threat to the standards of the New Sculpture more serious than either neoclassicism or historical anecdote', and laments 'his harsh simplifications and concern to echo the geometry of the masonry block'.[23]

In 1906, Holden won the competition for the new headquarters of the British Medical Association on the Strand (now Zimbabwe House). This was also clad in Portland stone, yet Holden began to hint at the steel frame within – which actually supported it – with the introduction of rather curious elongated Classical forms and further anti-rational Mannerist details. Again, the opportunity for sculpture was extremely constrained and poor Pibworth was finally cast aside, with the opportunity to contribute provided instead to a young American sculptor who had only just completed his studies in Paris, Jacob Epstein (1880–1959). Holden already knew exactly what he required in terms of sculpture for this prominent building and, having seen Epstein's *Girl with a Dove* in his studio in Stanhope Street, commissioned him to model 18 elongated figures at half life-size, to echo his architecture. Epstein modelled and cast his figures in plaster as he proposed to undertake the actual carving directly into the stone in situ (in the relatively brief period between the stone cladding being completed and the building itself being finished). The casts were all approved by their client, bar one (a rather fleshy female *Nature*), and represented all aspects of life and medicine including *Birth*, *Youth*, *Maternity*, *Age*, *Medicine* and *Chemistry*. Their style, while reminiscent of the last unfinished works of Michelangelo and of Rodin's sculpture, represented Epstein's first thoroughgoing attempt to break away from traditional European iconography in favour of elements derived from an alternative sculptural milieu – that of Classical India (fig.110). The female figures in particular may be seen deliberately to incorporate the posture and hand gestures of Buddhist, Jain and Hindu art from the Subcontinent, but as far as Edwardian London was concerned, they were simply perceived as unacceptably sexually explicit.

Their unveiling, once the scaffolding was removed from the building, caused an immediate storm of protest, with letters pouring into *The Times*, *Evening Standard* and *St James's Gazette*. They were described as 'statuary which no careful father would wish his daughter to see', but soon defended by everyone from the British Medical Association (who had approved and paid for them) to, rather astonishingly, Cosmo Lang, who was later appointed Archbishop of Canterbury. And so they survived – rather cramped within their stone slots, for many years streaked and stained, eventually largely decapitated and more recently cleaned along with the rest of the building and hardly noticeable. Looking back, however, in the words of Benedict Read, the figures had been 'offered to a public who, by their horrified reaction, indicated the arrival of the modern movement in sculpture in Britain'.[24]

110   The London debut of modern architectural sculpture: Jacob Epstein's (frost-damaged) nude figures on architect Charles Holden's British Medical Association building (now Zimbabwe House) on the Strand (1906–8)

6

THE CHANGING SCENE

King Edward VII died in Buckingham Palace on 6 May 1910 after only nine years on the throne. Outside the palace, the memorial to his mother's long reign was still not complete and it would fall to his son, George V, to unveil it in 1911. The Edwardian age was officially over and though few in the country yet realised it, Britain's position of global supremacy was now under threat. The empire's share of the world's GDP had fallen from around a quarter in 1870 to roughly a fifth by 1913, with the USA drawing level and Germany actually exceeding the UK's own domestic GDP, while Britain and Germany were also locked in a naval arms race which represented the first real challenge to Britain's control of the seas since the Battle of Trafalgar in 1805. The empire was creaking too, from within, with increasing industrial unrest in Britain and demands for independence, from Ireland and – worst of all – India, from where just less than half of the empire's total wealth was still generated. The reign of the new king would prove to be one of cataclysmic change.

The best of Britain's sculptors had raised their art to new heights and they had also brought architectural sculpture in from the cold, changing the perception of what had once been seen as a stonemason's craft to that of art of the highest level. Though Harry Bates had died in 1899 and Alfred Gilbert had withdrawn to Bruges (bankrupt, a victim of his own success, his professional and personal life in chaos, forced to leave the Royal Academy and not to return to England until 1926), Alfred Drury, Hamo Thorneycroft and George Frampton were fully occupied with the deaths of Gladstone, Tennyson and now Edward VII, providing a further flood of commissions for statues, in addition to their ideal and architectural work.

The Edwardian Baroque architectural style, to which they had contributed so much, remained popular. Having rippled out from the capital in waves during Edward VII's reign, it was now adopted for a wide variety of building types throughout the country and beyond, though generally with rather less of the original quality. In Manchester, it formed the basis of local architect Harry S. Fairhurst's Asia House, completed in 1909, Lancaster House (1910) and Bridgewater House (1912) – all of which were packing and shipping warehouses in a mixture of stone, brick and terracotta – and of Woodhouse, Willoughby and Langham's London Road Fire Station of 1906 (with some interesting glazed terracotta relief panels by local sculptor John Jarvis Millson, 1870–1914). Across the city, Clegg, Fryer and Penman completed their St James Buildings in 1912 in Portland stone and Charles Heathcote (1850–1938) provided the best of the bunch – a full-blown palazzo in Portland stone for Lloyds Bank at 53 King Street, in 1913 (fig.111). Appropriately, in addition to the bank's exuberant architecture, it was accompanied by architectural sculpture by the leading Manchester firm of architectural sculptors, Earp, Hobbs and Miller. Thomas Earp (1828–93), whom we encountered previously working with George Street on the Royal Courts of Justice, had taken Edwin Hobbs into partnership in 1864, with Hobbs establishing the Manchester business in response to the growing opportunities there, eventually adding Miller as a further partner to share the load. Their work on the Lloyds Bank building consisted of two allegorical groups on each corner of

111 Architect Charles Heathcote brought the Baroque to Manchester in the Lloyds Bank building of 1913

the building: *Britannia*, standing on a boat, supported by an impressively bearded male figure representing Britain, with a small boy standing in for the Colonies; and a female *Commerce*, also on a boat, flanked by a male Neptune and a boy carrying a fleece. While the sculptures are hardly Manchester's finest, the overall effect of the deeply modelled white architecture and its supporting sculpture still invest King Street with a blast of Edwardian confidence.

In London, the excesses of the Baroque were slowly slipping out of fashion and the influence of France and the École des Beaux-Arts was felt once more. This trend was led by the practice of Mewès and Davis (Charles-Frédéric Mewès, 1858–1914, and Arthur Joseph Davis, 1878–1951), both of whom had studied at the École. They had already completed the Ritz in 1906 and in 1911 they completed the Royal Automobile Club on Pall Mall, thus establishing it overnight as the most palatial of all the London clubs. Like numerous other contemporary London buildings, it was steel-framed, but appeared to be constructed of Portland stone, and notably, there was very little in terms of architectural sculpture, beyond several finely carved wreathed cartouches and some excellent console brackets. While its scale drew comparisons with nearby Buckingham Palace, the comparative restraint of its architectural style proved highly influential.

112 Architect Edwin Cooper at his most restrained in Marylebone Town Hall (1913–20)

Edwin Cooper, who had designed the grandiose Guildhall in Hull (complete with Albert Hodge's heroic sculptures), now produced the considerably quieter and more correct Marylebone Town Hall (now part of London Business School), on which work commenced in July 1914 with completion delayed until 1920 (fig.112). This represented something of a return to straight Classicism (though Cooper could not resist pairing the Corinthian columns of his portico), the central tower here concluding with a colonnade and stepped ziggurat cupola, familiar from the Greek tombs. While the carving of Corinthian capitals and matching urns above is particularly good, there is little further architectural sculpture beyond traditional winged cherubs and wreaths which cap two of the windows at high level above the portico, and wreathed brackets supporting the canopies of the side entrances which are topped with rather insignificant helmets. The portico itself is guarded by two stone lions which reinforce this new air of dignified calm.

When Harry Gordon Selfridge decided to build his new department store in Oxford Street, he had gone directly to the American Beaux-Arts-educated architect, Daniel Hudson Burnham (1846–1912), who had both overseen the design and construction of the World's Columbian Exhibition in Chicago (nicknamed 'The White City', which did so much to bring 'City Beautiful', namely Beaux-Arts, planning to civic America) and already completed stores for Gimbels, Filenes and Wanamakers in the US. Burnham (with assistance from local architect Robert Frank Atkinson, 1871–1923) produced the mighty Ionic temple to consumerism which remains the anchor store for the entire street, even today. But the contemporary commission which whetted the appetite of every local London architect was the building of the new London County Council Headquarters on one of the most prominent riverside sites in the city, directly opposite Barry and Pugin's Palace of Westminster. A competition was held for this prestigious opportunity in 1909, with both Sir Aston Webb and Richard Norman Shaw as assessors. The vast field was soon whittled down to a shortlist which included John Belcher, Edwin Lutyens, Henry Hare, Edwin Cooper and one of Aston Webb's employees, a young architect who had come second to Charles Holden in the competition for Bristol Library, Ralph Knott (1879–1929). Against all the odds, it was the 30-year-old assistant architect who snatched the prize from under the noses of his illustrious elders, and deservedly so. (Lutyens was almost inconsolable, having spent almost nine months on his design at his own expense.) Knott's design was much revised before construction commenced in 1911, with his proposed great hemicycle flipped from the land side, where it had served as the main entrance, to the riverside (as suggested by Professor C.H. Reilly in his entry). It stands, like a grand Beaux-Arts *analytique rendu*, facing the Thames and the Houses of Parliament, the river lapping against its giant, bronze, lion-head mooring rings (by Gilbert Bayes) which await the arrival of imaginary barges. Again, delayed by the First World War, it was not completed until 1922, by which time much of Knott's intended sculptural programme had been dramatically reduced, including the loss of six planned bronze groups by Bayes.

Most of the minor architectural sculpture (heraldic shields, caskets, torches, and so on) was carried out by Charles H. Mabey Jnr (1867–1965), the latest in a long line of talented London stone carvers, but the major sculptural groups, which were all delayed by the outbreak of the war, were assigned to the young, and then almost unknown, Ernest Cole (1890–1978) who was only 24 when he began working on the commission. It was originally intended that he should execute all the sculptures, but Alfred Hardiman (1891–1949) was eventually brought in to assist. Cole had attended the South Kensington Schools where he had been 'discovered' by architect Charles Ricketts (who had actually compared his talent to that of Alfred Stevens) and he started work on the sculptures in 1915, but was called up to serve his country in 1916. Despite this, he continued to progress the County Hall sculptures with an assistant on his weekends off. By the end of the war, he had completed five and a half of the eight groups required, and after visiting the United States for the first time, returned as 'a convert to modern art nonsense', as Ricketts now described him. (It is said that, from this point onwards, Ricketts could never hear Cole's name 'without a sort of rage possessing him'.[1]) His work then slowed to a snail's pace and he only produced one further group, which he failed to show Ralph Knott in plaster and which Knott rejected on being presented with the finished work in Portland stone, after which his commission (and brief career) was concluded by the Council.

Cole's largely naked completed sculptures divided opinion; some, including Lawrence Binyon of the British Museum, firmly believed 'that no other English sculptor living would have produced groups to match Cole's for bigness of conception and style', whereas Charles Marriot, the art critic of *The Times*, compared them unfavourably to Mabey's work, finding the contrast between the sculpture and the architecture too great (fig.113). They are certainly confused and indeed there is no record as to the subject matter of each group, but they are presumed to include *The Creation of Eve*, *Hero*, *Love*, *The Thames*, *The World Beyond*, *The Good Samaritan* and *Sacrifice*. Like Charles Wheeler's (1892–1974) later sculptures on Herbert Baker's (1862–1946) Bank of England (1921–33) (with which they have much in common stylistically) they proved to be hugely controversial with the public. Frankly, there was little to warm to amongst the contorted bodies and blank expressions of Cole's vaguely themed figures

113   One of Ernest Cole's paired sculptures on architect Ralph Knott's London County Hall (1911–33)

114 Like so many of his young contemporaries, Ernest Cole's principal aim appeared to be to 'shock the bourgeoisie'

Bank Hall in Glasgow in 1896. In 1904, he had beaten a field of London architects to win the commission to extend the British Museum and had moved to the capital to both oversee this major project and with the aim of establishing a new London practice. His proposal for the museum extension was a further grand Ionic colonnade which provided a new north face, a further building entrance and the Edward VII Galleries. Like Daniel Burnham, he had also studied under Jean-Louis Pascal at the École des Beaux-Arts in Paris, witnessed his fellow student Charles McKim's New York Central Station under construction, and was thus able to step back quite easily from his Baroque into the Beaux-Arts style when a commission such as the museum appeared to demand it. The building itself, unlike most of his previous work, has no architectural sculpture (though its stone detailing and carving is excellent), with only two free-standing imperial lions by his friend, George Frampton, flanking its entrance.

Burnet's hope of building a new London practice (in parallel to his practice in Glasgow who seemed completely alien to the strict Classical language of Knott's architecture (fig.114). Alfred Hardiman was employed to complete the groups in the late 1920s when he provided the figures on the northern facade in a similar style, though with clearly prescribed and rather more prosaic themes, such as *Town Planning* and *Recreation*. Cole's statues are, however, symptomatic of their period, of an increasing divergence between architecture and sculpture, and of the first, often painful and largely misunderstood, birth pangs of Modernism.

Architecture was affected by the new artistic currents too, though as usual it was slower to respond, with no architect's work expressing the pre-war confusion better than that of John James Burnet. We first encountered him working with George Frampton on his superbly confident Savings

115 Prolific architectural sculptor Albert Hodge assisted John James Burnet on the General Accident Fire and Life Assurance Corporation building (1909–11)

which continued under his ownership) proved to be rather an uphill battle against a strong field of well-established London competitors, but in 1908 he was finally commissioned by the General Accident Fire and Life Assurance Corporation to provide them with a new headquarters building on Aldwych (which was then being developed). Burnet's design for this difficult curving, sloping site proved a particularly elegant solution and also provided a return to a slightly more restrained version of his previous architecture, with three floors of rustication concluding in a long balcony, below three further floors of smooth ashlar Portland stone, topped off with one of Burnet's typical attic galleries (fig.115). The main entrance is a minor masterpiece, with a Doric order for the Crestola marble entrance screen behind two pairs of stone Ionic columns which are topped with black marble capitals. Each of the Doric columns is capped with a crouching figure representing *Strength*, *Prudence*, *Abundance* and *Prosperity*, on this occasion by his fellow Scot, the ever-industrious Albert Hodge. Above the architrave of the entrance, a central aedicule is flanked by two further crouching figures and two carved brackets, which support two further columns on the floor above, which are in turn topped by two further figures. To complete the composition, the two minor side entrances have typical Burnet broken pediments, which provide bases for pairs of rather lively cherubs. The building and its sculpture are superbly integrated, although Susan Beattie is generally critical of Hodge's work, suggesting that the final pair of figures which sit high above the entrance are as 'remote as cyphers from human experience'[2] but his sculptures work perfectly here within the context of what was the return to a more restrained and correct Classical architectural tradition, rather than within the more exuberant Baroque.

Burnet's next commission was for a London headquarters office for George Eastman's Kodak Corporation, and Burnet's response to this challenge represented something of a radical departure, not just for him, but also for British architecture. Burnet and Eastman considered numerous alternative

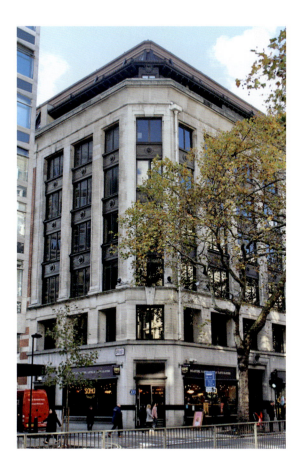

116 John James Burnet's contemporary Kodak building of 1910–11 was almost entirely devoid of architectural sculpture

designs for their corner site on Kingsway, which, though just a few hundred yards from the General Accident building on Aldwych, could not have been more different (fig.116). Burnet's selected solution was almost entirely stripped of traditional architectural detail and, though clad in stone, expressed its steel frame in thin stone pilasters which rose through four floors of glazed offices to terminate in an Egyptian-style cornice, below a recessed attic floor. Gone was the richly carved stone, the deep and enlivening shadows, the balconies, aedicules, pediments, capitals and, of course, the architectural sculpture. Burnet had reproduced (on a much smaller scale) what he had seen in New York at the behest of an American client, thus offering a first portent of what would soon appear throughout the streets of London and eventually every other British city.

As with Epstein's sculptures in the Strand (which had been revealed just three years previously), public reaction on the removal of the scaffolding on the Kodak building in 1911 was one of shock, revulsion and confusion, but for most critics, and even more for Burnet's younger fellow professionals, Kodak House provided a vision of the future. Though writing somewhat later, Nikolaus Pevsner expressed their views in phrases such as 'a new freshness', 'untried non-period forms' and 'a new distrust of ornament', and eulogised its 'straightforward expression of steel and concrete construction'.[3] For Burnet, it was a near total rejection of the Classicism that he had been educated in and so mastered. In responding to his American client, who wished to express his belief in the type of new technology which his company was promoting (and much encouraged by his junior partners, most notably Thomas Tait), Burnet, of all people, had tolled the death knell for traditional stone architecture and its architectural sculpture. Burnet followed up the Kodak building with his design for the Wallace Scott Tailoring Institute (1913–16) – a model factory in Glasgow in which he again expressed the building's structural frame, though here in brick and glass.

It was America that was now driving technical innovation in buildings – no longer imperial Britain. In 1852, the glass and steel construction of the Crystal Palace had represented the most daring building technology in the world, but since then, with its own burgeoning wealth and pioneering spirit, it was the United States which had taken up the challenge, producing the first steel-framed commercial buildings and the safety elevators that enabled them to be built higher and higher. Freed from many of the traditions of Old Europe (as Adolf Loos had identified), they were more relaxed about celebrating their technological progress in the external expression of their buildings, and their cities were soon witnessing buildings rising to what were then astonishing heights. The Singer Tower of 1908 in Manhattan, for example, rose from its stone rusticated base through 27 floors, with its steel frame expressed in the upper floors which were clad in terracotta. The United States appeared to be confidently marching forward, while Great Britain was showing the first signs of a crisis of national identity.

These first years of King George V's reign were a period of growing political division and unrest. A particularly well-led Liberal Party had secured the largest ever majority in the General Election of 1908, allowing them to bring forward a 'People's Budget' in 1909 which proposed both major social welfare initiatives and a significant hike in income taxes to pay for them. This was bitterly resisted in both Houses of Parliament and it took two further elections in 1910 and eventually the reform of the House of Lords to get the legislation finally approved. The Labour Party, too, was emerging from the rapidly growing Trade Union Movement and now had its own small contingent of MPs who were paid by donations from their members (MPs at this time did not receive a government salary). In 1909, the economy had also taken a turn for the worse, shattering confidence and leading to three of Edwin Lutyens's country house clients cancelling their projects on one morning. The Women's Social and Political Union had been formed in 1903 with the aim of achieving votes for women and it soon gained momentum, with organised marches throughout the country leading to violent protests, imprisonments and hunger strikes. By 1914, such were the fears of escalating industrial unrest that the Prime Minister Herbert Asquith suggested to the King that he should raise his profile by embarking on a series of 'Visits to Industrial Districts', adding that even his own position was now being questioned by many of the members of the Socialist Movement.

Attitudes to public sculpture were of course changing too, and the plea for 'no more frock coats and trousers' to be erected in town and city centres was becoming louder with each passing year. The public were also tiring of the conventional subjects of allegorical sculpture, and while public sculpture had always been subject to criticism, there was now a growing cynicism surrounding the portrayal of abstract themes and ideal virtues, with many new statues quickly becoming objects of ridicule. Lord Redesdale's much-quoted reaction to the two designs for a memorial to Edward VII in London produced by William Reynolds Stevens (1862–1943) was typical of this view – he suggested that the first design 'consisted of a pedestal adorned by a medallion portrait of King Edward in relief, surmounted by one of those conventional winged ladies who do duty as representing Peace, Victory, Science, Art, or any other abstract idea which the poverty-stricken mind of man can suggest', while the second design 'represented a boat out of the bows of which the King was represented as about to jump, apparently in order to escape from the same winged lady-of-all-work, who this time was serving in the wings as coxswain'.[4] An increasing proportion of the population shared his weariness with the traditional themes and subjects of symbolic representation which had by then been replicated over and over, with seemingly every town hall proclaiming the importance of Science, Art and Engineering and every bank celebrating Commerce, Prudence, Industry, Agriculture and Trade.

It was in this context that in June 1914 the heir to the Austro-Hungarian Empire, Archduke Franz Ferdinand, was assassinated by a terrorist in Sarajevo, leading to an international diplomatic crisis. Frantic efforts to avoid war continued throughout the summer, while the British economy slumped further, but they were all to no avail and as a result of a series of long-established interlocking international alliances between the great powers of Europe, what started as a retaliation against Serbia by Austro-Hungary soon brought first Russia and then Germany into conflict. France mobilised in support of Russia, Germany invaded Belgium, thereby violating the 1839 Treaty of London, and Britain subsequently declared war on Germany in defence of Belgium's neutrality. Soon the world would be at war, with few imagining that it would last four long years, during which the wealth and much of the youth of the vast British Empire would be poured into a long battle of attrition, fought largely in the mud of France and Belgium. Ironically, it would take the deaths of almost a million men from across the British Empire to emotionally engage the public once more in commemorative statuary.

The impact on British architects of the outbreak of war was immediate, with many of the projects which had survived the summer's economic downturn being cancelled overnight and valued architectural assistants immediately volunteering to fight. For projects which were under construction, the reaction was mixed, with Scottish architect James Miller, for example, seeing construction of his Gleneagles Hotel immediately halted, whereas numerous public projects (as already noted) continued to stagger along, coping with increasing shortages of labour and materials as the country moved onto a 'total war' footing. Miller's Glasgow practice was saved by his appointment to oversee the design and construction of one of the country's massive new Shell-Filling Factories in 1915, which eventually occupied a site of over 200 hectares by the end of the war. For Edwin Lutyens and Herbert Baker, the design and construction of the new imperial capital of India – New Delhi – kept the wolf from their doors. However, as the war dragged on, even this massive enterprise slowed almost to a stop, with their (and Reginald Blomfield's) commissions from the new Imperial War Graves Commission for war cemeteries and monuments filling the gap from 1916. John Burnet, like most other architects, soon had no active commissions and only survived the war by selling his collection of art, books and antiques.

Many of the younger sculptors enlisted: Alfred Hardiman, who would complete the London County Hall sculptures after the war, joined the Royal Flying Corps; William Reid Dick was to see action in France and Palestine; Gilbert Ledward joined the Royal Garrison Artillery, fighting in both France and Italy, and was 'mentioned in dispatches'; and Frederick

Wilcoxson served as an officer with the Royal Field Artillery in France (after which he was treated for severe shell shock). Charles Sargeant Jagger (1885–1934), who would go on to be perhaps the greatest of the memorial sculptors of the war, served in France with the Artists' Rifles (which attracted volunteers from the public schools and universities who generally trained with this regiment before taking up commissions as officers in other units), along with his fellow member sculptors, Frank Dobson (1886–1963), Jacob Epstein and poor William McMillan (1887–1977), who was emotionally scarred for life by his experience in the trenches.

Francis Derwent Wood, who at 41 was too old to enlist on the outbreak of the war, volunteered with the Royal Army Medical Corps in various London hospitals, and his exposure to the disfiguring injuries inflicted by the war's industrialised weapons eventually led him to open a special clinic: the Masks for Facial Disfigurement Department, located in the Third London General Hospital, Wandsworth. Instead of the rubber masks which were then used conventionally, Derwent Wood constructed masks of thin metal, which he (and soon several further artists, including William Bateman Fagan and Thomas Humphrey Paget) sculpted to match photographs of the men taken before their wounding, thus allowing the young men to return to their families and friends without their often-devastating injuries proving too shocking.[5] The ward stayed open for only two years, from 1917 to 1919, and while there is no record of the exact number of masks made, it must have made a substantial contribution to the lives of the 20,000 men who suffered severe facial injuries.

At the end of the war in 1918 – despite the monumental loss of both military and civilian life – there was considerable pride in yet another great victory for the British Empire (in fact, as a result of the Treaty of Versailles in 1919, Britain extended its empire even further with the acquisition of Palestine and Transjordan, Iraq, parts of Cameroon and Togo, and Tanganyika, thus reaching its territorial peak). The reality, however, was that the war had been an economic catastrophe for Britain, transforming the country from being the world's largest overseas investor to being its largest debtor, with interest payments (mostly to the US) that would consume around 40 per cent of the national budget for many years to come. Inflation more than doubled between 1914 and its peak in 1920, while the value of sterling fell by over 60 per cent. As a result of the scale of the loss of life amongst the young male population, certain trades, including building construction, were particularly adversely affected, with the cost of skilled labour increasing by a factor of three compared to 1914 prices, and increases in the cost of materials further compounding the problem. James Miller was soon advising his fellow architects that, in his view, 'the high cost of labour and material now prevailing, and so far as we can see, likely to prevail for an indefinite period, are such as will prevent what has been termed for lack of a better name the "luxury" type of building being carried out on any great scale for an indefinite period'.[6]

For a few architects and a much larger group of sculptors, however, the conclusion of the war brought a much-needed raft of commissions as the nation once more embarked on the commemoration of the dead on a scale never witnessed before or since. Subscriptions were sought throughout the country for city, town and village memorials, and while this resulted in a few commemorative buildings, the overwhelming majority of memorials took the form of free-standing monuments with or without sculpture. The quality of most of the sculpture was high, with much of it outstanding, and in several cases – such as Charles Sargeant Jagger – former soldier-artists brought a new and searing realism home from the front. The principal architects of the Imperial War Graves Commission – Baker, Blomfield, Holden and Lutyens – set the tone for much of the nation, with Lutyens developing the 'Elemental Classicism' of Herbert Baker's Boer War memorials in South Africa into works of high art. His best-known memorial, the national memorial – the Cenotaph in Whitehall – is almost devoid of sculpture, with just three carved stone wreaths (by

Derwent Wood) contrasting with the smooth stone and perfect proportions of his Portland stone pylon. Elsewhere, sculptors took the initiative and the outpouring of outstanding bronzes that were erected throughout the country in this period represent perhaps the finest group of war memorials in the world. Jagger's Royal Artillery Memorial on Hyde Park Corner (with stepped Portland stone base by architect Lionel Pearson) brought together the Classicism of Baker, Lutyens and Holden with a great stone howitzer, four bronze soldiers in full kit and carved reliefs of scenes of war. Others such as John Angel's in Exeter (1881–1960), who was then a pupil of Frampton, depicted a female *Victory* standing on a dragon and stretching heavenwards, high above four further beautifully modelled, rather pensive, bronzes representing a soldier, a sailor, a prisoner of war and a nurse, while many further depicted simply a lone soldier, either on guard or in action. In Birmingham, a Hall of Memory was built in the city centre in the form of a Baroque temple to commemorate the 12,320 local citizens who had lost their lives, complete with four excellent bronzes by sculptor Albert Toft (1862–1949) representing the Army, Navy, Air Force and (rather unusually for the period) Women's Services (fig.117).

After the conclusion of hostilities, the first claims on available building resources were for the completion of major projects which had commenced before the outbreak of the war. London County Hall and Marylebone Town Hall, we have already discussed, but the other major London public building which spanned the conflict was Edwin Cooper's monumental Port of London Authority building, begun in 1912 and not completed until 1922. After the war, Cooper (though hardly known today) was regarded as the leading architect of buildings for the City of London and his practice produced numerous bank and headquarters buildings as the economy recovered. His Port of London Authority building occupies an entire city block, with the corner nearest the Thames cut on the diagonal with a Corinthian portico forming the base to a ziggurat-like tower which steps onwards

117   Monument to those who served in the Navy by sculptor Albert Toft on the Hall of Memory in Birmingham (1923–5)

and upwards, via something resembling a triumphal arch, topped with a flat pedestal (fig.118). It was to mark something of a swansong for the Baroque. When Cooper won the competition for the project before the war, he was then working on Hull Guildhall with Albert Hodge, and it was Hodge to whom he turned again for a series of further colossal sculptural groups. Hodge had already sketched out two groups, *Exportation* and *Produce*, and a single figure of *Father Thames* when tragically he died in 1917 at the age of only 42. It fell to his assistant and leading stone carver, Charles Doman (1884–1944), the son of a Nottingham stone carver and monumental mason, to complete the sculpture on the building,

118 Few architects equalled the sheer bravado of Edwin Cooper in his Port of London Authority building of 1912–22, with sculpture by Albert Hodge and Charles Doman

119 Charles Doman's *Commerce* on the Port of London Authority building

and henceforth he also inherited Hodge's role of 'Sculptor in Chief' to Edwin Cooper.

The two statues of *Commerce* and *Navigation* by Doman are on either side of the main entrance portico at ground level and offer twice-life-size enthroned figures, with a male *Commerce* (with a basket of merchandise, measuring scales and a lamp of truth; fig.119) and a female *Navigation* (complete with ship's wheel, chart and globe). As with all the other sculpture on the building, these are Classical figures but with rippling muscles, protruding veins, fine voluminous drapery and, in the case of *Navigation*, bold bare breasts. They complement the Classical architecture superbly and with minor sculpture around the building such as swags, wreathed spandrels and relief tablets, the integration of sculpture and architecture is quite outstanding. But the major sculptural work is high above, with Hodge's magnificent and rather stern *Father Thames* occupying the principal arch of the tower. Here he stands on a plinth flanked once more by bows of a boat; with flowing beard and bulging muscles on a dramatically angled anchor, supporting a trident nonchalantly in his right arm, he points outward to the river and the distant sea with his left. To his sides and slightly lower are Hodge and Doman's two principal groups, with *Exportation* on his left – a winged male figure who is paddling out of his arch with the assistance of two sea horses (as in Hull) – and the more dramatic *Produce*, who simply bursts out of her arch, thrusting a flaming torch into the air while sitting atop a triumphal chariot drawn by another very fine ox (as on Burnet's Clyde Navigation Trust building by Hodge), accompanied by a lower male figure representing *Husbandry*. Being on the sides of the tower, as opposed to Hodge's groups in Hull which top the corner pavilions of the Guildhall, they lack some of their impact, but the compositions are more complex, even more successful, and beautifully executed by Doman. The entire building complex, including the sculpture, seems completely 'over-the-top' to us now, but for most Britons who viewed it in the 1920s, Cooper, Hodge and Doman had successfully and triumphantly celebrated the great river which flowed through the imperial capital and out to the waves which, most believed, Britannia still ruled.

Continuing the theme of projects interrupted by the war, in 1919 Gordon Selfridge proceeded with the next phase of his department store. With both Daniel Burnham and his London associate Frank Atkinson now dead, a fellow alumni of the École recommended John James Burnet who, having already completed

120 John James Burnet provided the setting for Gilbert Bayes's imperious *Queen of Time* of 1926–31 on the Selfridges building

tidal ebb and flow (the composition originally having been entitled *The Sea of Eternity*). It was cast in bronze and, typically for Bayes, gilt and inlaid with blue stoneware by Doulton's of Lambeth, before finally being installed in 1931.

With ten years of steady work in Oxford Street, Burnet rebuilt his London practice and it became much more successful and indeed fashionable after the war, as the economy finally stuttered into life. He was soon appointed by millionaire businessman Richard Tilden Smith to design Adelaide House (1921–5) on the north bank of the Thames, next to London Bridge, to provide office accommodation for his company and a penthouse complete with roof garden for Tilden Smith himself. Burnet's design (with considerable input from his junior partner, Thomas Tait) was a massive, steel-framed, stone-clad block with similar Egyptian styling to his earlier Kodak House.[7] The main elevations are also something of a reworking of his McGeogh's Warehouse in Glasgow of 1905–9 with its great vertical fins spanning from first-floor level to the recessed gallery below the curved cornice. The architectural sculpture was minimal and now hinted at Art Deco, with the highlight being the main entrance with its suave polished black marble columns, above which were seven blocks carved with coats of arms and a figure carved in high relief above the central block by one of Burnet's closest friends, sculptor William Reid Dick.

Reid Dick was another fellow Scot who, born into a working-class family in the Gorbals in Glasgow, was apprenticed to a firm of stonemasons at the age of 12 and commenced evening classes at Glasgow School of Art as soon as he was old enough. He was fortunate to be selected as one of the local sculptors to assist George Frampton on the Glasgow Art Gallery and Museum project, carving the exterior Scottish county crests and artists' names, after which he completed his apprenticeship with James C. Young and James Harrison Mackinnon, before moving to London in 1908 where he continued his studies at the SLTSA. He had already exhibited at the Royal Academy prior to the war and after returning

another mighty Ionic colonnade at the British Museum before the war, won the commission, thus rescuing him and his London practice from something close to penury. This huge project allowed Burnet to recover and also gave us Gilbert Bayes's famous *Queen of Time* sculpture over the main, central entrance. It was Selfridge himself who had selected Bayes, having admired his previous work, but Bayes and Burnet soon became good friends too (fig.120). Bayes's great winged female figure stands 11 feet high, below a great double clock on the prow of a stone ship, and is supported by four nymphs with two holding waxing and waning moons to represent the to London, he was commissioned to undertake several memorials, before Burnet gave him the opportunity to work on Adelaide House.

His unidentified statue on Adelaide House is a fascinating piece, directly carved in high relief – it is symmetrical apart from the slightly tilted globe which she holds. It combines a modern rather stylised minimalism with something of the ethereal in her aloof expression and hieratic stance (fig.121). She certainly works perfectly with Burnet and Tait's stripped-down, vaguely Art-Deco Classicism which must have appeared radically modern on its completion. It was another building which divided the critics and the public, with Burnet later referring to 'the argumentative storm which has centred around it',[8] but his fellow professionals praised his innovation once more. Reid Dick assisted again on Burnet's Vigo House on Regent Street (an even more unusual architectural concoction), providing a rather Athenian version of

121 The restraint of John James Burnet's Adelaide House is echoed in William Reid Dick's lone central figure

122 Alfred Oakley's *Mercuries and a Globe* above the main entrance to the Daily Telegraph building by John James Burnet (1928–30)

The Spinner as an appropriate symbol for this department store for tailor R.W. Forsyth of Glasgow.

By the time Burnet and Tait were appointed as consultants on the new Daily Telegraph building on Fleet Street (with Charles Ernest Elcock and Frederick Sutcliffe as architects, 1928–30), the architecture was full-blown Art Deco with a stylised colonnade within a vast proscenium arch, and the sculpture reduced to five small relief panels of swallows within the colonnade and a very lively rectangular carved relief panel with two figures of Mercury and a globe above the main entrance, which have all been attributed to Alfred James Oakley (1878–1959) (fig.122). High above all this, almost indistinguishable from ground level, are two further carved faces above windows on the two projecting side bays at attic level. These are by Samuel Rabinovitch (1903–91), a Manchester sculptor, who had studied there before the Slade School, London and in Paris – and represent *The Past* and *The Future* (fig.123). They were executed in situ, as was becoming the fashion, with the sculptor working high above Fleet Street on scaffolding. These two crude faces stare straight ahead with the distinctly African *Past*, in Rabinovitch's own words, representing a 'stern, glum, emaciated face . . . hollowed by age', while the mask representing

THE CHANGING SCENE

123   Samuel Rabinovitch's *The Future* carved directly into the parapet of the Daily Telegraph building

The Future was apparently a 'beaming face . . . young blank and fresh'. Despite their scale and position, they received considerable coverage, with the *Sunday Times* discussing them at length in its July 1930 edition, heaping praise on Rabinovitch, particularly for his return to direct carving which its critic admired.[9]

This was not Rabinovitch's first controversy, however, as he had been one of the team working under Jacob Epstein who had again provided architectural sculpture for Charles Holden, this time on the headquarters for London Underground at 55 Broadway in Westminster (1928/9). Other members of Epstein's team included Eric Gill (1882–1940), Allan Gairdner Wyon (1882–1962), Eric Aumonier (1899–1974) (whose father William had executed much of the architectural sculpture for Aston Webb on the Birmingham Law Courts), Alfred Horace Gerrard (1899–1998) and a young Henry Moore (1898–1986). Holden's office building was now stripped entirely of decoration and consisted of a series of stepped white stone blocks concluding in a massive clock tower; and (though such is the monumental scale of the building that they are almost lost) it is accompanied by a programme of ten external sculptures, with two figures representing *Day* and *Night* by Jacob Epstein and eight figurative reliefs that represent *The Winds* for each cardinal point (with *Day* located eight feet above the secondary entrance portal on the south-east facade and *Night* in the same position on the north-east facade). Epstein's two figures are in an avant-garde style – quite unlike his earlier emaciated sculptures on Holden's British Medical Association building – with both *Day* and *Night* being heavy, brooding masses in a much more primitive idiom. The sculpture representing *Day* takes the form of a seated, smiling, adult male with a young boy, whose body is twisted unnaturally to allow his penis to become a focal point of the work (fig.124). The adult male has a threatening physical presence, aggressive facial expression, and surrealistic elongated arms, in contrast to the female figure which represents *Night* who takes the form of a shrouded woman with a mournful expression cradling a frail-looking child, and evoking an even darker, more solemn mood.

124   Jacob Epstein's controversial sculpture, *Day* on Charles Holden's London Underground Headquarters building (1927–9)

159

As to *The Winds* which were carved on pediments above the sixth floor on each of the eight principal faces of the cruciform building, all eight are nude figures of different genders, positioned horizontally and facing the direction of the wind that they represent (fig.125). Gill's three works (two female, one male) adopt animated, sexually charged poses (and are broadly representative of many of Gill's other works, such as his 1922 engraving *The Nuptials of God*). Aumonier's *South Wind* relief opts for a more formalised Art Deco arrangement, with a male figure carved with sharp geometric features and flowing lines. Gerrard also employs geometric shapes, in the forms of waves protruding from his female figure as she holds her hair, and it is sculpted in a more abstract manner. Rabinovitch's relief is also an elongated, full-figured female nude within the Art Deco tradition, while Wyon's *East Wind* is a dynamic and more naturalistic depiction of a male figure squeezing a balloon. Finally, we have the first public commission of Henry Moore, a female relief representing the *West Wind* which is the closest to Epstein's figures in style and gives little hint that here is the man who will ultimately dominate 20th-century British sculpture.

As the sculptors had fully intended, their work shocked the public and was attacked by the press, with demands that the sculptures be removed (with Epstein eventually forced to carry out some further direct carving to modify the size of the penis on *Day*). Apart from the nudity (which was hardly new), it was not the fact that these young artists' work was 'abstract' that caused the public so much irritation, but the fact that it:

> came somewhere between the abstract and the recognizable – works in which the artist used recognizable natural things but had distorted or even rearranged them according to what he felt his work needed. This really infuriated the public of that time. Purely abstract work they could ignore as having no pictorial or illustrative interest . . . Distortion, particularly of the human figure, left the average person no answer except ridicule.[10]

125   Eric Gill's *North Wind* on the London Underground Headquarters

While Epstein, Gill and Moore continued their experiments in Modernism – in something that was now beginning to resemble a parallel universe – there were three architects who dominated most of the contemporary new building in the City of London at this time, Edwin Cooper, Edwin Lutyens and Herbert Baker, all three of whom were knighted during the 1920s for services to architecture, and all three of whom now adopted a rather severe, particularly restrained and very elegant late Classicism in which they clad steel frames in traditionally detailed Portland stone, much to the delight of their conservative clients.

It was really only after the war, with his appointment to design New Delhi with Baker and with the huge popularity of his Cenotaph in Whitehall, that Lutyens finally managed to break out of his typecasting as a country house architect. The 1920s saw a raft of commercial projects (mostly undertaken in collaboration with other architects) which commenced with Britannic House on Finsbury Circus for the Anglo-Persian Oil Company (later British Petroleum). This immense block of office accommodation had its main elevation to Moorgate, but it is its great curved elevation to Finsbury Circus which is best known and which was to prove extremely influential throughout the following decade. There is no hint of a departure from the Classical tradition here, and while Charles Holden, Thomas Tait and most young British sculptors were now experimenting with Modernism, Lutyens and most of his fellow British establishment architects were staring resolutely backwards and revelling in a particular fascination with the architecture of 16th-century Italy.

From its rusticated base, Lutyens's Britannic House rises like a sheer cliff of white Portland stone, with windows simply punched into the wall plane below a massive, two-storey colonnaded attic. Within this framework Lutyens distributed further minor features in something of a Mannerist style, with recessed columns and decoration to several of the principal first-floor windows, carved and decorated keystones here and there, and several

126   Edwin Lutyens, Britannic House (1924–7), with outstanding architectural sculpture by the firm of Broadbent and Company

figurative sculptures almost concealed in various corners around the building. Within the context of Classicism, it was an extraordinarily inventive composition which was raised to another level by the sheer perfection of Lutyens's proportions and razor-sharp details. Previously, Lutyens had included little sculpture in his buildings – a decorated architrave here or a richly carved fireplace there – but in Britannic House, for the first time, he produced an extensive and beautifully integrated programme of sculpture (fig.126). He turned to Derwent Wood for the figurative sculptures, and he echoed Lutyens's restraint in several suitably oriental figures, including *Indian Water-Carrier*, *Persian Scarf Dancer* and *Spring*, which stand on plain stone blocks in first-floor recesses, and two *Britannias* on the corners of the building, which make a modest contribution to this overall work of art. It is actually the decorated keystones and minor details by local architectural sculptors Broadbent and Company that have the greatest impact, however, as they contrast so sharply and beautifully with Lutyens's sheer white planes of stone. These are mainly human heads surrounded with fruit or leaves, representing the company's span around the globe, but also include monograms of the company and its subsidiaries. The style is both livelier and richer than Derwent Wood's figures and they match perfectly Lutyens's own exquisite details. Reflecting the changing scene, this and the other Portland stone-clad, steel-framed contemporary buildings would soon be much criticised for their failure to express their structure (Ruskin again), with Sir John Summerson describing Britannic House in 1937 as 'about as relevant to modern office design or to Persian oil as this article is to the Nicene Creed';[11] but at the time, far from there being disappointment or criticism, there was instead considerable admiration for this new contribution to the development of the architecture of the City.

Lutyens followed this with a series of Midland Bank buildings, starting with his brick and stone tribute to Sir Christopher Wren in the perfect cube of the branch in Piccadilly, before being invited to design new headquarters for the Midland Bank in 1924 on a site on Poultry, right in the heart of the City, within yards of the Bank of England. This is widely regarded as Lutyens's finest urban building and it is certainly his most 'correct' work. He went to extraordinary lengths to refine its proportions, even to the extent of reducing the bands of rustication (which here cover the entire building) by an eighth of an inch with each band. The sculpture here is very limited, being restricted almost entirely to decorated keystones (by Broadbent and Company once more) and two fine (but in the context, insignificant) small sculptures of a boy with a goose (reflecting the building's address)

by William Reid Dick, which were finally added in 1937 (with some wit suggesting that they were 'laying the golden eggs'). With each of his further bank buildings the sculpture became less and less significant, until finally, his Midland Bank in Manchester of 1929–32 (which was perhaps the most extreme example of what had become a stepped Elemental Classicism in the style of Charles Holden) was almost entirely devoid of sculpture or architectural detail, with the exception of a tiny cartouche atop each of its four almost identical elevations.

Sir Edwin Cooper sailed effortlessly through these apparently choppy architectural waters as if drawn by a team of Neptune's sea horses, entirely unaffected by the growing trends towards simplification and abstraction. Cooper, like his City clients, valued tradition, and he regarded any young architects who had omitted the study of the works of Peruzzi, Sanmicheli and Sangallo as a disgrace to their profession. As for the emerging trends of the 1920s and 1930s, they made him 'oft times depressed . . . when I look around and see what is going on – freak buildings devoid of scale and proportion. Elementary and elephantine forms in stone called Sculpture.'[12] Fortunately, for now his views were in the majority, and he remained, along with many of his more minor peers, active in producing what the public perceived to be 'real architecture' which was enhanced by 'real sculpture'.

In 1925, the brokers of Lloyd's invited him to design their new building in Leadenhall Street (of which only the facade remains, having been replaced in 1986 by Richard Rogers's Lloyd's building). Cooper's design provided another example of correct Classicism in the style of the Beaux-Arts, but he also employed the flat planes of ashlar championed by Lutyens in what was probably his finest building. The great arch of its main entrance, complete with coffered vault and recessed, richly sculpted architrave, was topped with an attic floor with five deeply recessed windows, flanked by circular wreaths above tablets, below a traditional triangular pediment with sculpture (fig.127). This was by Charles Doman once more.

127 Edwin Cooper, Lloyd's building (1925–8), Beaux-Arts portico with pediment sculpture by Charles Doman

He provided a three-dimensional frieze which is centred on a globe on which a rather nonchalantly seated female figure representing *Commerce* leans (supported by a lion for courage and a beehive representing industry). On its other side is *Shipping*, represented as an equally languorous helmeted male figure (with a boat's prow and an owl for wisdom), with both figures holding either end of a garland which encircles the lower part of the central globe. While the composition is almost Athenian, the bold modelling in three dimensions (rather than being in relief), combined with the very natural relaxed poses of the main figures, gives the sculpture a rather more contemporary feel. Cooper also used sculpture lavishly throughout the interior of the building and in this Doman was assisted by Henry Charles Fehr (parts of which survive, dotted around the interior of the new Richard Rogers building).

Just a few years later, in 1929, Cooper designed the National Provincial Bank at 1 Princes Street on the acute corner with Poultry, next door to Lutyens's headquarters for the Midland Bank and opposite the Bank of England. It is quite the equal of Lutyens's effort. It is similarly bold (interestingly with full-height rustication that echoes its neighbour), with a strong, dentiled, overhanging cornice above the arched ground floor, below a floor of offices which provide the base for a deep three-storey colonnade on both the Poultry and Princes Street elevations, and this is brought to a climax on the concave corner of the building where the colonnade becomes a recessed bay below a rooftop sculptural group (fig.128).

128   Ernest Gillick's delightful allegorical group is centred on *Britannia*, who is supported by *Mercury*, *Truth* and both *Higher* and *Lower Mathematics*, on Edwin Cooper's National Provincial Bank of 1929–31

Doman's work here is two very well-behaved sculptures of *Integrity* and *Prosperity* which stand in two niches adjacent to the main entrance at ground level, where their intricate carving can be appreciated by passers-by. These are Classical in inspiration once more, but despite their formal setting and theme have all the strength and powerful muscularity of the best of his old master Albert Hodge's work. Unusually, the allegorical group high on the corner of the building is not by Doman but by Ernest Gillick (1874–1951), who had contributed several sculptures on the V&A Museum back in 1901 and also a sculptural group on the City Hall in Cardiff. Again, the theme and garb is Classical, but this is a particularly animated group, which is centred on *Britannia* complete with Greek helmet. Beside her we have *Mercury*, representing commerce, *Truth* with his flaming torch, and unusually, though entirely appropriately, *Higher Mathematics* and *Lower Mathematics* represented by two naked females. *Lower Maths* has a pen and large book with which to protect her modesty and is accompanied by an owl as wise tutor, while *Higher Maths* holds a magic square, complete with numerical acrostic, with both maidens not only baring their breasts but also a considerable quantity of thigh. It is an utterly delightful group – witty, fresh, well composed and beautifully carved – and proves that, even in the early 1930s, there was still much life left in British 20th-century Classicism. Unlike the efforts of Epstein and others, it was well received by public and press alike, with the *Daily Herald* (14 March 1932) suggesting that its elevated position confirmed it as 'High Art'. But while Cooper, Lutyens and Burnet would all build bank headquarters in the area in the 1920s, it was to be Herbert Baker who would pick the plum, being appointed by the mighty Bank of England to rebuild 'The Old Lady of Threadneedle Street' on the other side of the road.

At the time of the Bank's approach to Baker, he was having a testing time attempting to work with Edwin Lutyens on the construction of imperial New Delhi (and indeed, when his great rival Lutyens heard of Baker's selection, he was apparently 'inconsolable'). Baker's initial appointment in 1921 was to advise the Bank as to whether they should retain Soane's great encircling wall and rebuild within it, or instead clear the site for an entirely new building. To their surprise, Baker, who had a very high regard for his predecessors' existing contributions on the site (which included Robert Taylor and Charles Cockerell, as well as John Soane), proposed not only that the outer wall should be retained, but also as many of the existing banking halls behind it as possible, and that the model of top-lit banking halls behind the wall should actually be extended around most of the building's perimeter, with new, higher buildings in the centre of the site and a new Garden Court created to light them. For Baker, this was not just a sensitive and practical approach but also symbolic of the Bank's extraordinary history and, hopefully, great future. The Bank's Court of Directors were far from convinced – as several had anticipated a new building and a new image for the Bank, along the lines of the New York Federal Reserve Bank which had been completed just before the war – and Baker was asked to think again, but he eventually convinced the doubters and was soon instructed to prepare drawings of his proposals for the widest possible consultation.

The press, public and professional reaction to Baker's strategy was almost entirely positive, with most (including the Trustees of the Soane Museum) acknowledging that the existing rabbit warren of courts and banking halls which had grown up unplanned over the previous 200 years was no longer suitable for the needs of a modern bank. The Bank was both delighted with the public reaction and grateful for its architect's astute and sensitive advice; and thus, on 1 March 1923, Baker was appointed to proceed with his proposals, with the Bank's resident architect, Francis Troup, appointed as an adviser. As if the project wasn't already complex enough, with the retention and conservation of so many existing buildings, the moving of Robert Taylor's Court Room to a new position on site and the construction of the new seven-storey offices and six floors of new vaults and basements, the Bank also informed Baker that it wished to remain on site throughout construction, along with its reserve of gold bullion, thus making one of the most complex architectural projects of the post-war period also a logistical nightmare. Baker succeeded not only in managing this process, but also in successfully orchestrating the contributions of dozens of artists and craftsmen to produce one of the finest examples of the integration of British craft, art and architecture of the 20th century.

Baker had been senior assistant in Ernest George's office in the late 1880s, during which time he had regularly attended meetings of the Guild and drunk deeply at the well of artistic collaboration. Despite his early switch from Arts and Crafts architecture (or in his case, Cape Dutch) to Classicism, his belief in the crucial role that his fellow artists could play in his work was never diminished. In South Africa he had encouraged various local craftsmen, including stone carvers and metalworkers, to contribute to his buildings (it was also Baker who had involved local artists in the decoration of the state buildings in New Delhi). Having secured his own position with the Bank, he was determined to have the young Charles Wheeler appointed as sculptor for the buildings. Baker had worked with a number of sculptors in South Africa including John Tweed and John Swan (and indeed the first casting of George Frederic Watts's equestrian statue, *Physical Energy*, had been given central stage on Baker's Rhodes Memorial in Cape Town). But after coming across Wheeler's memorial to Kipling's son in the local church at Burwash, he invited him to contribute to his school memorial at Winchester College, for which Wheeler produced a sculpture of St Mary for a niche above the entrance. He had then involved him in the design of his war memorials in France, and by the time that he won the Bank commission had decided that their working relationship would be for life, as he described in his autobiography: 'I formed the opinion that an architect should as far as possible work in close and continuous collaboration with the same artists and craftsmen. By working together year by year they may attain that full sympathy and understanding which is needed for any approach to perfection of thought, design, and execution'; and of Wheeler: 'we two have enjoyed intimate mutual understanding and the ready interpretation of ideas and the transformation of them into the fullness of art'.[13] In 1925 the Court of Directors approved Wheeler's appointment and (as Cecil Rhodes had done for Baker many years previously) Baker took his protégé on a grand tour of the Classical sites of Europe at his expense, prior to starting work together on the Bank.[14]

Wheeler's task was extensive, as Baker intended that sculpture should be integral to both the building's exterior, including the courtyards, and the major interior spaces. His challenges therefore ranged from the major sculptures to the portico above the main entrance, to carved portrait keystones (including his own and Baker's image), Greek inscriptions, a head of Pythagoras surrounded by a mist of numbers, a winged Pegasus plaque, a new *Lady of the Bank*, twin lions supporting a column (*The Pillar of the House*), new bronze main entrance doors, crests of previous Governors of the Bank, a gilt bronze *Ariel* atop Baker's new domed circular banking hall (fig.129), plaques of deities and even circular bronze light fittings with lions and eagles, representing the pound and the dollar 'in eternal chase'. Baker's interiors, unlike the lavishly decorated exteriors, have a restrained and powerful Roman gravitas and provide the perfect canvas for the work of his fellow artists. Wheeler's sculptural work was just a part of an immense overall decorative programme – the like of which has never been seen again in Britain – and it included mural paintings by a group of artists under the leadership of Sir David Cameron, mosaics by Boris Anrep and carved plaques and metalwork by Lawrence Turner and Joseph Armitage. As an orchestrated work of art in the spirit of the Guild, the interiors are quite the equal of Sedding's Holy Trinity or Collcutt's Lloyd's Register of Shipping, and it is a tragedy that, for security reasons, they are so rarely seen.

Wheeler's principal sculptures, however, were to be the figures below Baker's new portico and a *Lady of the Bank* within its pediment (fig.130). These took the form of two female nude caryatids (their lower parts screened by drapery) and four male telamones, who are completely naked and look inwards towards the two central female figures while carrying a range of symbolic accessories including chains and keys. Wheeler produced one-third-size models of these, which were approved by Baker and his client, after which Wheeler carved them directly on the building. For an architect as conservative as Baker, he must have had great faith in his young protégé, as the figures were executed in the Modern style that, in architecture, Baker abhorred. Though nothing like as abstract as Epstein's contemporary work (and almost certainly influenced by the Swede Carl Milles, whose figurative sculptures such as his *Sun Singer* of 1926 had been exhibited in London during the 1920s), nevertheless, these were much reduced in detail, distinctly heavy, frozen in position and, it has to be said, entirely out of sympathy with their very traditional setting. High above, *The Lady of the Bank* was in a similarly lumpen style, though with more than a hint of Art Deco in her stylised crown and billowing cloak. If Baker had sought to distract

129   Charles Wheeler's gilt bronze *Ariel* atop Herbert Baker's new domed banking hall which formed part of his rebuilding of the Bank from 1925 to 1938

130   Charles Wheeler's *Lady of the Bank* on the portico of Herbert Baker's Bank of England

131 One of Charles Wheeler's female caryatids which caused such controversy on their unveiling

from any architectural criticism of his new portico, he could not have succeeded more fully, as when the scaffolding was finally removed, Wheeler's statues caused a further storm (fig.131).

They were immediately linked with Epstein's work in the popular press, and while more erudite publications such as *The Banker* (no doubt prompted by the Bank) suggested that they reflected the 'Roman vigour' of Soane, Wheeler and Baker were soon on the back foot. The press had a field day, with 'Elephantine' once more the most popular description, and if the style was not sufficient to offend, then their nudity on this national institution did the trick. The *Evening News* was particularly scathing about *The Lady of the Bank*, suggesting that she 'appears to be in the act of removing her bath-robe; but in case of the cake of soap that she should by rights be fondling she is dangling on her knee what looks like a small Greek temple. This may be her bath salts . . .'.[15] Baker enlisted the support of William Reid Dick (and even his other close friend, T.E. Lawrence) to convince the Directors of the Bank that no-one had blundered. They were soon onside, with the Governor himself, Montagu Norman, defending them both in the press and at the Bank's council meeting in 1931 – at which the figures were described as 'very extraordinary monstrosities', and rather more wittily, 'The Seven Vamps of Architecture'.[16] Interestingly, although Baker supported Wheeler fully (he could hardly do anything else), Wheeler's later work on the Bank project, such as the figurative keystones and his bronze *Ariel*, were much more traditional in style and, frankly, are more sympathetic to Baker's architecture, and there were to be no further abstract figures on any of Baker's future buildings.

By 1930, Baker and Lutyens were applying the final touches to the state buildings of New Delhi, the new imperial capital of India, from where it was intended that the Viceroy would continue to direct his native subjects; King George V still presided over a vast empire, and despite both real and artistic revolutions on the Continent, the great ship *Britannia* sailed on, its passengers looking increasingly fondly backwards.

7
A HOUSE DIVIDED

The first years of the 1930s were overshadowed by the Great Depression, which had started in the US with the Wall Street Crash of 1929. This soon became a global event, sending shares, levels of manufacturing and Britain's exports crashing, in common with every other advanced economy. There were few architects who had an immense project such as Herbert Baker's rebuilding of the Bank of England to see them through the next few years and the opportunities for major new buildings were therefore severely curtailed. However, in this economic winter, as has so often been the case, theoretical developments advanced while practical experiments were constrained and, as sculpture had followed painting, British architecture would soon witness true Modernism, rather than Elemental Classicism or Art Deco. The wind of change was now blowing from the Continent and it carried the seeds of a radical new architecture to Britain, where over the next decade they would slowly, eventually, take root.

The influence of American commercial architecture had already been seen in Britain with the expression of the structural frame in several buildings, such as in Burnet's Kodak House; we have witnessed the increasing reduction of architectural detail in the work of Charles Holden and others, and this, combined with the asceticism of the Arts and Crafts architecture, provided fallow ground for what were much more radical, Continental manifestos. By the early 1930s, Le Corbusier had published his seminal *Vers une architecture* in English (in 1927), with its seductive images of cars and ocean liners and his new definition of a house as 'a machine for living in'; Walter Gropius had completed his Bauhaus buildings (1926–7) which became the workshop for many of Europe's most innovative artists and teachers; Gunnar Asplund's Stockholm International Exhibition had brought Modernism to Scandinavia, and Willem Dudok's hugely influential Hilversum Town Hall building was completed in 1931. Epstein and his cohort from Holden's London Underground building were emerging as an exciting new wave of British sculptors and, with the addition of Wheeler, Barbara Hepworth (1903–75) and Ben Nicholson (1894–1982, to whom Hepworth was briefly married), they would go on to dominate British sculpture during the next 50 years, while, at the same time, through their increasingly limited contributions to architectural sculpture, would return it to a minor tributary of their art.

Despite the majority of British architects being largely unconcerned with the development of Modernism during the 1930s, there had already emerged one or two small groups of heroic pathfinders. By the turn of the decade, New Zealander Amyas Connell (1901–80) had completed the white, flat-roofed, concrete-framed, High and Over in Amersham (rather ironically, for a professor of archaeology), and Thomas Tait and Charles Elcock's Art Deco Daily Telegraph building on Fleet Street now had a new neighbour emerging from its scaffolding – the Daily Express building by architects Ellis and Clark with engineering by Sir Evan Owen Williams (1890–1969). As historian Owen Hopkins noted: 'The original proposal was for a conventional steel-framed and stone-fronted building, but this was supplanted by Owen Williams's idea of using a concrete frame to double the unobstructed width

132   Ellis and Clark, Daily Express building, Fleet Street (1932). A new architecture in which sculpture played no part

of the printing hall in the basement. The result was the first true curtain-walled building in London with its facade of black Vitrolite and transparent glass set into chromium strips – all wonderfully smooth' (fig.132).[1] It was a genuinely Modern building – sleek, shining and utterly devoid of any historical detail or sculpture (although the entrance lobby did develop into something of an Art Deco fantasy by Robert Atkinson with reliefs by Eric Aumonier) – and it was soon replicated for the Daily Express in Glasgow (1937) and Manchester (1939). Owen Williams continued his pioneering buildings with his Boots Factory in Nottingham (1930–32), where the concrete frame was not only expressed but here exposed, with walls of steel-framed glass lighting the production areas. In 1933, the Modern Architecture Research Group (MARS) was formed by a number of young British architects to engage in their noble battle against the suffocating forces of historicism and tradition. They too were soon producing further modern buildings including Wells Coates's Lawn Road Flats in Hampstead (Isokon building), Torilla in Hertfordshire by F.R.S. Yorke (both 1934), and Maxwell Fry's Kensal House in Ladbroke Grove, London (1937), all of which were, of course, stripped of any ornamentation or sculpture.

The Guild had a brief reincarnation as 'Unit One' – a group of Modern artists formed by the painter

Paul Nash in 1933, which included architects Wells Coates and Colin Lucas, as well as painters Ben Nicholson and Frances Hodgkins and sculptors Hepworth and Moore, although their collective aim was the promotion of all the Modern arts, rather than collaboration across their respective fields. But for most British architects, never mind their clients, this was all just too extreme and they were much more interested in producing further Art Deco architecture for the Jazz Age, rather than embracing the New Machine Age, with Harry Stuart Goodheart-Rendel's (1887–1959) St Olaf House (1930–31), on the south bank of the Thames, being a typical example of the style (fig.133). It is a rather strange (though not inelegant) building and further represents the slow and far from complete transition from tradition to modernity, with a steel frame still clad in Portland stone, but here stripped of any traditional stone detail. On the road side, two smooth stone towers enclose horizontal bands of windows (which express its frame in an entirely Modern way), with a rather minimal black and gold mosaic outline figure of St Olaf on one of the curved corners, by Frank Dobson. Dobson, the son of a painter, had painted himself until the outbreak of war (in which he had served as a member of the Artist's Rifles), and it was around this time that he turned to sculpture, exhibiting with the short-lived Vorticist movement.

In complete contrast to the road elevation of St Olaf House, is the river frontage, which expresses the structural grid vertically and horizontally above a black granite base, against which is applied a three-storey high, square black and gold relief in gilded metal and terracotta within a black marble frame. This is then echoed with the words 'Hays Wharf' in gold and black on the plain Portland stone cornice. The inspiration for the relief is probably the American architect Raymond Hood's slightly earlier Ideal House on Great Marlborough Street which had brought a little New York pizazz to London in 1929.

In similar vein, though less confused and more convincing, was George Val Meyer's contemporary Broadcasting House, on which construction was underway at the start of the decade. (Meyer had actually been the site landlord's architect and successfully managed to convert himself into also being the leaseholder's.) Its architecture drew on the Elemental Classicism of Holden and others, to which was added a dash of Art Deco curved ocean-liner styling, with the entire composition then provided with the comfort blanket of traditional Portland stone. As the BBC's Director General Lord Reith had identified the BBC's values as to 'Inform, Educate and Entertain', it was thought appropriate that their new headquarters on Langham Place should include some art, and their Arts Correspondent recommended Eric Gill for the job of providing the sculpture. Meyer provided a niche above the main entrance for a statue and the Governors of the Corporation decided that

133 Harry Stuart Goodheart-Rendel, St Olaf House (1930–31), with the faintest of reliefs by sculptor Frank Dobson on its curved corner

134   Eric Gill's famous and recently vandalised sculpture of *Prospero and Ariel* on architect George Val Meyer's Broadcasting House (1930–32)

Shakespeare's *Prospero and Ariel* (Ariel being the spirit of air) would be a suitable subject (fig.134). Gill (despite having contributed to Holden's London Underground Headquarters) had little time for architectural sculpture because, in his view and words, the sculptor was only 'called in by the architect to titivate a building which, it is supposed, would otherwise be too dull or plain',[2] but despite this view, he regarded the commission for *Ariel* as a free-standing statue and therefore worthy of his time. Even so, his cynicism regarding his client's motives ran deep, as he wrote in his biography, suggesting that architectural sculpture merely 'proclaims who the building belongs to and what game they think they are playing at', and that 'The Governors of the BBC imagine they are playing a very high game indeed.'[3] Despite Gill's reservations, his sculpture actually works well with the rather severe stone planes of the architecture, with the draped and bearded *Prospero* standing on a stone sphere which represents the globe and serves to unite the two arts. Gill chose to ignore the Governors' source and decided to make *Prospero* 'God the Father' and *Ariel* 'God the Son', and thus Ariel has his arms raised as if on the cross and both his hands and feet carry the marks of the stigmata. This all proved of little consequence, however, compared to the controversy (yet again) surrounding the prominence and size of Ariel's genitalia. As with Epstein's *Day* on Holden's earlier building, there were calls for the statue to be removed, and once again, in an effort to respond to the criticism, the genitalia were subject by further direct carving to reduce their proportions.[4]

Gill also carried out two further reliefs of Ariel with angels which are beautifully composed (fig.135), and another of Ariel leading children in dance with his pipe which is rather more prosaic and a relief for the entrance hall – *The Sower*. Gilbert Bayes was commissioned to provide six relief panels depicting Classical subjects for the concert hall within, and Eric Aumonier executed the BBC's coat of arms in relief above the fourth-floor balcony on the building's main elevation on Portland Place, which is deeply modelled with their motto 'Nation Shall Speak Peace Unto Nation' carved on projecting blocks (which invests it with more than a hint of the old USSR).

As Gombrich had described of the 19th-century French Realist painters (see Chapter 1, p.12), the long held 'unity of tradition' between artists and their public had been broken by this new generation of

135 Eric Gill's *Ariel between Wisdom and Gaiety* on Broadcasting House

sculptors who, far from seeking public acclaim for their work, now appeared more interested in causing public offence. Many did everything they could to distance themselves from the majority whom they held in utter contempt, with Gill regularly talking of 'the complete mess which the men of business have made of the modern world' and their 'beastliness', leading to his fleeing the 'commercialism' of London for a commune in Sussex.[5] As Gombrich had described of their fellow-artist painters of a century before: 'it became an acknowledged pastime to "shock the bourgeois" out of his complacency and to leave him bewildered and bemused. Artists began to see themselves as a race apart' and 'stressed their contempt for the conventions of the "respectable"', while the 'artist who sold his soul and pandered to the taste of those who lacked taste was lost'.[6] In this context, architects were generally regarded as the lackeys of 'the men of business' and as architecture was increasingly regarded as a profession rather than an art; as Gill had made clear, it was of little interest to this new generation of sculptors who would go on to lead British sculpture, and in several cases forge international reputations.

The 'Conservative Modernism' of Broadcasting House became increasingly popular amongst British architects as the decade progressed and the principal Continental influences on British architecture were less the radical architecture of Le Corbusier, Walter Gropius and Mies van der Rohe, and more the brick De Stijl of Willem Dudok in Hilversum and (rather ironically as he introduced Modernism to Scandinavia with his Stockholm Exhibition of 1930) the Nordic Classicism of the Swede Gunnar Asplund, whose exhibits at the 1925 Paris Exhibition were categorised as 'Swedish Grace'. So popular was his work amongst British architects that when the competition was held to design the new headquarters for the Royal Institute of British Architects, just a little further up Portland

Place from Broadcasting House, the entries for the competition were described by George Gilbert Scott as more suitable for the headquarters of the 'Institute of Swedish Architects'. The competition was won by George Grey Wornum (1888–1957) who emerged blinking in the limelight of his professional success from a small, until then largely unknown, London private practice. His design was an austere white Portland stone block with a glazed triple-height slot in the principal elevation to Portland Place marking the main entrance, which was announced at pavement level by two free-standing columns, topped by male and female naked figures representing *The Spirits of Architecture* by James Arthur Woodford (1893–1976) (fig.136).

Nottingham-born Woodford's studies at the city's School of Art had been curtailed by the First World War, in which he served, but he continued his training after the war at the Royal College of Art and as a Rome Scholar. His two column capital sculptures here both look upwards and shield their eyes, with their bent arms turned into a curved conclusion to the column. They have a fascinating tension, appearing to be carved in relief, but actually emerging from the confines of the column shaft. High above them is the subject of their gaze above the great glazed slot – a further figure, by South African-born Edward Bainbridge Copnall (1903–73), representing *Architectural Aspiration* who also looks onward and upward, with a collection of temples, churches and bridges at his feet. This is more abstract than Woodford's figures below and has something of the angularity of the Futurists about it. Interestingly, as with Woodford's figures,

136 George Grey Wornum, Royal Institute of British Architects headquarters (1932–4)

it is partly incised and partly in relief, making it somehow even more integral to the architecture. Again, as in the two nudes below, he shields his eyes from the rays of an imaginary sun with oversized arms and enormous hands. Around the corner on Weymouth Street, almost lost above Grey Wornum's very elegant first-floor windows and long balcony, are a set of further figures by Copnall representing *Sir Christopher Wren* (presumably selected as Britain's greatest architect) and a supporting cast which includes *The Painter*, *The Sculptor*, *The Artisan* and, to bring it all up to date, *The Mechanic* (fig.137). These are all in the same, popular, flat-relief style of the period, with just their supporting blocks and side slots up to the start of their boots or clothing incised. Woodford also produced the excellent bronze front doors whose panel reliefs show scenes of London, including numerous examples of its architecture and bridges. As one might have expected of the majority of British architects of the 1930s, it is very polite, rather reserved and all in the best possible taste.

While many of these Moderne stone buildings were in London (William Curtis Green's Scottish Widows building in Cornhill, with sculpture by William McMillan, being another good example), the regional cities were also well represented. In Liverpool, Herbert James Rowse (1887–1963) produced the George's Dock building of 1934, which was designed to conceal one of the principal ventilation shafts of the new Mersey Tunnel. Partly in response to the unusual challenge that he had been set, Rowse moved away from the style of his earlier (and very successful) Classical buildings such as the India Buildings (1923–30) and Martin's Bank (1927–32) on Water Street, to what Gavin Stamp described as 'a smooth streamlined style with Art Deco ornaments, American in inspiration'.[7] Rowse appears to have seen architectural sculpture as a key element in his mission to conceal the vast ventilation shaft, and he appointed the local firm of Thompson and Capstick to undertake all the work on the building. Edmund Charles Thompson (1898–1961), the son of a stone carver, was originally from

137   Edward Copnall's *Sir Christopher Wren* – one of five relief figures carved on the RIBA headquarters building

Belfast, but like so many other young sculptors, had served in the war, before settling in Liverpool where he studied sculpture at the Liverpool School of Art prior to setting up a studio with George Thomas Capstick (1901–64). Thompson had already worked with Rowse on the India Buildings on which he had provided several carved head keystones in Classical style along with two Neptune crest reliefs which had more of a contemporary feel. His work

138 George Capstick's relief of *Modern Mercury* on architect Herbert Rowse's George's Dock, Liverpool (1934)

on the George's Dock building was quite different, with all his contributions, within what was a very significant programme of sculpture, in a rather formal, symmetrical Art Deco which perfectly complemented the plain geometric blocks of Rowse's architecture.

Above the main entrance is *Speed – The Modern Mercury*, a figure in high relief whose attenuated vertical lines suggest extreme acceleration, with what appears to be a motorbike wheel at its base and a helmeted *Mercury* above, complete with helmet and goggles, and shoulders hunched as if over handle-bars, all this resting on a base with two stylised winged horses – both referring to *Mercury* and as symbols of old-fashioned modes of transport (fig.138). It is very finely conceived and carved, relevant, witty, and must have been one of the first examples in Liverpool of 'streamlined moderne'. *Night* and *Day*, two free-standing, cross-legged, seated statues, appear in fluted niches on either side of the main entrance. These are in smooth polished black basalt and their curved lines are in complete contrast to *Mercury* (fig.139). They symbolise the tunnel's 24-hour operation, with *Night* supporting a star and *Day* a sun disc. Four fine shallow relief panels decorate the corner pavilions and represent *Civil Engineering*, *Construction*, *Architecture* and *Decoration*, the disciplines required to construct the tunnel. These are beautifully composed with central male seated figures in loin cloths holding a symbol of their trade, art or profession. They are supported by flanking female figures with either stylised hair or headdresses, who carry further tools of the trade (with the inherent sexism of master and servant somewhat offset on the realisation that the women depicting in *Civil Engineering*, for example, are toting pneumatic drills). Each male figure sits on a block inscribed with a circle, square, triangle or, in the case of *Civil Engineering*, a circle imposed on a triangle, with each of the female figures having one foot on the block on either side of the man's feet. Within each panel the symmetry is broken only by the differing tools which the female figures hold, such as the sculptor's mallet and chisel or the painter's palette and brushes within *Decoration*, and this considerably enlivens a composition which might otherwise appear almost funeral.

Thompson and Capstick's largest scale contributions to the building are in vast relief panels on each of the four faces of the ventilation shaft entitled simply *Ventilation*. These are decorated with a zigzag pattern representing blown air above three rows of wave shapes representing

A HOUSE DIVIDED

the Mersey and flanked by two fluted columns, each topped by Liver Birds with raised wings. The sculptors also provided the Mersey Tunnel coat of arms, flanked by two winged bulls, on the Queensway tunnel entrance. In all, they are a fascinating collection of carvings (and far superior to Rowse's architecture), and while drawing on traditional precedents such as *Mercury*, they reflect the very modern purpose of the building they adorn and emphasise that public sculpture still had much to contribute in the modern world.

Rowse and his sculptors worked together again on the Liverpool Philharmonic Hall (1936–9), but sadly, this brick, ocean liner-style building had little external architectural carving beyond six small abstract capitals to the brick columns between the foyer windows, although internally Thompson provided several interesting plaster relief panels. Thompson and Capstick did work for other architects including Gunton and Gunton on their Exchange Buildings in 1939, but again, their contribution was limited to two bas reliefs of *Neptune* and *Mercury* over the entrance doors in a sharp geometric Art Deco style similar to their excellent work on the George's Dock building.

In Glasgow, James Miller had established himself as the 'go-to' architect for city-centre banks with his mighty Union Bank of Scotland Headquarters completed in 1927, and his smaller Commercial Bank of Scotland in West George Street which opened in 1931 (with beautifully stylised Ionic capitals in relief by Gilbert Bayes); and in 1934 he was again commissioned by the Commercial Bank to provide them with a further banking hall in Bothwell Street. What Miller produced for them is one of the finest British banks

139 George Capstick's *Night* oversees the main entrance to the Mersey Tunnel in Liverpool

177

140 James Miller, Commercial Bank, Glasgow (1934)

of the 1930s. Like so many other buildings of the period, it was essentially a white block of Portland stone, but here raised on a plinth of polished black marble and, like the RIBA headquarters, with a mighty slot carved out of the block for the main entrance (fig.140). But here, Miller's great chasm is deeply recessed and its lintel supported by two enormous Corinthian columns that look as if they might have been salvaged from some ancient Greek or Roman temple. Its few high-level windows are simply punched into the stone block and between its third-floor windows are exceptionally fine shallow carved reliefs, which continue between the windows on the side of the building to form a frieze (fig.141). These are again by Bayes (who seems to have developed a working relationship with Miller following Albert Hodge's death in 1917) and they depict *Commerce*, *Industry*, *Contentment*, *Justice*, *Prudence* and *Wisdom*, with the title of each panel incised (and often partly obscured) behind the figures' heads. The scenes, which combine Classical and medieval garb, are brilliantly conceived and carved to produce layer upon layer of activity portrayed within what is, in reality, a few inches of depth. One is reminded of Frampton's spandrels in the city's art gallery – *Commerce* overlays a slave, upon a sheep, upon two men with sacks of corn, one behind the other, in front of a ship; *Contentment* offers a baby carried in front of its mother, who shows it proudly to its father, who stands in front of a mighty bullock, whose rectilinear yoke contrasts with the human and animal forms. This was Bayes in his element and in his *Modelling for Sculpture* he detailed his historic precedents:

> the incised, so often used by the Egyptians, the bold though severe Assyrian, the freer Greek ranging from the early archaic through the metope friezes, the wingless Victory, the Renaissance work including the subtle reliefs of Desiderio da Settignano, Donatello, and the school of their time, and the bolder work of the Della Robbias . . . add to these the lessons to be learnt from the deep pierced reliefs of China and Japan and the deep incised work of India, Java and Ceylon and you have a store to meet almost any requirement.[8]

Miller's architecture and Bayes's sculpture work perfectly together here, both drawing on the well of historic precedent while still producing a work of art which is entirely contemporary, powerful and yet extremely refined, making it one of the outstanding examples of the integration of architecture and sculpture of the 1930s.

As if to complicate this contemporary architectural scene even further, Classicism simply refused to die. In the early 1930s construction started on Unilever House on the north bank of the Thames, with architect James Lomax-Simpson (1882–1977) providing a palatial, eight-storey Classical headquarters building for Lever Brothers, which swept around the corner from Victoria Embankment to New Bridge Street. Lomax-Simpson had been appointed to lead Lever Brothers' in-house architectural team in 1910, becoming a director of the company in 1917. Up until 1930, almost all of his

141   One of Gilbert Bayes's exquisite reliefs on James Miller's Commercial Bank depicting *Industry*

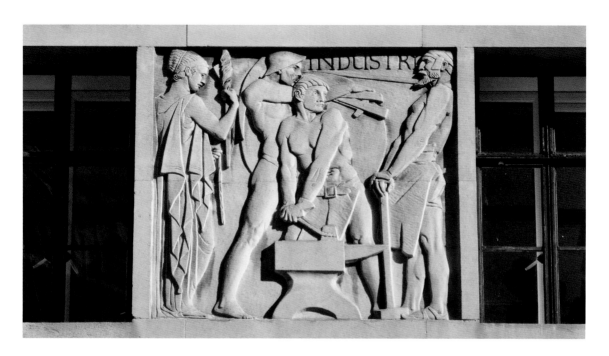

142 William Reid Dick's *Controlled Energy* on James Lomax-Simpson's Unilever House (1930–32)

architecture had been domestic, either contributing further housing to Port Sunlight model village or carrying out alterations and extensions to Lord Leverhulme's own residences in Hampstead and Stornoway. Consequently, an aged Sir John Burnet was called in to advise on this major city-centre project, and unsurprisingly sculptor William Reid Dick soon appeared alongside him on the scene. Lomax-Simpson (who had a passion for horses and counted the equestrian painter Alfred Munnings among his closest friends) had always intended that the concave corners which concluded his mighty colonnade should frame two equine statues, and these fell to Reid Dick.

The statues, entitled *Controlled Energy*, each consist of a large, powerful horse with its head bowed but still straining forward, restrained by discreetly draped muscular figures, one male and one female, who are using their full but lesser weight to pull back on the reins (fig.142). The stone beneath the horses has been only partially cut away and then rough-hewn, thus linking the legs of both horse and human, and adding further strength to the composition. Despite the power rippling through the equine and human muscles, the composition still retains something of the flatness that typified the architectural sculpture of the 1930s, with some distinctly Art Deco styling in the horse's neck, muscles and mane, and in the maiden's rather fashionable bob hairstyle. Unlike Wheeler's telemones at the Bank, these groups work well within the sheer ashlar planes of the concave corners of the building in which they have been carefully placed, and act almost as two emphatic full-stops to the considerable energy created by Lomax-Simpson's sweeping colonnade.⁹

There was great public interest in the progress of the Unilever sculptures, with preliminary models released to the press and Reid Dick also playing to the crowd by providing photographs of both 'Victor' (reputedly the largest horse in the world), who was his model, and also the two rather more lithe human models, posing in his studio. When it was suggested that restraining Victor was a little more than could be expected of 'one of the fairer sex', he responded that 'these days women are controlling affairs nearly, if not quite, as much as men' – a statement which must have gone down well with at least half the readers.¹⁰ Bronze models of the groups were also made (as rather sturdy bookends), with Lord Leverhulme presenting one set to the Lord Mayor of London at the official opening and further pairs being distributed amongst the design team. Gilbert Ledward (1888–1960) was also appointed to carry out the minor architectural sculpture and this included rather contorted Art Deco versions of a *Merman* and *Mermaid* over the two side entrance doors, as well as a series of keystones in similar style featuring women's heads and a cartouche with the Unilever monogram over the main entrance. This is elegantly lit by two particularly fine bronze Art Deco lamp standards by Walter Gilbert (1871–1946) decorated with the rather jazzy diagonal patterns that were so popular at the time (fig.143).

This continuation of the Classical tradition came as something of a shock to the young German art historian Nikolaus Pevsner (1902–83) when he arrived in Britain in 1933. With all the moral zeal of a true believer, he pronounced that British architects' 'rejection of the Zeitgeist' was 'symptomatic of a diseased society'. Despite rather admiring Hitler's achievements, Pevsner had been sacked from his teaching post at the University of Göttingen when his family's Jewish connection was revealed, and he became one of the first of what was soon a flood of German and Russian academic and artistic refugees who sought safety in Britain. These included one of the heroes of Modernism, Walter Gropius, the founding director and architect of the Bauhaus, as well as the Expressionist architect Erich Mendelsohn, a fellow teacher from the Bauhaus, Marcel Breuer, and soon also two Russians, Serge Chermayeff and Berthold Lubetkin. The impact of their arrival was considerable with them immediately being given teaching roles, providing public lectures and soon receiving architectural commissions, with Mendelsohn and Chermayeff designing the De La Warr Pavilion in Bexhill (1934–5), Berthold Lubetkin, Highpoint in Highgate, London (1935) and the Finsbury Health Centre in London (1938), and Gropius, the

143   One of Walter Gilbert's pair of bronze lamp standards which light and guard the entrance to Unilever House

Impington Village College in Cambridgeshire (1938) as well as a considerable number of zoo buildings (with several British clients only too happy to have these revolutionaries experimenting on animals rather than humans). All their buildings were white, concrete-framed and flat-roofed, with horizontal steel windows and (despite the cross-fertilisation of ideas between the arts promoted at the Bauhaus) almost no decoration or architectural sculpture. With the English architects who were already established in the MARS Group, these new reinforcements in the war against tradition further strengthened the forces of British Modernism, but it would take another world war for them to achieve their strategic objective.

Meanwhile, life continued much as normal for most Britons, with a new monarch – Edward VIII – on the throne (briefly), a distinct upswing in the economy and record-low interest rates in the latter part of the decade leading to something of a housing boom, with 'Mock-Tudor' the predominant style. For architects, while their budgets rarely reached the level of pre-war buildings, there was plenty of work again. Civic architecture, once the source of considerable interest to architectural sculptors, was now dominated by the flat brick planes of Willem Dudok's Hilversum Town Hall, with just the occasional stone relief panel or decorated door surround (such as Hornsey by Reginald Uren of 1934–5 and Clifford Culpin's Greenwich Town Hall of 1938–9), with Thomas Tait, Burnet's younger partner, being a leader of this new style.

Tait's Royal Masonic Hospital in Hammersmith, which was selected by the RIBA as the best new building of 1933, had all the trademark elements – horizontally grouped and banded windows, projecting concrete door canopies, cantilevered balconies, the almost playful balancing of horizontals and verticals in its massing and, of course, the now ubiquitous verticals of two flagpoles above the main entrance. The entire building complex had only two pieces of external sculpture – relief statues of *Hebe* and *Aesculapius* by Gilbert Bayes which topped two concrete piers

144   Gilbert Bayes's *Hebe* on Thomas Tait's Royal Masonic Hospital (1933)

below the flagpoles (fig.144). Interestingly, these are in carved concrete, which Bayes and one or two other sculptors, including William Doyle-Jones (1873–1938), had experimented with as the material was becoming used more and more in building construction. (In fact, Bayes probably pioneered its use in his Concrete Utilities building at the Empire Exhibition at Wembley in 1924.) Bayes's technique was to model the sculptures in clay from which a cast was made for the concrete. This was then poured and allowed to almost set, at which point he would carry out further surface carving adding detail directly, before the final work was cured and installed on the building. There were initially great hopes amongst many architects that the production of sculptures and sculptural detail in concrete 'at practically no increase in cost over plain work' would allow architectural sculpture to be produced much more cost-effectively, but sadly the reality was that, if a reasonable quality of finish was required, it remained an expensive, labour-intensive process. By the end of the decade, the number of new civic buildings which still offered a significant sculptural programme were now very few and far between.

Perhaps unexpectedly, one of these emerged in the rather sleepy north-eastern London Borough of Walthamstow with its remarkable new town hall building. Its architect, Philip Dalton Hepworth (1888–1963) – the one-time partner of Grey Wornum who had designed the RIBA headquarters building – had won the competition for the new town hall in 1932 with a very conservative design in the Classical style of Lutyens. However, by the start of construction (which had been delayed until 1937), his proposals had undergone something of a metamorphosis to emerge as a further Portland stone, Nordic Classical building in the style of Gunnar Asplund. Often mis-described as 'Fascist Architecture', at the time Hepworth's stripped-down Classicism offered a radical vision of civic munificence for this predominantly working-class community. The Town Hall, with its elegant portico, faces a circular pond (once used for bathing and model boating) with a new civic hall by Hepworth to its right and Law Courts to its left, beneath an elegant copper clock tower which has more than a hint of Stockholm City Hall. (Unfortunately, the court building was much delayed and eventually carried out in a Brutalist concrete style in the early 1970s.) It was always Hepworth's plan that (as at the RIBA headquarters) the severity of the architecture should be contrasted with architectural sculpture, and Hepworth was successful both in persuading his clients of the civic and social value of this public art, and also that it should fall to John Francis Kavanagh (1903–84), the Irish sculptor (fig.145).

Yet another fascinating architectural sculptor, Kavanagh had suffered a serious accident when he was 16, leaving him almost unable to walk at the time. He had spent his convalescence making clay models, and so much were they admired that he commenced a training in sculpture at the Crawford School of Art in Cork in 1919, going on to study at Liverpool School of Art and eventually the Royal College of Art, where he worked under Gilbert Ledward, Henry Moore and Charles Sargeant Jagger (whom he went on to assist, including carving the stone elephants that mark the entrance to Lutyens's Viceroy's House in New Delhi). This was followed by a two-year Rome Scholarship, and on his return to

145   John Kavanagh's bas-reliefs on the columns of Philip Dalton Hepworth's Walthamstow Town Hall (1937–42)

England he exhibited at the Royal Academy and was soon appointed Head of the School of Sculpture and Modelling at Leeds College of Art. At Walthamstow, he provided a series of relief sculptures within panels on the side of the columns of the entrance portico depicting local trades and industries in a rather geometric style which perfectly echoed the architecture. On the outside of the council chamber, between high-level windows (still visible, but rarely seen), he carved five relief figures – *Recreation*, *Motherhood*, *Fellowship*, *Education* and *Work* – which stand in elegant, stepped niches (fig.146). These share the same geometric style as the panels which gives them a distinctly Futurist feel (with more than a hint of Fernand Léger's paintings and Umberto Boccioni's sculptures), and it is regrettable that they are situated on the rear, north side of the building and so rarely catch the sunlight in which his relief panels are often bathed. They are quite remarkable and, far from being dominated by the architecture, their intricate composition and precise and almost mechanical carving inject just the vitality which I am certain Hepworth had hoped for. Kavanagh also modelled a *Tragedy* and *Comedy* for Hepworth's adjacent Civic Hall and, like so many earlier town halls, construction of both buildings was delayed by war, not finally reaching completion until 1945. Although both architect and sculptor continued their successful careers, Philip Dalton Hepworth was never to win another commission on this scale, nor to have the opportunity to work again with John Kavanagh.

In Edinburgh, Thomas Tait had won the commission for St Andrew's House (1933–9) on one of the most prominent sites in the city centre. It was to provide a new home for the Scottish Office and the Secretary of State for Scotland, effectively becoming the most important government building in the country. Tait's design is outstanding: in its response to the dramatic and historic location in the very heart of the city (below Playfair and Cockerell's National Monument on Calton Hill – see p.66); in the brilliance of his massing and detailing which builds to a crescendo above the main central entrance; and in his evocation of a contemporary Scotland which looks both back with pride, and forward with hope. Like so many important public and commercial buildings of the period it is steel-framed but clad in stone, which links this modern addition to the historic architectural heritage of Scotland's capital city. It was originally intended to be clad in Portland stone but was executed in a more interesting (and appropriate) grey Northumbrian Darney stone, and this, combined with a generous budget, provided an opportunity for architectural sculpture. Given Burnet and Tait's long-standing relationship with William Reid Dick and his then position as Scotland's most famous sculptor, he was appointed to lead a team of sculptors to suitably embellish Tait's building and once more celebrate the country's values in stone. Reid Dick himself was responsible for six half-length sculptures that act as capitals to the square pillars that imply a Classical portico above the main entrance to the building. (These have a distinct echo of the portico on David Bryce's exquisite former Bank of Scotland in nearby St Andrew's Square, 1846–51.) Reid Dick's figures represent *Architecture*, *Statecraft*, *Health*, *Agriculture*, *Fisheries* and *Education* and are in a simplified Classical style, looking straight ahead and holding relevant accessories (*Health* – snake and bowl, *Agriculture* – sickle, and so on), with Tait's plain cornice providing the perfect backdrop. They are accompanied by a series of carved heraldic devices, modelled by Alexander Carrick and Phyllis Bone, and carved by local sculptor John Marshall. A truly magnificent *Coat of Arms of Scotland* by Carrick (1882–1966, one of the many Scottish sculptors who had contributed to Robert Lorimer's Scottish National War Memorial in Edinburgh Castle), on a rectangular panel above the main entrance doors, rests on Tait's stylised stone thistle columns, which in turn frame excellent bronze doors designed by Walter Gilbert, depicting scenes from the life of St Andrew (executed by H.H. Martyn) (fig.147). The interiors are equally fine, with panelled meeting rooms and principal offices, elegant stone fireplaces and metalwork by Thomas Hadden.

146   John Kavanagh's *Education* – one of five figures on the exterior of the council chamber of Walthamstow Town Hall

147 Alexander Carrick's magnificent *Coat of Arms of Scotland* above the main entrance to St Andrews House

Throughout, the sculpture and architecture are as one and Reid Dick's restrained half-statues, Bone's heraldic devices and Carrick's coat of arms work perfectly with Tait's architecture which, despite its Moderne styling and wonderfully sharp detailing, is essentially still a Classical building in its organisation and composition.

By the end of the decade the economy had largely recovered from the Depression and there was no shortage of both opportunities and new building types – cinemas, underground stations, power stations, apartment blocks and airports – but beyond the occasional relief panel, incised lettering or coat of arms, they were now almost entirely devoid of sculpture. Both Hepworth and Kavanagh's Walthamstow Town Hall and Tait and Reid Dick's Scottish Office were to be amongst the last examples of a decorative tradition – as old as architecture itself – that was now drawing to a close.

George VI now reigned during the country's six long years of the Second World War, during which the generation of architects who had dominated British architecture since the First World War passed away one by one – Sir Edwin Cooper died in 1942, as did Sir Reginald Blomfield, followed by Sir Edwin Lutyens in 1944 (with work already abandoned on his great Liverpool Roman Catholic Cathedral), with only Sir Herbert Baker surviving to see victory before his own death in 1946, having already acknowledged that the outbreak of hostilities had signalled his retirement. They were another six years with little building except munitions factories, Nissen huts, aircraft hangars and control towers, and another generation of young architects and sculptors were soon drawn into the conflict.

Though Britain and its empire emerged victorious, the effects of 'Total War' were profound, both at home and abroad. Much of Europe – whose empires had dominated the world for so long – was in ruins, and host to the armies of the United States and the Soviet Union who now held the balance of global power. Britain was left essentially bankrupt, with insolvency only averted in 1946 by the negotiation of a $US 4.33 billion loan from the United States (the last instalment of which was repaid in 2006). At the same time, independence movements were on the rise in the colonies of all the European nations, with the situation complicated further by the increasing Cold War rivalry of the United States and the Soviet Union. In principle, both nations were opposed to European colonialism but in practice, American anti-communism prevailed over anti-imperialism, and therefore the United States supported the continued existence of the British Empire in the short term, if only to assist in keeping Communist expansion in check.

Just two months after the end of the war in 1945, Clement Attlee's Labour Party was elected in a landslide victory over Winston Churchill's Conservatives, thus providing the new government with a platform to introduce the most radical programme of social change since that of Henry Campbell-Bannerman and Herbert Asquith's Liberal governments prior to the First World War. The National Health Service was created and unemployment benefit was introduced, as was town planning legislation controlling land development; National Parks and Areas of Outstanding Natural Beauty were created; the independence of India, Pakistan, Burma, Ceylon and Jordan was granted; the State of Israel was created; and a fifth of the country's economy, including the coal, electricity, water, gas, steel and railway industries was nationalised. It was to be a new and very different type of Britain, and investment would be made by the government where it was perceived to be needed – not left to the vagaries of the market – resulting in ambitious programmes of public housing, school and hospital building; and they were to be built in the architecture of the future, not the past. Modernism had emerged triumphant and would soon be taught in every School of Architecture, demanded by every progressive government department, town council and forward-looking commercial enterprise, and, in the words of historian David Watkin, it would become 'a morally, socially, politically, and artistically cohesive package from which no one must be at liberty to abstain'.[11] The rules were soon established; materials had to be contemporary – glass, steel, concrete, sheet metal, composite panels (with stone condemned as inherently reactionary and elitist); details must be functional, clean, efficient, straightforward and mass-produced, with any type of individualism or ornament now a crime; most historic buildings, towns and cities were regarded as unfit for the modern world and must be radically redeveloped; functions within urban areas must be zoned by use and a new profession of town planners set to work to pursue Attlee's promised 'New Jerusalem'.

In contrast to the widely held desire to erect memorials to the fallen after the First World War, there seemed little interest in any more 'useless lumps of stone' and most towns and cities simply added lists of names to their First World War memorials, with the very few statues raised to those lost in the Second World War taking a very long time to be erected. But worse than this, there were also calls to remove many of the existing public statues, with the former members of the royal family, military heroes and local citizens commemorated now unrecognisable to most people (indeed, Manchester had come very close to melting down all their bronze public statues as part of the war effort). The *Manchester Guardian* warned against sweeping away much of the city's history in what it described as 'a gale of Philistine Modernism'.[12] In Glasgow, Douglas Percy Bliss, the Director of the Glasgow School of Art, wrote an article in the *Glasgow Herald* in which he referred to two of Paul Raphael Montford's magnificent figure groups from the Kelvin Way Bridge, which had been dislodged by a German bomb and now lay at the bottom of the River Kelvin, describing how he 'often regarded them down in the river bed and moralised inwardly on the decline and fall of sculpture in our city'.[13] As to historic architectural sculpture, it was simply an integral element of an irrelevant architecture, its allegorical subjects generally mocked, and in most cases, it was simply smashed to pieces along with the buildings it had adorned.

This is not to suggest that there was any corresponding public enthusiasm for Modern sculpture. While critics such as Pevsner (who had by then become established as the ultimate arbiter of British taste) might think that Henry Moore was the greatest living sculptor and that his sculpture offered 'an immensely suggestive interplay of solids and voids',[14] the majority of the public just saw a series of bronze shapes which only vaguely related to the human form – and for thinking thus were condemned as philistines. British sculpture had become an intensely personal art, with Moore, for example, continuing an exploration of biomorphic abstraction through the three themes that were to dominate his career: the mother and child, the family group and the reclining figure. By the end of the Second World War few understood his work, but nevertheless (with the boost of the international prize for sculpture at the Venice Biennale in 1948) he was well on his way to achieving the extraordinary feat – for a sculptor – of being recognised by the general public. And he was far from alone, with Barbara Hepworth soon achieving a similar prominence with her abstract sculpture and a new generation of sculptors including Reg Butler, Lynn Chadwick and Kenneth Armitage helping to achieve real distinction for British sculpture internationally, largely despite the public's reaction to their work.

Architectural sculpture was once more returning to the artistic backwater from which it had emerged, and even for those sculptors who had an interest in collaboration with an architect there were few opportunities after the war, with the sharp, clean, unadorned Modern International Style being adopted for almost all new building.

Everything was conspiring against the art, and even on the relatively rare occasions that sculpture was proposed for a new building, the sculptors involved invariably merely provided a version of their studio work at the size required, with the initial selection of a sculptor by the architect often representing the only real element of what might be described as collaboration. Examples of architectural sculpture from the late 1940s and early 1950s are therefore few and far between, not least because all private sector building was severely restricted, and thus Siegfried Charoux's (1896–1967, an Austrian who had settled in England after the war) series of male nudes on architects Gunton and Gunton's (now demolished) St Swithin's House of 1951 is one of very few contemporary examples. These included a group of five figures representing *The Arts*, high above street level below the building's parapet, consisting of two pairs of reclining figures which face each other and flank a central standing nude, along with a number of individual standing figures at intervals at second-floor level representing *Manual Labour*. These are all rather lumpen and listless, with the representatives of *The Arts* looking rather bored, while the postures of the various workers suggest that they may be on strike – although, one has to say, they are all in sympathy with Gunton and Gunton's dull, Portland stone building. St Swithin's House was denied listing in 1999 which would have saved it, as in the view of English Heritage neither the sculpture nor the architecture was of sufficient quality.

Like the steel and coal industries, the art of architecture had also been 'nationalised', with various public bodies setting up their own 'in-house' teams to execute their buildings. The London County Council Architects' Department soon became the largest architects' office in the country and attracted many of the country's best young architects, who were given considerable responsibility at an early age, including Sir Hugh Casson, Sir Leslie Martin, Colin St John Wilson, Sir James Stirling, Alison and Peter Smithson, Patrick Hodgkinson and John Partridge. These were the men and women who would strive to build the 'Land Fit For Heroes' that Prime Minister Clement Attlee had offered his supporters, and to expand this vision of a Socialist future even further, it was proposed that the Great Exhibition of 1851 should be commemorated with a Festival of Britain in 1951.

Unlike the Great Exhibition, which celebrated Britain's newly acquired status as global leader, the Festival of Britain was to offer a country, exhausted by war and austerity, the promise of a better, fairer, more equal, social democratic future; it was to encourage its citizens to look forward with hope and excitement rather than backwards with nostalgia and longing; and it was to provide a model for the redevelopment of the country's shattered towns and cities. As Mark Girouard recounted in his biography of James Stirling, London in 1950 was still:

> dingy and dilapidated. Meat, butter and sweets were still rationed. Swathes of London had been flattened by bombing, and were still wastelands of flowering weeds and shattered walls. There were gaps in the streets everywhere, and the buildings between the gaps were down-at-heel... Few people had telephones or cars, no one had a television... In clothes, in food, in restaurants, there was not much choice and little sense of style.[15]

Also in contrast to the Great Exhibition, this was to be a national celebration, with events held throughout the country. King George VI (now no longer Emperor of India, of course) thus declared it open in a broadcast from the steps of St Paul's Cathedral following a Service of Thanksgiving at Westminster Abbey; and then, later in the afternoon, the King and Queen attended a service of dedication led by the Archbishop of Canterbury at the newly completed Royal Festival Hall. Despite the nationwide programme of events during that summer of 1951, the centrepiece of the Festival was the exhibition on the South Bank of the Thames, with Hugh Casson as its Director of Architecture.

This was organised in two major parts on either side of Hungerford Railway Bridge, with the main exhibition area, which was centred on the Dome of Discovery, to the west and the new Festival Hall and more minor exhibits to the east. The Dome of Discovery (designed by architect Ralph Tubbs) was a vast, shallow dome which appeared to float above its lightweight steel lattice structure. It was accompanied by the equally futuristic Skylon (designed by Hidalgo Moya, Philip Powell and Felix Samuely) – an aluminium-clad column which was suspended in mid-air by a cable structure – and these were surrounded by various pavilion buildings, linked by high-level walkways and landscaped gardens, which contained exhibits based on various themes (devised by Ian Cox) including *The Land of Britain*, *Minerals of the Island*, *Power and Production*, *Sea and Ships*, *Health*, *The Seaside* and *Television*. For many visitors it was their first experience of Modernism, and what became known as 'The Festival Style' was hugely influential, as the art critic William Feaver described: 'Braced legs, indoor plants, lily-of-the-valley sprays of lightbulbs, aluminium lattices, Cotswold-type walling with picture windows, flying staircases, blond wood, the thorn, the spike, the molecule',[16] and with it, typography, product and industrial design were elevated to join the higher arts such as sculpture, which was also well represented.

As with the architecture, all the sculpture was Modern, with Barbara Hepworth offering *Contrapuntal Forms*, Henry Moore a *Reclining Figure*, Lynn Chadwick providing a *Hanging Mobile*, Jacob Epstein *Youth Advances*, Reg Butler his metal *Bird and Cage*, Frank Dobson *London Pride* and Daphne Hardy-Herion *Youth*. The nearest to architectural sculpture came in the form of *The Sunbathers* by Peter Lazlo Perry on a wall at Station Gate and *The Islanders* by Siegfried Charoux, which was displayed against a white rendered wall (fig.148). Considering that the Festival represented an almost unique and quite extraordinary collaboration of the various arts, the almost total absence of architectural

148 Siegfried Charoux's *The Islanders* below the towering Skylon at the Festival of Britain, 1951

sculpture confirmed that it had little to offer British Modernism. This message was rammed home in the other major building on the site to the east of Hungerford Bridge – the new Royal Festival Hall designed by Leslie Martin, Peter Moro and Robert Matthew of the London County Council Architects' Department (fig.149). Martin, who was only 39 when he was appointed to lead the design team, described the structure as 'an egg in a box' with his curved auditorium space separated from its surrounding building to insulate it from the sounds from the adjacent railway line. It is an elegant building with a sparkling, fully glazed first-floor foyer facing the river which appears to float

above the recessed ground floor entrances. Crisp, clean, functional and devoid of any unnecessary detail, decoration or sculpture, in 1951 it offered a glimpse of a bright future – it was a new type of architecture for a new type of society and it remains both a lasting symbol of the aesthetic of the exhibition and its only survivor.

Like its predecessor, the Great Exhibition, the Festival was hugely popular with the public, with 8.5 million visitors to the main South Bank site and, as noted, this was accompanied by numerous further events throughout the country, ranging from the selection of Trowell in Nottinghamshire as the 'Festival Village', to an exhibition on 'Industrial Power' in Glasgow and an arts festival in Belfast, with the Festival ship, HMS *Campania*, taking a travelling exhibition to various ports around the country throughout the summer. But it was not without its critics. Sir Thomas Beecham likened the new Festival Hall to a 'giant chicken coop',[17] and for many the whole enterprise was inextricably linked to the Labour Government – Winston Churchill described it as 'three-dimensional Socialist propaganda'[18] and ensured that almost every element of it, including the great Dome of Discovery and Skylon (which was toppled into the Thames), was demolished shortly after his return to power in 1952.[19]

While the Festival site was being cleared, many of this new generation of leading British artists who had collaborated to produce it were busy creating one lasting final expression of their shared ideals in the Time and Life building on New Bond Street in London (1951–3). Its architect was Michael Rosenauer (1884–1971) who had studied sculpture in Vienna before making London his home in the 1920s. He was employed by the London County Council prior to the war to advise on public housing and it was there that he encountered both Hugh Casson and Misha Black (1910–77), who designed the interiors of the building. But it was on the exterior, in a concrete screen wall to a second-floor terrace above the street, that Rosenauer worked with Henry Moore on one of Moore's very

149 Portland stone brings a civic gravitas to the London County Council Architects' Department's Festival Hall of 1949–51 – now stripped of all sculpture and other decoration

few examples of integrated architectural sculpture (fig.150). The screen is formed of four colossal abstract figures within shaped, near rectangular openings, with the outer faces towards New Bond Street more deeply modelled than the flatter rear faces. As Moore said himself: 'The fact that it is only a screen with space behind it, led me to carve it with a back as well as a front, and to pierce it, which gives an interesting penetration of light, and also from Bond Street makes it clear that it is a screen and not a solid part of the building.'[20] Moore later had the idea of trying to make the four components of the frieze revolve, but the building work was too advanced and the concept also proved

150 Henry Moore's sculpture on the Time and Life building in London

too expensive to carry out. Within, the reception area had a further relief, *The Spirit of Architecture* by Ben Nicholson, and a further welded iron sculpture, *Complexities of Man* by Geoffrey Clarke (1924–2014), murals in the sixth-floor cafeteria by the architect Oliver Cox (1920–2010) depicted the various courses of a meal, and the interiors of the executive dining room and anteroom were designed by Leonard Manasseh (1916–2017, who had designed the '51 cafe at the Festival of Britain). It remains both one of the last great examples of the integration of architecture and sculpture in London and a fitting tribute to the men and women who created the Festival.

While this generation of post-war architects would go on to lead their profession in Britain through the next few decades, they were to be mostly followers rather than leaders in the development of Modern architecture; but as for the sculptors who had contributed to the Festival, including Henry Moore, Barbara Hepworth, Ben Nicholson and others, they would lead their art internationally, exhibiting and carrying out commissions around the globe and being mentioned in the same breath as Brancusi, Giacometti, Archipenko and Calder. But their obsessions with the depiction of negative and positive space were divorced from the art of architecture and while their work often sat within Modern architectural spaces, the buildings invariably merely provided shelter, enclosure or a backdrop for their work. There seemed to be no place for architectural sculpture as a collaborative art form in this Brave New World.

EPILOGUE

Of course, there were rare exceptions to prove the rule, such as Wilfred Dudeney's (1919–84) *Newspapermen* of 1955 – both in relief and free-standing adjacent to Richard Seifert's Pemberton House in London – and Charles Wheeler et al.'s figurative sculpture on Victor Heal's New Change Buildings for the Bank of England of the same year. But the Portland stone buildings which these sculptures graced now appeared like a throwback to the pre-war days of the 1930s and were soon surrounded by towering office slabs in glass, steel and concrete. In the 1960s, abstract concrete reliefs enjoyed a particular vogue – such as Frederick Bushe's precast concrete panels on the Liverpool University lecture rooms of 1965 and William Mitchell's panels on Federation House in Liverpool of 1965–6 – while in the 1970s almost every new shopping development was graced by at least one example of public art, such as Manchester's famous Arndale Centre which sported *Totem* by Franta Belsky in 1977 (in aluminium-filled, glass-reinforced resin on a steel frame), or Neil Livingstone's bronze *Kentigern* of the same year which celebrated the pedestrianisation of Glasgow's Buchanan Street (both of which, interestingly, have been removed to council storage).

By the 1980s and through the 1990s, Postmodernism brought both a renewed interest in the creation of a richer public realm and the first glimmers of a modest Classical revival, with both strands of development rekindling artistic relationships between architects and sculptors. As Glasgow reinvented itself as a city of culture, so the repair of the city centre commenced with a number of sensitive and imaginative developments such as the Italian Centre by architects Page & Park of 1988–90 (fig.151). This included several architectural sculptures, including one of Alexander Stoddart's (1959–) first commissions, the Neo-Classical *Italia* and *Mercury* which crown the attic floor and their brother-in-arms *Mercurius* in bronze at ground level. These are accompanied by a series of *Guardians and Mythological Figures* in galvanised steel by Jack Faulds Sloan which provide both a frieze to the inner courtyard and several abstracted figures within the steel structure of the canopy, all of which complement the Postmodern Classical architecture and add a further layer of meaning to this celebration of the local Italian community's contribution to the commercial life of the city. In total, eight per cent of the entire project budget was dedicated to the various art works included within it, and the architects are to be commended for ensuring that the various artists' contributions are so well integrated within the architecture.

Local sculptor Alexander Stoddart, who was educated at both Glasgow University and Glasgow School of Art (where his undergraduate thesis was on the life and work of John Mossman), has gone on to establish himself both as a critic of most contemporary art (describing Tracy Emin, for example, as 'the high priestess of societal decline', *The Guardian*, 6 June 2009) and as the go-to sculptor for traditional civic public figurative sculpture, including statues of both *David Hume* (1996) and *Adam Smith* (2008), the philosophers of the Scottish Enlightenment, on the Royal Mile in Edinburgh.

151 Jack Faulds Sloan's galvanised steel shutters representing *Apollo with the Setting Sun and Rising Moon* on Page & Park's Italian Centre (1988–90)

He is also a Classical architectural sculptor working with contemporary Classical architects such as John Simpson, for whom he produced a series of friezes on Homeric themes for the Queen's Gallery in Buckingham Palace (2002), Robert Adam, for whom he produced a bronze frieze depicting an allegory of traditional and Modernist values for the Sackler Library in Oxford (2001), and most notably Craig Hamilton, to whose Chapel of Christ the Redeemer at Culham (2017) he contributed both the statue of *Christ the Redeemer* in marble and extensive further architectural sculpture. Perhaps, with sculpture always having formed such an integral element within the Classical architectural language, it is hardly surprising that it is only really within this minor tributary of contemporary architecture that the art of architectural sculpture currently retains a few faint gasps of life.

So let us conclude with these glowing embers amongst the ashes, and the further hope that someday soon sculptors and architects will once again recognise the contribution which they can make to each other's art and once more together produce further works of richness, complexity and technical virtuosity which communicate contemporary ideas and ideals and, in the meantime, fortunately, we may still relish their predecessors' extraordinary shared achievements.

NOTES

INTRODUCTION

1 John P. Seddon, 'The Relation of Architecture to Painting and Sculpture', *The Builder*, 22 March 1851, p.180.

I TO THE VICTOR THE SPOILS

1 *Queen Victoria's Journal*, 1 May 1851, vol.31, p.211.
2 Martin J. Daunton, *Progress and Poverty: An Economic and Social History of Britain 1700–1850*, Oxford University Press, Oxford, 1995.
3 E.H. Gombrich, *The Story of Art*, 12th edn, Phaidon Press, London, 1972, p.380.
4 As Benedict Read pointed out, the production of commemorative sculpture in Victorian Britain achieved an almost industrial scale: 'The pattern included national commemoration of national heroes, local commemoration of national heroes, local commemoration of local heroes, of specific local ties or achievements; parallel to this was a pattern of choice of sculptors – national artists doing national and local heroes, local artists doing national and local figures, let alone locally born national artists executing local commemorations of national figures; in Scotland and Ireland there was a further distinction in the choice between major national artists who had stayed at home and those who had been lured away, for instance, to the "wealth and blandishments of Babylon", as was said of Foley, who had gone to London to pursue his career.' Benedict Read, *Victorian Sculpture*, Yale University Press, New Haven and London, 2nd Printing, 1983, p.85.
5 *The Complete Works of John Ruskin*, Vol.XXXVI, 'The Letters of John Ruskin 1827–1889', p.347.
6 Many sculptures were reduced in size for larger production runs in bronze or ceramics using the 'Cheverton Reducing Machine' (or similar others) which was developed to accurately reduce the scale of a sculpture to domestic size. Sculptors would then often sell the rights to a foundry or in many cases to a ceramics firm such as Minton, Doulton or Wedgewood, who would then mass-produce the piece.
7 Bernard Porter, *The Battle of the Styles: Society, Culture and the Design of a New Foreign Office 1855–61*, Bloomsbury, London, 2011, p.95.
8 Alexandra Gordon Clark, 'A.W.N. Pugin', in Peter Ferriday (ed.), *Victorian Architecture*, Jonathan Cape, London, 1963, p.140.
9 Notably *Contrasts; or a Parallel between the Noble Edifices of the Fourteenth and Fifteenth Centuries and Similar Buildings of the Present Day; shewing the Present Decay of Taste: Accompanied by an Appropriate Text*, a pamphlet published in 1836 in which he explored what he saw as the decline of architectural standards since the Middle Ages.
10 A scene captured by J.M.W. Turner in *The Burning of the Houses of Lords and Commons October 16th, 1834*, now held by the Philadelphia Museum of Art.
11 It was widely acknowledged that: 'There was no other architect (*other than Pugin*) who could provide such details, fine and intricate, rich in colour and noble in scale, the Perpendicular tracery, the pinnacle *flèches* of the ventilation ducts, panelled ceilings, broadly patterned flock wallpapers,

encaustic tiles, even coat stands and light fittings.' Alexandra Gordon Clark, 'A.W.N. Pugin', in Ferriday, *Victorian Architecture*, pp 150–51.
12 *Illustrated London News*, no.xli, 30 August 1862.
13 Read, *Victorian Sculpture*, p.70.
14 Rupert Gunnis, *Dictionary of British Sculptors, 1650–1851*, Harvard University Press, Cambridge, MA, 1954, p.389.
15 Alfred Barry, *The Architect Of The New Palace At Westminster. – A Reply To A Pamphlet By E. Pugin, Esq., Entitled "Who Was The Art-Architect Of The Houses Of Parliament?"*, 2nd edn, John Murray, London, 1868, pp 92–3.
16 Interestingly, Garland went on to state that: 'I never to my knowledge ever saw Mr. Pugin' (Barry, *The Architect Of The New Palace At Westminster*, p.93).
17 Read, *Victorian Sculpture*, p.146.
18 F.H.W. Sheppard (ed.), *Survey of London, Vol. XXXVIII. The Museums Area of South Kensington and Westminster*, Greater London Council, 1975, p.170.
19 Musgrave Lewthwaite Watson, for example, claimed that he gave both Sir Francis Chantrey and Sir Richard Westmacott eight hours each per day, and he continued this for over a decade before he was in a position to establish his own studio.
20 Belt won the case, nevertheless, as there was no legally prescribable limit as to how much of any work of art could be carried out by an assistant.
21 A.M.W. Stirling, *Victorian Sidelights: From the Papers of the Late Mrs Adams-Acton*, Ernest Benn Ltd, London, 1954, p.219.

2 ONE TRUE CHRISTIAN STYLE

1 John Ruskin, *The Stones of Venice*, The New Universal Library Edition, George Routledge & Sons, London, 1907, p.28.
2 John Ruskin, *The Stones of Venice, Vol.1*, Smith Elder, London, 1851, Appendix 12, p.372.
3 Ruskin, *The Stones of Venice*, pp 25–6.
4 Ruskin, *The Stones of Venice*, p.26.
5 John Ruskin, *The Seven Lamps of Architecture*, The New Universal Library Edition, George Routledge & Sons, London, 1907, p.157.
6 Ruskin, *The Seven Lamps of Architecture*, p.167.
7 Ruskin, *The Seven Lamps of Architecture*, p.37.
8 Ruskin, *The Seven Lamps of Architecture*, p.182.
9 Ruskin, *The Seven Lamps of Architecture*, p.82.
10 John Ruskin, *The Stones of Venice, Vol.II*, The New Universal Library Edition, George Routledge & Sons, London, 1907, p.169.
11 Ruskin, *The Stones of Venice, Vol.II*, p.181.
12 Ruskin, *The Stones of Venice, Vol.I*, p.47.
13 Ruskin, *The Seven Lamps of Architecture*, p.108.
14 Ruskin, *The Stones of Venice, Vol.I*, p.228.
15 Ruskin, *The Seven Lamps of Architecture*, p.55.
16 Ruskin, *The Seven Lamps of Architecture*, p.17.
17 Ruskin, *The Seven Lamps of Architecture*, p.181.
18 Ruskin, *The Seven Lamps of Architecture*, p.40.
19 Ruskin, *The Seven Lamps of Architecture*, p.42.
20 Amy Woolner, *Thomas Woolner, R.A., Sculptor and Poet – His Life in Letters*, E.P. Dutton & Company, New York, 1917, p.213.
21 H.S. Goodhart-Rendel, 'Victorian Public Buildings', in Peter Ferriday (ed.), *Victorian Architecture*, Jonathan Cape, London, 1963, p.95.
22 The town hall, more than the railway stations, churches or country houses, was perhaps the greatest symbol of the emergence of the new wealthy British middle class during the second half of the 19th century, and Godwin was committed to applying Gothic to this building type as well. He was not short of inspiration with both the Lombardic and Hanseatic Leagues offering numerous Gothic precedents from the 12th century onwards.
23 Charles L. Eastlake, *A History of the Gothic Revival*, Longmans, Green, and Co., London, 1872, p.354.
24 *Hampshire Telegraph and Sussex Chronicle*, 3 December 1853.
25 Charles Handley-Read, 'William Burges', in Ferriday, *Victorian Architecture*, p.210.
26 Fiona Pearson, *Goscombe John at the National Museum of Wales*, National Museum of Wales, Cardiff, 1979, pp 77–8.

27 Handley-Read, 'William Burges', in Ferriday, *Victorian Architecture*, p.210.
28 During the 1840s and 1850s he averaged around half a dozen new and half a dozen restored churches every year.
29 Sir George Gilbert Scott, *Personal and Professional Recollections by the Late Sir George Gilbert Scott. Edited by his Son, G. Gilbert Scott*, Sampson Low, Marston, Searle & Rivington, London, 1879, p.226.
30 Emma Hardy, *Farmer and Brindley: Craftsmen Sculptors 1850–1930*, Victorian Society, London, 1993.
31 F. Leighton, Report of Committee of Enquiry on the National Art Training School, 1889, London, 16 July 1889.
32 David Cole, 'Sir Gilbert Scott', in Ferriday, *Victorian Architecture*, p.181.
33 Scott required that the pre-eminent sculptors employed to execute the groups should do so in strict accordance with Armstead's models, in contrast to Ruskin's doctrine of individual contribution. F.H.W. Sheppard, *Survey of London, Vol.XXXVIII, The Museums Area of South Kensington and Westminster*, Greater London Council, 1975, p.153.
34 Handley-Read, 'William Burges', in Ferriday, *Victorian Architecture*, pp 192–3.
35 Statues to Albert abounded throughout the empire – the Memorial in Manchester of 1861–7 by Thomas Worthington is also particularly fine, with Albert and various supporting statues executed by local sculptor Matthew Noble and the architectural sculpture by local firm T.R. & E. Williams.
36 Scott, *Personal and Professional Recollections*.
37 Cole, 'Sir Gilbert Scott', in Ferriday, *Victorian Architecture*, p.181.
38 Scott, *Personal and Professional Recollections*, p.178.
39 Scott, *Personal and Professional Recollections*, pp 214–15.
40 Scott, *Personal and Professional Recollections*, p.215.
41 Scott, *Personal and Professional Recollections*, p.271.
42 Scott, *Personal and Professional Recollections*, p.272.
43 Joseph Kinnard, 'G.E. Street, The Law Courts and the Seventies', in Ferriday, *Victorian Architecture*, p.228.
44 'Some recollections of the late Mr Street on the building of the Law Courts', *The British Architect*, 1 December 1882.
45 H.S. Goodhart-Rendel, *Victorian Public Buildings*, lecture given at the Victoria and Albert Museum in 1952.
46 David B. Brownlee, *The Law Courts: The Architecture of George Edmund Street*, MIT Press, Cambridge, 1984, p.326.
47 Kinnard, 'G.E. Street', in Ferriday, *Victorian Architecture*, p.233.
48 Mark Girouard, *Alfred Waterhouse and the Natural History Museum*, Yale University Press, New Haven and London, 1981, p.17.
49 Advertisement, *The Builder*, 13 January 1849, p.4.
50 Benedict Read, *Victorian Sculpture*, Yale University Press, New Haven and London, 2nd Printing, 1983, p.228.
51 Girouard, *Alfred Waterhouse and the Natural History Museum*, p.56.
52 It was originally planned that Adam and Eve should surmount the parapet to the main entrance, to symbolise both that humankind was the crowning glory of God's work and that the entire collection was a part of His creation of the earth. Sadly, Eve was never produced and Adam later fell and smashed on the pavement during a bombing raid in the Second World War.
53 'The Natural History Museum at South Kensington', *The Builder*, 22 June 1878.

3   ET IN ARCADIA EGO

1 Edward Gibbon, *The History of the Decline and Fall of the Roman Empire, Vol.1*, John Murray, London, 1862, p.77.
2 E.M. Dodd, 'Charles Robert Cockerell', in Peter Ferriday (ed.), *Victorian Architecture*, Jonathan Cape, London, 1963, p.108.
3 Dodd, 'Charles Robert Cockerell', in Ferriday, *Victorian Architecture*, p.113.
4 The redoubtable Catherine was clearly not an employer to tangle with, as in 1856 she took

apprentice Matthew Taylor to court for disobeying her orders, as the *Leeds Mercury* of Thursday 21 February 1856 reported: 'On Saturday (19 February 1856), at the Leeds Court House, Mrs Mawer, widow of the late Mr Mawer, stone-mason, near the new Town-hall, summoned one of her apprentices to show cause why he did not obey her lawful command to go into the country to work. Mr. Horsfall appeared for Mrs Mawer, and Mr. Ferns for the apprentice. The case was brought into Court for the purpose of deciding the legality of the apprentice's claim for 2s. a week for expenses when from home performing his employer's work. It appeared that Mrs Mawer paid him 8s. per week, and by reason of his proficiency in his business he was frequently sent into the country to carve stone in churches and churchyards, and on such occasions his railway fare was paid, and 6d. per night allowed for lodgings. Mr. Horsfall called several master stone-masons, who proved that the custom of the trade was to allow 6d. per night only when apprentices or journeymen were sent into the country to work. Mrs Mawer had, however, made occasional presents to the apprentice; but he now claimed 2s. per week for expenses. Mr J. Hope Shaw decided that, although the apprentice's indenture compelled him to obey all the lawful commands of his employer, yet, if the means were withheld whereby he could perform such command, he could not be punished for refusal. It was the same when a witness was subpoened; if a reasonable sum were not tendered to him for expenses, he could not be punished if he failed to obey the command. The sum of 2s. per week for expenses when an apprentice was away from home, the Bench considered a reasonable sum; and that not having been paid, they were of opinion that it was not a disobedience requiring punishment. The summons was therefore dismissed.'

5   See *British Architect*, vol.28, 1887, p.130.
6   Records of the Society of Arts, London, 1865.
7   First lecture delivered to the Haldane Institute in Glasgow by Alexander Thomson in 1874, Ronald McFadzean, *The Life and Works of Alexander Thomson*, Routledge and Kegan Paul, London, Boston and Henley, 1979, pp 261–2.
8   McFadzean, *The Life and Works of Alexander Thomson*, p.262.
9   Lecture to the Glasgow Architectural Society, 7 May 1866, McFadzean, *The Life and Works of Alexander Thomson*, p.202.
10 Second lecture delivered to the Haldane Institute in Glasgow by Alexander Thomson in 1874, McFadzean, *The Life and Works of Alexander Thomson*, p.265.
11 Andor Gomme and David Walker, *Architecture of Glasgow*, rev. edn, Lund Humphries, London, 1987, p.33.
12 McFadzean, *The Life and Works of Alexander Thomson*, p.85.
13 John Tweed, *Tweed's Guide to Glasgow and the Clyde*, Scholar's Choice, Rochester, NY, 2015, p.6.
14 Ray McKenzie, *Public Sculpture of Glasgow*, Liverpool University Press, Liverpool, 2002, p.151.
15 In 1984, the head of John Fielding was removed by vandals. Unfortunately, it was later found and restored.
16 Fiona MacCarthy, *William Morris: A Life for Our Time*, Faber & Faber, London, 1994, pp 111–12.

4   HARMONY ATTAINED

1   Marion Harry Spielmann, *British Sculpture and Sculptors of Today*, Cassell, London and New York, 1901, p.1.
2   Frederic Watts's equestrian statue entitled *Physical Energy* – which he started work on in the early 1880s as a 3.5 ton gesso grosso model (plaster mixed with glue size and hemp) – could also make this claim, but it was not cast until 1902, shortly before his death, despite encouragement from Millais in 1886, and therefore failed to make the impact of Leighton's *Athlete* at the time.
3   Benedict Read, *Victorian Sculpture*, Yale University Press, New Haven and London, 2nd Printing, 1983, p.289.
4   Susan Beattie, *The New Sculpture*, Yale University Press, New Haven and London, 1983, p.3.

5 W.R. Lethaby, *Philip Webb and His Work*, Oxford University Press, Oxford, 1935, p.75.
6 National Association for the Advancement of Art and its Application to Industry, *Transactions*, 1888, p.356.
7 Despite the catalogue of sculptural riches within Holy Trinity, it was also intended that there would be further statues of the Apostles on the nave columns by Hamo Thorneycroft, further carvings by Armstead in the arcade spandrels and a painted ceiling to the nave.
8 Lethaby, *Philip Webb and His Work*, p.76.
9 Charles Allen (like Harry Bates) carved in stone and wood for Farmer and Brindley before the start of his formal education and joined Thorneycroft to work on the Accountants' Hall, staying with him as the wealthy Thorneycroft's chief modelling assistant until 1894, when he moved to Liverpool to take up the position of Instructor in Sculpture at the newly opened Liverpool School of Architecture and Applied Art, and also established his own studio. Glaswegian John Tweed, who had studied at the Glasgow School of Art, had just arrived in London and joined Thorneycroft's team as a 20-year-old, before going on to study in Paris, work in South Africa for Herbert Baker, and eventually establish his own studio in London.
10 Royal Institute of British Architects, *Transactions*, vol.8, 1892, pp 49–50.
11 Beattie, *The New Sculpture*, p.72.
12 George T. Noszlopy, *Public Sculpture of Birmingham*, Liverpool University Press, Liverpool, 1998, pp 49–50.
13 Philip Ward-Jackson, *Public Sculpture of the City of London*, Public Sculpture of Britain, vol.7, Liverpool University Press, Liverpool, 2003, p.461.
14 Beattie, *The New Sculpture*, p.86.
15 Frampton, *Art Journal*, 1897, p.321.
16 Despite their outstanding body of work, Frampton is still best known for his statue of *Peter Pan* in Kensington Gardens of 1912, and Gilbert for *Eros* (actually *Anteros*) in Piccadilly Circus.
17 Association for the Promotion of Art and Design in the City of Glasgow, *Kelvingrove Art Gallery and Museum: Selected Design*, Glasgow, 1892, p.2.
18 Letter from Alfred Waterhouse to Glasgow City Council, 29 October 1897.
19 Glasgow City Archive, F12/2 (Box 2), Letter from William Shirreffs to J. Shearer, 28 July 1897.
20 Alastair Service, *Edwardian Architecture: A Handbook to Building Design in Britain 1890–1914*, Thames & Hudson, London, 1977, p.50.
21 James Betley and Nikolaus Pevsner, *Essex: Buildings of England*, Yale University Press, New Haven, 2007, pp 276–7.
22 Beattie, *The New Sculpture*, p.106.
23 Henry Curry Marillier, *Dekorative Kunst*, vol.12, p.369.
24 G.A. Bremner, *Building Greater Britain: Architecture, Imperialism and the Edwardian Baroque Revival, c.1885–1920*, Yale University Press, New Haven, 2022, p.1.

5   THE POWER AND THE GLORY

1 Simon Heffer, *The Age of Decadence*, Windmill Books, London, 2017, p.30.
2 Alexander Stuart Gray, *Edwardian Architecture: A Biographical Dictionary*, Gerald Duckworth & Company, London, 1985, p.54.
3 Gray, *Edwardian Architecture: A Biographical Dictionary*, p.7.
4 Joseph Boehm, who had been the Queen's favourite for many years, had already provided the most reproduced piece of sculpture in Britain by modelling the famous 'Jubilee Head' of Victoria for her coinage.
5 Following the announcement of Webb's selection, a number of Brock's contemporaries demanded to know why there had been no similar competition for the appointment of the sculptor, but to no avail.
6 Susan Beattie, *The New Sculpture*, Yale University Press, New Haven and London, 1983, p.230.
7 Benedict Read, *Victorian Sculpture*, Yale University Press, New Haven and London, 2nd Printing, 1983, pp 377–8.
8 *Liverpool Daily Post*, 14 May 1901.

9. Alastair Service, *Edwardian Architecture: A Handbook to Building Design in Britain 1890–1914*, Thames & Hudson, London, 1977, p.142.
10. Beattie, *The New Sculpture*, p.117.
11. The building has recently been converted into a hotel and apartments, and the sculpture cleaned and restored.
12. A. Lys Baldry, 'Alfred Drury, A.R.A.', *The Studio*, vol.37, February 1906, p.14.
13. Drury went to great lengths to accurately depict his subjects, including draping wet blankets over his poor models' heads.
14. Public Record Office, Works 12, 91/20.
15. Gray, *Edwardian Architecture: A Biographical Dictionary*, p.15.
16. *Builder's Journal and Architectural Record*, 20 August 1902, p.3.
17. Rickards's personal brilliance attracted many friends, with Arnold Bennet placing him, along with H.G. Wells, as 'the two most interesting, provocative and stimulating men I have yet encountered'.
18. Beattie, *The New Sculpture*, p.131.
19. Having succeeded in capturing much of the world, the sleeping lion had become an imagined symbol of British foreign policy which, rather than now being expansionist, simply aspired to provide *Pax Britannica* for all those who were fortunate enough to live within the protection of the empire – but along with the gentle reminder that if roused from its slumber, it would defend its pride ferociously.
20. Much of the carving was executed by Alexander Young, c.1867–1915, who actually died on 22 January 1915 while working in situ on the sculptures.
21. Henry Poole went on to contribute to many further building projects including, notably, his quite remarkable high-level frieze to Liberty House on Regent Street in London, to which he added three onlookers who gaze down at his sculpture from above the parapet.
22. Adolf Loos, 'Ornament and Crime', *Les Cahiers d'Aujourd'hui*, no.5, June 1913.
23. Beattie, *The New Sculpture*, p.131.
24. Read, *Victorian Sculpture*, p.386.

6 THE CHANGING SCENE

1. Cecil Lewis (ed.), *Self Portrait: Letters and Journals of Charles Ricketts, collected and compiled by T. Sturge Moore*, Peter Davies, London, 1939, p.275.
2. Susan Beattie, *The New Sculpture*, Yale University Press, New Haven and London, 1983, p.131.
3. Nikolaus Pevsner, 'Nine Swallows – No Summer', in Nikolaus Pevsner and J.M. Richards (eds), *The Anti-Rationalists*, The Architectural Press, London, 1976, pp 203–4.
4. Report by Lord Redesdale upon proposals for a memorial to Edward VII in the Memorial Park at Shadwell.
5. Each mask required many weeks of work on the part of Wood and the other sculptors, starting with a plaster cast being taken of the subject's face after the wounds and subsequent surgery had healed. This was then used as the foundation for the prosthetic restorative work, with the sculptor working to replace the missing components of the face with the shapes from the opposing side. The mask itself was made from a thin galvanised copper sheet to facilitate painting after forming, with each mask finished while the patient wore it in order to most accurately match the tone of the flesh with the enamels.
6. James Miller, 'The Business Side of Architecture', *RIBA Journal*, 25 June 1921.
7. Burnet had been appointed by the Imperial War Graves Commission to design the war cemeteries and memorials in Palestine and Gallipoli, and sent Tait there on the pretext of a site visit, but which was actually a study tour of Egyptian architecture.
8. A. Trystan Edwards, *Sir John Burnet and Partners Architects*, Masters of Architecture, Geneva, 1930.
9. Rabinovitch soon abandoned sculpture, abbreviated his name to Sam Rabin and began a successful career as a boxer, winning a bronze medal at the Olympics of 1928 in Amsterdam.
10. http://www.visual-arts-cork.com/sculpture/british-modern.htm#history
11. John Summerson, 'Architect Laureate', *Night and Day*, 28 October 1937.

12. Lecture to the RIBA in June 1931 on acceptance of their Royal Gold Medal, RIBA Collection.
13. Herbert Baker, *Architecture and Personalities*, Country Life Limited, London, 1944, p.167.
14. Baker also successfully proposed the young engineer Oscar Faber as engineer for the project, despite its extraordinary complexities, and was well rewarded in his choice.
15. *Evening News*, 23 October 1930, Editorial.
16. *The Times*, 20 March 1931.

7 A HOUSE DIVIDED

1. Owen Hopkins, *British Architecture, 1926–1945*, talk given at the Newcastle City Centre on 15 June 2016 celebrating 90 Years of British Architecture.
2. 'Prospero and Ariel', *The Listener*, 15 March 1933, p.397.
3. Eric Gill, *Autobiography*, Devin-Adair Company, New York, 1941, p.248.
4. There have now been more recent calls for the statue to be removed completely following the publication of Fiona McCarthy's biography of Gill which confirmed that he engaged in both paedophilia and bestiality, and as can be seen in the illustration, in 2021 it was damaged in a hammer attack by a protester against child abuse.
5. Gill, *Autobiography*, p.211.
6. E.H. Gombrich, *The Story of Art*, 12th edn, Phaidon Press, London, 1972, pp 397–8.
7. Gavin Stamp, 'Charles Reilly and the Liverpool School of Architecture, 1904–1933', *Journal of the Society of Architectural Historians*, vol.56, no.3, September 1997, pp 345–8.
8. Gilbert Bayes, *Modelling for Sculpture: A Book for the Beginner*, Winsor and Newton, London, 1930.
9. Horse-tamers are, of course, part of the Classical tradition which dates back to the Dioscuri groups on the Quirinal Hill in Rome, and there were a number of further contemporary examples including Alfred Turner's (1874–1940) version atop Herbert Baker's Delville Wood South African War Memorial in France (1925–6) which features Castor and Pollux together restraining a war horse and symbolising the two races – British and Dutch, not black and white – of the recently united South Africa.
10. Philip Ward-Jackson, *Public Sculpture of the City of London*, Public Sculpture of Britain, vol.7, Liverpool University Press, Liverpool, 2003, p.278.
11. David Watkin, *Morality and Architecture*, Clarendon Press, Oxford, 1977, p.95.
12. *Manchester Guardian*, 24 July 1948.
13. Douglas Percy Bliss, 'Sculpture in Glasgow', *Glasgow Herald*, 20 February 1954, p.3.
14. Nikolaus Pevsner, 'Thoughts on Henry Moore', *Burlington Magazine*, vol.86, no.53, February 1945, p.47.
15. Mark Girouard, *Big Jim: The Life and Work of James Stirling*, Chatto & Windus, London, 1998, p.50.
16. William Feaver, 'Festival Star', in Mary Banham and Bevis Hillier (eds), *A Tonic to the Nation: The Festival of Britain 1951*, Thames & Hudson, London, 1976, p.54.
17. *The Times*, 21 November 1950, p.6.
18. Robert Anderson, 'Circa 1951: Presenting Science to the British Public', talk given at Oregon State University, 29 October 2007.
19. As lead architect, Sir Hugh Casson confirmed this view, stating that the designers saw the Festival as 'the advance guard of Socialism'. See Becky E. Conekin, *The Autobiography of a Nation: The 1951 Festival of Britain*, Manchester University Press, Manchester, 2003.
20. Henry Moore, *Volume II: Sculpture and Drawings 1949–54*, Lund Humphries and Co., London, 1965.

BIBLIOGRAPHY

Baldry, Alfred Lys, *Modern Mural Decoration*, George Newnes Ltd, London, 1902

Barry, Alfred, *The Architect Of The New Palace At Westminster. – A Reply To A Pamphlet By E. Pugin, Esq., Entitled "Who Was The Art-Architect Of The Houses Of Parliament?"*, 2nd edn, John Murray, London, 1868

Bayes, Gilbert, *Modelling for Sculpture: A Book for the Beginner*, Winsor and Newton, London, 1930

Beattie, Susan, *The New Sculpture*, Yale University Press, New Haven and London, 1983

Betley, James, and Nikolaus Pevsner, *Essex: Buildings of England*, Yale University Press, New Haven, 2007

Bremner, A., *Building Greater Britain: Architecture, Imperialism and the Edwardian Baroque Revival, c.1885–1920*, Yale University Press, New Haven, 2022

Cavanagh, Terry, *Public Sculpture of Liverpool*, Liverpool University Press, Liverpool, 1997

Chappell, Edgar, *Cardiff Civic Centre: A Historical Guide*, Priory Press Ltd, Cardiff, 1946

Daunton, Martin J., *Progress and Poverty: An Economic and Social History of Britain 1700–1850*, Oxford University Press, Oxford, 1995

Davey, Peter, *Arts and Crafts Architecture*, Phaidon Press Ltd, London, 1995

Eastlake, Charles L., *A History of the Gothic Revival*, Longmans, Green, and Co., London, 1872

Ferriday, Peter (ed.), *Victorian Architecture*, Jonathan Cape, London, 1963

Gill, Eric, *Autobiography*, Devin-Adair Company, New York, 1941

Girouard, Mark, *Alfred Waterhouse and the Natural History Museum*, Yale University Press, New Haven and London, 1981

Gombrich, E.H., *The Story of Art*, 12th edn, Phaidon Press, London, 1972

Gomme, Andor, and David Walker, *Architecture of Glasgow*, Lund Humphries, London, new and completely revised edition, 1987

Gray, Alexander Stuart, *Edwardian Architecture: A Biographical Dictionary*, Gerald Duckworth & Company, London, 1985

Gunnis, Rupert, *Dictionary of British Sculptors, 1650–1851*, Harvard University Press, Cambridge, MA, 1954

Hamilton, Alec, *Arts and Crafts Churches*, rev. edn, Lund Humphries, London, 2021

Heffer, Simon, *The Age of Decadence*, Windmill Books, London, 2017

Irvine, Louise, and Paul Atterbury, *Gilbert Bayes Sculptor 1872–1953*, Richard Dennis, Somerset, 1998

Lethaby, W.R., *Philip Webb and His Work*, Oxford University Press, Oxford, 1935

Lewis, Cecil (ed.), *Self Portrait: Letters and Journals of Charles Ricketts, collected and compiled by T. Sturge Moore*, Peter Davies, London, 1939

Londsdale, Henry, *The Life and Works of Musgrave Lewthwaite Watson, Sculptor*, George Routledge & Sons, London, 1866

MacCarthy, Fiona, *William Morris: A Life for our Time*, Faber & Faber, London, 1994

McFadzean, Ronald, *The Life and Works of Alexander Thomson*, Routledge & Kegan Paul, London, Boston and Henley, 1979

McKenzie, Ray, *Public Sculpture of Glasgow*, Liverpool University Press, Liverpool, 2002

Marsden, Jonathan (ed.), *Victoria & Albert: Art & Love*, The Royal Collection, London, 2010

Middleton, Robin, and David Watkin, *Neoclassical and 19th Century Architecture*, Faber & Faber, London, 1987

Morris, William, *The Prospects of Architecture*, Works, Volume XII, Cambridge University Press, Cambridge, 2012

Noszlopy, George T., *Public Sculpture of Birmingham*, Liverpool University Press, Liverpool, 1998

Pearson, Fiona, *Goscombe John at the National Museum of Wales*, National Museum of Wales, Cardiff, 1979

Pevsner, Nikolaus, and J.M. Richards (eds), *The Anti-Rationalists*, The Architectural Press, London, 1976

Read, Benedict, *Victorian Sculpture*, Yale University Press, New Haven and London, 2nd Printing, 1983

Rossetti, William Michael, *Fine Art, Chiefly Contemporary, 1867*, Kessinger Publishing Company, London, 2008

Ruskin, John, *The Seven Lamps of Architecture*, The New Universal Library Edition, George Routledge & Sons, London, 1907

Ruskin, John, *The Stones of Venice I & II*, The New Universal Library Edition, George Routledge & Sons, London, 1907

Scott, Sir George Gilbert, *Personal and Professional Recollections by the Late Sir George Gilbert Scott. Edited by his Son, G. Gilbert Scott*, Sampson Low, Marston, Searle & Rivington, London, 1879

Service, Alastair, *Edwardian Architecture: A Handbook to Building Design in Britain 1890–1914*, Thames & Hudson, London, 1977

Spielmann, Marion Harry, *British Sculpture and Sculptors of Today*, Cassell, London and New York, 1901

Stanton, Phoebe B., *Pugin*, Thames & Hudson, London, 1971

Stewart, John, *Sir Herbert Baker: Architect to the British Empire*, McFarland, North Carolina, 2022

Stewart, John, *The Life and Works of Glasgow Architects James Miller and John James Burnet*, Whittles, Dunbeath, 2021

Stirling, A.M.W., *Victorian Sidelights: From the Papers of the Late Mrs Adams-Acton*, Ernest Benn Ltd, London, 1954

Toft, Albert, *Modelling and Sculpture: A Full Account of the Various Methods and Processes Employed in these Arts*, Seeley, Service & Co. Limited, London, 1929

Ward-Jackson, Philip, *Public Sculpture of the City of London*, Public Sculpture of Britain, vol.7, Liverpool University Press, Liverpool, 2003

Watkin, David, *Morality and Architecture*, Clarendon Press, Oxford, 1977

Webster, Christopher (ed.), *Episodes in the Gothic Revival*, Spire Books Limited, Reading, 2011

Woolner, Amy, *Thomas Woolner, R.A., Sculptor and Poet – His Life in Letters*, E.P. Dutton & Company, New York, 1917

Wyke, Terry, with Harry Cocks, *Public Sculpture of Greater Manchester*, Liverpool University Press, Liverpool, 2004

WEBSITE

British Empire Timeline, oxfordreference.com

INDEX

Note: *italic* page numbers indicate figures.

Adelaide House, London 156, 157, *157*
Admiralty Arch, London 113, 116, *116*
Albert Memorial, London 24, 41, *42*, 43, 44, 81, 115
Allen, Charles John 40, 84, 85, 92, 111, 116, 117, *117*, 127
Alliance Bank, Liverpool 63
Angel, John 153
Armitage, Joseph 22, 166
Armstead, Henry Hugh 41, 44, *82*, 83
Art Workers' Guild, London 8, 81
Ashbee, Charles Robert 141
Ashton Memorial, Lancaster 122, *122*
Asplund, Gunnar 169, 173
Athenaeum Club, London 17, 57, *57*
Athenaeum, Glasgow 94
Atkinson, Robert Frank 146, 155, 170
Aumonier, Eric 159, 172
Aumonier, William 89, 102, *103*

Baily, Edward Hodges 25
Baker, Sir Herbert 26, 147, 151, 152, 153, 161, 165, 166, *167*, 168, 169, 185
Bank of England, London 147, *167*, 169, 193
Barry, Sir Charles 17, 19, 21, 25, 39, 48, 57, 63
Bartels, Carl Bernard 127
Bates, Harry 40, 80, 83, 84, 87, *87*, 88, 89, 92, 130, 144
Bayes, Gilbert 7, 135, *156*, 156, 172, 177, 178, 179, *179*, 182, *182*
Behnes, William 25
Belcher, John 64, 81, 84, 85, *85*, 87, 104, 105, 106, *108*, 109, 111, 112, 113, 121, *121*, 122, 122, 123, 132, 146
Belfast City Hall 105, *105*, 106, *107*, 111

Bell, Edward Ingress 87
Bell, John 14, 15, *15*, 17, 21, 41, 80, 81
Bell, Robert Anning 102
Bentley, John Francis 104
Birmingham Council House 71–2, *73*
Birmingham Hall of Memory 153, *153*
Birmingham Law Courts 159
Bishopsgate Institute, London 101, *102*
Black Friar Public House, London 102, *104*
Blanchard, M.H. 52, 53
Blomfield, Sir Reginald 84, 86, 151, 152, 186
Bodley, George Frederick 138
Boehm, Joseph Edgar 80, 93
Bolton Town Hall 72, *73*, 81, 123
Bone, Phyllis 185, 186
Bonehill, Joseph 63
Boucher Alfred 83
Boulton, Richard Lockwood 34, 35, 36, 51
Bowden, J. William 76
Bramwell, Edward George 99
Bridgeman, Robert 104
Brindley, William 24, 40, 47
Bristol Central Reference Library 141, *141*
Britannic House, London 161, *161*
British Linen Bank, Glasgow 100
British Medical Association HQ, London 143, *143*, 159
Broadcasting House, London 171, *172*, *173*, 173
Brock, Thomas 25, 79, 80, 106, 113, *114*, 115, *115*, 116, *116*, 130
Broderick, Cuthbert 57, *58*, 59
Brown, William Kellock 95

Brydon, John 118, *118*
Burges, William 26, 33, 36, *37*, 38, 39, 69, 101, 127
Burne-Jones, Edward 83
Burnet, John James 7, 26, 70, *71*, 93, 94, *94*, 95, *95*, 96, 121, 134, *134*, 135, 148, 149, *149*, 150, 151, 155, 156, *156*, 157, *157*, 158, *158*, 165, 169, 180, 182, 185
Burnham, Daniel Hudson 113, 146, 148, 155
Burton, Decimus 17, 57, *57*
Bushe, Frederick 193
Bute, 3rd Marquis of (John Patrick Crichton-Stuart) 36, 127

Callcott, Frederick 102, *104*
Capstick, George Thomas 175, *176*, 177, *177*
Cardiff Castle 36, 37, *37*, 38, *38*, 39, 127
Cardiff City Hall *128*, 130, 131, *131*, 132, 138
Cardiff Law Courts 130, 131, *131*, 132, *132*, 133
Cardiff Technical College 136
Caroe, William Douglas 132
Carpeaux, Jean-Baptiste 79
Carrick, Alexander 185, 186, *186*
Cassidy, John 104
Casson, Sir Hugh 188, 189, 190
Castell Coch 37, 39
Cathays Park, Cardiff 127, 132
Cenotaph, Whitehall, London 152, 161
Central Criminal Court, the Old Bailey, London 123, *123*, *124*, 125
Chantrey, Sir Francis 25, 69
Chapel of Christ the Redeemer, Culham 194

INDEX

Charing Cross Mansions, Glasgow 94, 94
Charoux, Siegfried 188, 189, *190*
Church of Our Most Holy Redeemer, Clerkenwell, London 83
Church of the Holy and Undivided Trinity with Saint Jude, Chelsea, London 81, *82*, *83*, 84
Clapperton, Thomas J. 135
Clayton and Bell 43
Clyde Navigation Trust 70, *71*, 94, 134, *134*, 155
Cockerell, Charles 8, 17, 18, *18–19*, 56, 66, 67, 165
Colchester Town Hall 105
Cole, Ernest 147, *148*
Collcutt, Thomas Edward 106, *108*, 109, 111, 166
Collitt and Company 57
Commercial Bank, Bradford 60
Commercial Bank of Scotland, Glasgow 177, *178*, *179*
Cooper, Sir Edwin 135, *135*, 146, *146*, 153, *154*, 155, 161, 162, 163, *163*, *164*, 165, 186
Copnall, Edward Bainbridge 174, 175, *175*
Crane, Walter 89, 101
Creswick, Benjamin 91
Crewe, Municipal Buildings and Public Baths 126
Crystal Palace 9, 17, 29, 76, 150

Daily Express Buildings, London, Glasgow, Manchester 169–70, *170*
Daily Telegraph Building, Fleet Street, London 158, *158*, *159*, 169
Dalou, Aimé-Jules 79, 90
Dean, Thomas Newenham 31
Dick, William Reid 7, 26, 100, 151, 156, 157, *157*, 162, 168, 180, *180*, 181, 185, 186, *186*
Dobson, Frank 152, 171, *171*, 189
Doman, Charles 153, *154*, 155, *155*, 163
Doulton & Company 41
Doyle, James Francis 111
Doyle-Jones, William 182
Drury, Alfred 84, 90, *90*, 92, 113, 115, 119, *119*, *120*, 121, 125, 144
Dudeney, Wilfred 193
Dujardin, Edouard Romain 54, *55*

Earp, Hobbs and Miller 144
Earp, Thomas 48, 49, *50*, 144
Elcock, Charles Ernest 158, 169
Electra House 121, *121*, *122*, 123
Ellis and Clark 169, *170*
Ellis, Peter 77, *77*
Elmes, Harvey Lonsdale 17, *18–19*, 57
Epstein, Jacob 8, 143, *143*, 150, 152, 159, *159*, 160, 161, 168, 169, 172, 189
Evans, David 135
Ewing, James Alexander 75

Fabbrucci, Aristide 99
Fairhurst, Harry S. 144
Farmer, William 40
Farmer and Brindley 39, 43, 44, *47*, 51, 52, *52*, 54, 60, 74, 83, 84, 87, 102, 104, 106
Fehr, Henry Charles 116, 130, 132, 139, *139*, 140, *140*, 163
Ferris, Richard 101
Festival of Britain 8, 189, *190*, *191*
Foley, John Henry 14, 15, 21, 41, *43*, 79, 81
Ford, Edward Onslow 80, 84, 117
Foreign Office, Whitehall, London 41, 43, 44, *45*
Frampton, Sir George 7, 36, 80, 84, 90, *90*, 92, 93, 95, 96, 97, *98*, 99, *99*, 100, 104, 109, *109*, 110, *110*, 111, 113, 115, 117, 120, 121, *121*, 122, 125, 135, 140, 144, 148, 153, 156, 179
Free Trade Hall, Manchester 63
Frith, W.S. 89, *89*, 90, 92
Fuchs, Emil 113
Fuller-Clark, Herbert 102

Garbe, Richard 135, *136*
General Accident Fire and Life Assurance Corporation, London 149
George, Ernest 78, 113, 165
George Adam & Son 96
George's Dock building, Liverpool 175, *176*, 176
Gerrard, Alfred Horace 159, 160
Gibbs and Canning Limited 54
Gibson, James Glen Sievewright 139, *139*
Gibson, John 21, 63, *65*
Gilbert, Alfred 36, 80, 92, 115, 144
Gilbert, Walter S. 78, 181, *181*, 185

Gill, Eric 8, 159, 160, *160*, 161, 171, 172, *172*, 173, *173*
Gillespie, John Gaff 100
Gillick, Ernest *164*
Gingell, William Bruce 60, *61*
Glamorgan County Council building, Cardiff 133, *134*
Glasgow Art Gallery and Museum 96, *98*, 102, 121, 130, 156
Glasgow City Chambers 72, 74, *74*, 106, 119
Glasgow Fine Arts Institute 24, 70
Glasgow Savings Bank 95, 97, 148
Glasgow School of Art 24, 69, 95, 99
Glasgow University 48, 96
Godwin, Edward William 33, *33*, 35, 36, 72
Good, Edward 76
Goodhart-Rendel, Harry Stuart 33, 39, 171, *171*
Gosse, Edmund 80, 112
Grasby, Charles 76
Great Exhibition, The Crystal Palace, Hyde Park, London 8, 9, *10–11*, 12, 13, *13*, 17, 41, 53
Gunton and Gunton 177, 188

Hadden, Thomas 185
Hamilton, Craig 194
Hampton, Herbert 123
Hancock, John 64, *65*
Hardie, George 85, 87
Hardiman, Alfred 147, 151
Hare, Henry Thomas 126, *126*, *127*, 141, 146
Harris, Vincent 133
Hatfield, John Ayres 13, 14
'Hatrack', 144 St Vincent Street, Glasgow 100, 101
Heathcote, Charles 144, *145*
Hemms, Harry 44
Hepworth, Barbara 169, 171, 188, 189, 192
Hepworth, Philip Dalton 183, *183*, 185, 186
Hill, William 72
Hitch, Nathaniel 102, *104*
Hobbs, Edwin 48, 144
Hodge, Albert Hemstock 7, 22, 133, 134, *134*, 135, 146, 149, 153, *154*, 155, 164, 177

Holden, Charles Henry 141, *141*, 142, *142*, 143, *143*, 146, 152, 153, 159, *159*, 161, 162, 169, 171, 172
Hope, George 57
Horniman Museum, Forest Hill, London 101, 102, *103*
Hull Guildhall 146
Hutchesontown District Library, Glasgow 95

Ingle, William 58, 60
Ingram House, London 127
Institute of Chartered Accountants' Hall 64, 84, 85, *85*, 87, *87*, 91, 92, 99, 105, 106, *108*, 109, 111, 112, 121, 132
Islington Central Library, London 126, 127
Italian Centre, Glasgow 193, *194*

Jagger, Charles Sargeant 152, 153, 183
Jenkins, Frank Lynn 111
Joass, John James 85, 121, *121*, 122, *122*
John, William Goscombe 39, 84, 90, 92, 121, 132, 135

Kavanagh, John Francis 183, *183*, *184*, 186
Keller, Johan 99
Kingston upon Hull Guildhall 135, *135*
Kitson, John William 40
Knott, Ralph 146, 148, *148*
Kodak Corporation building, London 149, *149*, 150, 169

Lambeth School of Art 40
Lancaster Town Hall 123
Lanchester, Henry Vaughan 136
Lanchester, Stewart and Rickards *128*, 130, *131*, 132, *137*
Law Society Library, London 142, *142*
Lawson, George Anderson 74, 75, *75*
Ledward, Gilbert 151, 181, 183
Leeds Town Hall 57, *58*
Leighton, Frederic 79, 80, *80*, 85
Liverpool Philharmonic Hall 177
Liverpool Union Bank 63
L.J. Watts & Co. 105
Lloyds Bank, Manchester 144, *145*, 162
Lloyd's Register of Shipping, London 106, *108*, 111, 121, 166

Lomax-Simpson, James 179, 180, *180*
London Underground Headquarters, Westminster, London 159, *159*, 160, 169, 172
Longden & Co. 96
Lucy and Littler 63
Lutyens, Sir Edwin 146, 150, 151, 152, 153, 161, *161*, 162, 163, 165, 186
Lysaght, Thomas Royse 60, *61*

Mabey, Charles Henry 64, *65*, 147
MacKinnon, James Harrison 76, 100, 156
Magnoni, Carlo Domenico 140
Manchester Assize Courts 32, 51
Manchester Town Hall 24, 51, *52*, 76
Marochetti, Baron Carlo 15, 71, 81, 93
Marshall, John 185
Marshall, William Calder 21, 41, 72, *73*, 81, 123
Marylebone Town Hall 146
Mawer, Catherine 58, *59*, 60
Mawer, Charles 58
Mawer, Robert 57, 59
McGill, Donald 130, 132, 133, *133*
McGillvray & Ferris 101
McKissock, Peter, and Sons 97
McMillan, William 152, 175
Mersey Tunnel, Liverpool 177, *177*
Mewès and Davis 145
Middlesex Guildhall, London 139, *139*, *140*
Midland Hotel, London 41, 44, *46*, *47*
Miller, Felix Martin 14, 63
Miller, James 7, 134, 151, 177, 178, *178*, 179, *179*
Milles, Carl 166
Millson, John Jarvis 144
Mitchell, William 193
Moira, Gerald 126, 127
Montford, Paul Raphael 130, 131, 132, *132*
Moore, Henry 8, 159, 160, 161, 171, 183, 188, 189, 190, 192, *192*
Morris, William 78, 88
Morrison & Mason 74
Mossman, J. & G. 24, 26, 70, 74
Mossman, J., G. & W. 69
Mossman, John 68, 69, 70, *70*, 71, *71*, 75, 80, 94

Mountfield, J.R. *118*, 119
Mountford, Edward William 91, *92*, 123, *123*, 124, 125, 126, 141
Munro, Alexander 32

National Gallery of Scotland, Edinburgh 17, 66
National Monument of Scotland, Edinburgh 66
National Museum and Galleries of Wales, Cardiff 135, *136*
National Provincial Bank of England, London 63, *65*, 163, *164*
Natural History Museum, London 51, *53*, *55*, 60, 89
Nesfield, William Eden 78
New Delhi, India 136, 151, 161, 165, 168
Nicholl, William Grinsell 8
Nicholls, Thomas 26, 36, *37*, 38, 39, 80
Nicholson, Ben 169, 171, 192
Noble, Matthew 51, 76
Northampton Town Hall 33, *33*, 34, *34*, *35*, 72

Oakley, Alfred James 158, *158*
Old War Office, Whitehall, London 119, *119*, 120
Oriel Chambers, Liverpool 77, *77*
O'Shea, James and John 31, 32, 36, 39, 51, 52
Oxford Town Hall 126, *126*
Oxford University Museum of Natural History 30, 31, *31*, 32, 39, 53

Page & Park 193, *194*
Palace of Westminster, London 17, 18, 20, 21, 23, 25, 27, 59, 62, 63
Paxton, Joseph 9, 76
Payler, Benjamin 58
Pegram, Alfred Bertram 10, 135
Pemberton House, London 193
Perry, Peter Lazlo 189
Philip, John Birnie 41, 44
Pibworth, Charles James 141, *141*, 142, *142*, 143
Pite, Beresford 85, 121
Playfair, William 17, 66, *66*
Pomeroy, Frederick William 83, 84, *84*, 90, 91, *91*, 92, 102, 106, *107*, 122, *122*, 123, 124, *124*, 125, 126, 132

INDEX

Poole, Henry 104, 130, 131, *131*, 132, 136, *137*, *138*
Port of Liverpool Building 127
Port of London Authority Building *154*, 155
Pugin, Augustus Welby Northmore 18, 21, 22, 27, 48

Rabinovitch, Samuel 158, *159*, 159, 160
Raggi, Mario 91
R.A. McGillvray & Sons 100
Rhind, John 76, *76*, 94, *94*, 95
Rhind, William Birnie 99
Richard Lockwood Boulton & Sons 72, *73*
Richmond, Sir William 126
Rickards, Edwin Alfred 130, 136
Ricketts, Charles 147
Rosenauer, Michael 190
Rowse, Herbert James 175, *176*, 177
Royal Automobile Club, London 145
Royal Courts of Justice, London 33, 48, *49*, *50*
Royal Festival Hall, London 190
Royal Institute of British Architects Headquarters, London 173, *174*, 175
Royal Masonic Hospital, London 182, *182*
Royal Scottish Academy, Edinburgh 66, *66*
Ruskin, John 16, 27, *28*, 32, 33, 35, 39, 47, 52, 55, 56, 67, 77, 81, 84, 85, 141

Saint Fin Barre's Cathedral, Cork 36
Salmon, James 100, 101
Samuely, Felix 189
Schenck, Frederick E.E. 126, *127*
Scott, George Gilbert 24, 33, 39, 40, 41 *42*, *43*, 44, *45*, *46*, 47, *47*, 48, 50, 81, 87, 96, 113, 138, 174
Scott, Giles Gilbert Scott 138
Sedding, John Dando 81, *83*, 84, 91, 166
Seifert, Richard 193
Selfridge, Henry Gordon 113, 146, 155, 156
Selfridges building, Oxford St, London 156, *156*
Shaw, Richard Norman 78, 81, 83, 84, 104, 105, 111, 113, 146
Sheffield Town Hall 91, *91*, *92*, 123
Shirreffs, William 96, 97, 99, 100

Simpson, John William 96, 97, 194
Simpson, Willink & Thicknesse 116
Skipwith, Frank Peyton 139, *139*
Sloan, Jack Faulds 193, *194*
Smith, Arnold Dunbar 135
South Kensington Museum, London 88, 89, *90*, 96
Sparks, John Charles Lewis 41
St Andrew's House, Edinburgh 185–6 *186*
St George's Hall, Liverpool 7, 18, *18–19*, 57, 58, 72
St Olaf House, London 171, *171*
St Swithin's House, London 188
St Vincent Street Church, Glasgow 68, *68*, 69
Stevens, Alfred 8, 79, 80, 120, 147
Stevens, William Reynolds 151
Stockport Town Hall 106, 183
Stoddart, Alexander 193
Street, George Edmund 33, 48, *49*, *50*, 78, 144
Swan, John 165

Tait, Thomas 150, 156, 158, 161, 169, 182, *182*, 185, 186
Taylor, Matthew 58
Thicknesse, Philip Coldwell 127
Thomas, Alfred Brumwell 105, *105*, 106
Thomas, John 21, 22, 25, 59, *59*, 60, 62, *62*, 63, 80
Thomas, Percy 136
Thomason, Yeoville 71, *73*
Thompson and Capstick 175, 176, 177
Thompson, Edward Charles 175, 177
Thomson, Alexander 'Greek' 26, 67, 68, *68*, 69, 70, 77
Thorneycroft, Mary 13, 60, 85
Thorneycroft, Thomas 41, 85
Thorneycroft, William Hamo 71, 80, 81, 84, 85, 86, *86*, 87, 91, 92, 106, 111, 113, 144
Time and Life building *192*
Todmorden Town Hall 64
Toft, Albert *131*, 153, *153*
Townsend, Charles Harrison 101, *102*, *103*
Turner, Alfred 125, *125*
Tweed, John 71, 75, 85, 165
Tweed, William 76, 92

Unilever House, London 179, *180*, *181*

Val Meyer, George 171, *172*
Vickers, William 100
Victoria and Albert Museum, London 113
Victoria Law Courts, Birmingham 88, *88*, 89
Victoria Memorial, Liverpool 117
Victoria Memorial, London *114*, 115, 123, 127
Villard de Honnecourt 39

Walters, Edward 63
Walthamstow Town Hall, London 183, *183*, *184*, 186
Waterhouse, Alfred 32, 33, 40, 48, 50, 51, 52, *52*, 53, *54*, 55, *55*, 60, 76, 87, 88, 89, 96, 105, 130
Watts, George Frederic 79, 130
Webb, Sir Aston 87, 88, *88*, 89, 90, 96, 113, *114*, 115, 130, 146, 159
Weekes, Henry 32, 41, *43*
Wesleyan Central Convocation Hall, London 136, *137*
West of England and South Wales District Bank, Bristol 60, *61*, 62
Westminster Roman Catholic Cathedral, London 104
Wheeler, Charles 26, 147, 165, 166, *167*, 168, *168*, 169, 193
Whelan, Edward 31, 32
Whitechapel Art Gallery, London 101
Whiteley, Thomas 58
Williams, Sir Evan Owen 169, 170
Wilson, Henry 81
Winter, J. Edgar 106
Wood, Francis Derwent 100, 101, 115, 152, 153, 162
Woodford, James Arthur 174, 175
Woodhouse, George 72
Woodward, Benjamin 31
Woolner, Thomas 32, 51, 64
Wornum, George Grey 174, *174*, 175, 183
Wren, Sir Christopher 123, 162
Wyon, Allan Gairdner 159, 160

Young, James Charles 100, 156
Young, William 74, *74*, 119, *119*

PICTURE CREDITS

1 Author's Collection; 2 Royal Collection Trust / © His Majesty King Charles III 2023; 3 Public Domain; 4 Peter Clarkson; 5 Public Domain; 6 Tony Hisgett; 7, 8 Author's Collection; 9 Public Domain; 10, 11, 12, 13, 14, 15, 16 Author's Collection; 17 Redstone Hill; 18 Robin Denton; 19 Public Domain; 20 James Beard; 21, 22 Philip Wright; 23, 24, 25, 26 Author's Collection; 27 Tim Green; 28, 29, 30, 31 Author's Collection; 32 Gary Chatterton; 33 Sally Whyte; 34 Philip Wright; 35, 36, 37, 38 Author's Collection; 39 David M. Gray; 40, 41, 42 Roger Edwards; 43 Author's Collection; 44 Robert Linsdell; 45, 46, 47 Roger Edwards; 48 Louise Jayne Munton; 49 Peter Clarkson; 50, 51, 52, 53, 54, 55, 56, 57, 58 Author's Collection; 59, 60 Philip Wright; 61 PunkToad; 62, 63, 64, 65, 66, 67 Roger Edwards; 68 Author's Collection; 69 Keith Bowden; 70, 71 Author's Collection; 72 David Brossard; 73 Jennifer Boyer; 74, 75, 76, 77 Author's Collection; 78 Peter Clarkson; 79 Author's Collection; 80 David Ardron; 81, 82, 83, 84 Author's Collection; 85, 86 Maggie Jones; 87 Ken Fawcett; 88, 89, 90, 91, 92, 93, 94, 95, 96, 97, 98 Author's Collection; 99 Roger Edwards; 100 Philip Wright; 101, 102, 103, 104, 105, 106, 107, 108, 109, 110 Author's Collection; 111 Malcolm Jones; 112, 113, 114, 115, 116, 117, 118, 119, 120, 121, 122, 123, 124, 125, 126, 127, 128, 129, 130, 131 Author's Collection; 132 Nigel Turner; 133, 134, 135, 136, 137 Author's Collection; 138 Shaun Brierley; 139 Alan Cookson; 140, 141 Roger Edwards; 142, 143 Author's Collection; 144 Maggie Jones; 145, 146 Author's Collection; 147 gre99qd; 148 Public Domain; 149 Ewan Munro; 150 John Oram; 151 Roger Edwards